AMERICAN ENERGY

AMERICAN ENERGY

ENERGY
The Politics of
21st Century
Policy

Walter A. Rosenbaum
University of Florida

Los Angeles | London | New Delhi
Singapore | Washington DC

Los Angeles | London | New Delhi
Singapore | Washington DC

FOR INFORMATION:

CQ Press
An Imprint of SAGE Publications, Inc.
2455 Teller Road
Thousand Oaks, California 91320
E-mail: order@sagepub.com

SAGE Publications Ltd.
1 Oliver's Yard
55 City Road
London, EC1Y 1SP
United Kingdom

SAGE Publications India Pvt. Ltd.
B 1/I 1 Mohan Cooperative Industrial Area
Mathura Road, New Delhi 110 044
India

SAGE Publications Asia-Pacific Pte. Ltd.
3 Church Street
#10-04 Samsung Hub
Singapore 049483

Copyright © 2015 by CQ Press, an Imprint of SAGE
Publications, Inc. CQ Press is a registered trademark of
Congressional Quarterly Inc.

Printed in the United States of America.

Library of Congress Cataloging-in-Publication Data

Rosenbaum, Walter A.
American energy : the politics of 21st century policy /
Walter A. Rosenbaum, University of Florida.

pages cm

Includes bibliographical references and index.

ISBN 978-1-4522-0537-3
(pbk. : alk. paper)—ISBN 978-1-4833-1068-8 (web pdf)
1. Energy policy—United States—History—21st century.
2. Energy consumption—United States—History—
21st century. I. Title.

HD9502.U52R6397 2014
333.790973—dc23   2013037022

This book is printed on acid-free paper.

Acquisitions Editor: Charisse Kiino
Associate Editor: Nancy Loh
Editorial Assistant: Davia Grant
Production Editor: Stephanie Palermini
Copy Editor: Patricia Sutton
Typesetter: Hurix Systems Pvt. Ltd.
Proofreader: Susan Schon
Indexer: Teddy Diggs
Cover Designer: Candice Harman
Marketing Manager: Amy Whitaker

MIX
Paper from
responsible sources
FSC® C014174
www.fsc.org

14 15 16 17 18 10 9 8 7 6 5 4 3 2 1

CONTENTS

BOX, TABLE, AND FIGURES   **vii**

PREFACE   **ix**

CHAPTER 1 THE POLITICS OF POLICY   **1**

The "Well From Hell"   2

Making Energy Policy: A Primer   9

Policy Drivers   22

What Follows: American Energy in Transformation   33

CHAPTER 2 MANAGING ENERGY: A POLICY PRIMER   **34**

From Abundance to Insecurity   34

Governing and Choice: Energy Policy Options   46

Conclusion: The Governed Energy Marketplace   59

**CHAPTER 3 CARBON POLICY: PETROLEUM AND
NATURAL GAS**   **60**

An Era of Transformation   60

Petroleum   61

Governing Petroleum: Seeking a Policy Future   67

Natural Gas: A Mix of Rewards and Risks   81

Conclusion: The Foundation of Energy Policy   89

CHAPTER 4 CARBON POLICY: COAL   **91**

The Troubled Future of Future Gen   92

The Resource: "A Saudi Arabia of Coal"   93

The Politics of Coal Policy   98

Governance: Coal Policy and the Future   102

Coal, Climate Warming, Deadlock, and Improvisation   112

Conclusion: Coal at the Crossroads   116

CHAPTER 5 NUCLEAR ENERGY   **119**

A Rising and Fading "Renaissance"   119

The Commercial Nuclear Power Industry Today   122

Governance: Confronting the "Nuclear Option"   134

Conclusion   141

**CHAPTER 6 RENEWABLE ENERGY AND
ELECTRIC POWER**   **143**

A Path Not Yet a Highway   144

Renewable Energy: The Resource   145

Governance: The Policy Challenge of Renewables   153

Electric Power   165

Conclusion   174

CHAPTER 7 AMERICAN AND GLOBAL ENERGY   **176**

Rising Global Energy Demand   177

Global Climate Change   181

Improving Energy Security   186

"Riding the Wave" of Technology Innovation   188

Conclusion: The Global Imperative   191

ENDNOTES   **195**

INDEX   **211**

ABOUT THE AUTHOR   **217**

BOX, TABLE, AND FIGURES

BOX

7-1   Global Climate Change Impacts in the United States:
      Key Findings   182

TABLE

6-1   Top Ten States in Wind Potential   151

FIGURES

2-1   US Energy Production, 2010: Percent of
      Total Btu by Source   35
2-2   US Energy Consumption, 2010: By Energy Source   36
2-3   State Gasoline Tax Rates (Cents Per Gallon), 2013   51
2-4   Historical Average of Annual Energy Subsidies   53
2-5   Federal Energy Subsidies by Type: 2010 and 2007   54
3-1   United States Petroleum Consumption by Sector, 2012   62
3-2   US Imports and Exports of Petroleum
      Products, 1991–2012   63
3-3   US Net Imports of Petroleum as a Proportion of
      All Domestic Petroleum Consumption, 2012   63
3-4   US Natural Gas End Use, 2012   83
3-5   US Dry Natural Gas Production by Source, 1990–2040   84
3-6   US Shale Oil Formations, 2011   85
4-1   Top Coal Producing States, 2011   95
4-2   US Coal Production by Mining Method, 2009   96

5-1   Commercial US Nuclear Power Reactors, Location
      and Age, 2012   123
5-2   State Commercial Nuclear Reactor
      Waste Storage, 2010   129
6-1   Projected Primary Energy Use by Fuel, 1980–2035   145
6-2   Total US Energy Production, 2012   146
6-3   Renewable Energy Production: Percent of
      Total US Electric Supply, 2012   147
6-4   US Electricity by Source, 2010   167
6-5   State Renewable Portfolio Standards, Mandates,
      or Goals, 2010   173
7-1   OECD Versus Non-OECD Cumulative
      Demand Growth, 1996–2012   178
7-2   Projected Oil Consumption for the United States,
      China, and India, 2010–2030   179
7-3   Global CO_2 Emissions From Fossil Fuel Combustion and
      Some Industrial Processes, 2008 [million metric tons]   184
7-4   US Crude Oil Imports by Country of Origin, 2011   187

PREFACE

Not too long ago, the mayor of a small Louisiana parish reflected upon the sudden prosperity that seemed almost miraculously to attend some of his neighbors. The lucky ones, he observed, "went to bed one night poor and woke up the next day rich, enabled to buy a Cadillac and pay cash . . . It was kind of like the show *The Beverly Hillbillies*. Parish homeowners, he said, could typically earn "signing bonuses of $350 to as much as $30,000 an acre from gas companies, as well as royalties that can last for decades."[i]

This prosperity has a name. It is shale oil "fracking," a technology rapidly altering state and local economies across America, about which much will be said in coming chapters. Fracking is an example of what an increasing array of energy experts believe to be a remarkable and compelling change underway across the US energy economy. This book concerns this transformation and its impact upon America's traditional governance of its vast energy resources. Because this change is forcing a rethinking and revision of American energy policy, this narrative has two interrelated themes. The discussion gives necessary attention to traditional foundations of national energy policy, such as energy taxes, subsidies, environmental and market regulation. The narrative also focuses in every chapter upon recent technological innovations and economic events reshaping, sometimes profoundly, the substance of current energy

---

[i] Clifford Krauss and Tom Zeller, Jr., "When a Rig Moves In Next Door," *New York Times,* November 7, 2010, BU:1.

policy—technical innovations, such as fracking and wind farms, or economic transformations, such as the recent surge in US energy exports.

There can be uncertainties, of course, when riding the wave of predictions about America's changing energy future now increasingly frequent among energy professionals and policymakers—experts can miscalculate. However, the early evidence of many predicted changes in America's energy economy is already apparent; it compels the attention of current energy policymakers and requires recognition in any interpretation of current US energy politics and policy.

These important transformations in the American energy economy are "remarkable" in several respects. The change has been so recent that a book written about contemporary US energy policy only a few years ago would now be surprisingly outdated. The changes underway are also notable for the anticipated scope of their impact. The decision of the Obama administration in 2011 to move ahead aggressively with regulation of domestic CO_2 emissions from electric utilities, for instance, is predicted to alter the long-term economic future and market competitiveness of the domestic coal and natural gas industries.

The reader will note the interplay between themes of change and continuity in each of the following chapters, which focus upon American energy governance in different perspectives. The first chapter introduces institutions, actors, and settings essential to understanding the US energy policymaking process. Chapter 2 is a concise "primer" describing traditional policy instruments commonly encountered in energy governance. The following four chapters explore current politics and policy issues in four important energy domains: petroleum and natural gas, coal, nuclear energy, conservation and electric power. Each of these chapters has a common format:

- The Energy Source: Its Significance and Changing Status
- Currently Significant Resource Policies and Politics
- Contending Issues
  - Flashpoints of Current Controversy
  - Policy Alternatives

The final chapter, 7, explores important issues arising from US engagement in the global energy marketplace.

I am indebted to my reviewers and editors for their very important contribution to the creation and writing of this book and herewith absolve them of any responsibility for mistakes of commission or omission which—alas!—are my own. My able reviewers include: Christopher Burdett, Virginia Commonwealth University; Fred Curtis, Drew University; Greg Gangi, University of North Carolina, Chapel Hill; Marjorie Randon Hershey, Indiana University; Susan Hunter, West Virginia University; W. Henry Lambright, Syracuse University; Robert Lifset, University of Oklahoma; Daniel Press, University of California, Santa Cruz; and Allan Stoekl, Pennsylvania State University. The very helpful editorial oversight and chapter preparation were provided by Charisse Kiino, Davia Grant, Stephanie Palermini, and Patrice Sutton. Oh, yes, a word of appreciation to my two cats, Karma and Dharma, who purred contentedly at my side, looking absolutely confident about my ability, while I struggled many an hour for the proper ideas and the right words for the following narrative.

THE POLITICS OF POLICY

"You never want a serious crisis to go to waste," [Rahm] Emanuel, the incoming White House chief of staff, said at a *Wall Street Journal* conference last month. "And what I mean by that is an opportunity to do things that you think you could not do before. . . . What used to be long-term problems, be they in the health care area, energy area, education area—things . . . that were long-term are now immediate and must be dealt with."

NPR News, December 23, 2008[1]

Shortly before 10:00 p.m. on April 20, 2010, the massive drilling platform straddling the deepest drilling well in the world, a symbol of America's quest for energy security, exploded in the Gulf of Mexico fifty miles offshore. The fireball hurling thousands of feet into the tropical night unleashed the worst environmental disaster in US history and the second worst oil spill in world history. What followed the explosion of the Deepwater Horizon drilling platform was a human and ecological tragedy rapidly transformed into a signature event in the narrative of American energy regulation.

The Deepwater tragedy unfolded on the threshold of a decade now predicted to transform profoundly the way Americans use energy. Before 2017, it is expected that the United States will

- overtake Saudi Arabia and Russia to become the world's leading oil producer after decades of increasing dependence upon imported oil,

- become a net exporter of natural gas while natural gas increasingly displaces coal as the major fuel for producing electricity,
- experience a gradual decline in coal production as the electric power industry turns increasingly to natural gas for fuel,
- rely on renewable energy as a significant source of electric power,
- witness the failed revival of the commercial nuclear power industry, and
- enact new regulation to reduce significantly US global climate warming emissions.

The Deepwater explosion itself left a triple legacy. First, the decision to permit the platform and the incompetent regulation that facilitated the disaster were issues of energy governance, and the tragedy intensified an already embittered policy conflict over the future of American offshore energy exploration. Moreover, Deepwater added another disputed matter in the greater national controversy concerning how to govern all the nation's richly abundant energy resources—a deeply contentious and enduring debate pervading the whole history of American energy development. These matters are the substance of future chapters.

This chapter concerns the remaining legacy. Deepwater also created a political arena. The national media swiftly converged on the unfolding disaster to produce, before a huge national audience, a stage throwing into sharp relief many of the actors, institutions, and events inherent to the nation's energy policymaking and destined to appear among others throughout the chapters to follow. Deepwater provides a short but practical introduction to this chapter, which concerns the actors, institutions, and setting of American energy policymaking.

THE "WELL FROM HELL"

The drilling platform, managed by Transcon Corporation for British Petroleum (BP), the world's largest energy corporation, had operated inconspicuously for seven years before the explosion. What followed was a horrific spectacle. The aftermath became a gripping human tragedy staged before a huge national audience produced when national cable and network television devoted more than half their daily airtime to the disaster for more than a month.

"I Had No Idea It Could Do What It Did"

The disaster began when dangerously high methane gas pressure, building up in the underwater borehole, breached the elaborate safety equipment designed to prevent a gas blowout. First, an enormous volume of mud and oil rushed up the pipeline, erupted through the drilling platform, and cascaded down on the rig. A suffocating mist of methane gas rapidly followed, spread across the rig, and ignited. "Crew members were cut down by shrapnel, hurled across rooms and buried under smoking wreckage," reported the *New York Times*. "Some were swallowed by fireballs that raced through the oil rig's shattered interior. Dazed and battered survivors, half-naked and dripping in highly combustible gas, crawled inch by inch in pitch darkness, willing themselves to the lifeboat deck."[2] The crew had been meticulously prepared for the most plausible disasters. This one was wholly unimagined. "I had no idea it could do what it did," later remarked one veteran crew member.

In the furious fire consuming the drilling platform, eleven crew members died. The disaster left 126 survivors, including many badly injured crew members and four executives from BP and Transcon who were visiting the rig to celebrate its seven-year safety record. In little more than a day, the Deepwater platform incinerated, rolled over, and sank, beginning a frantic, eighty-nine-day struggle to cap the well and suppress the steady stream of crude oil leaking into the Gulf.

A Massive Impact

It is an axiom of modern energy politics that energy and environmental issues have become inseparably bonded. The media abundantly demonstrated this reality and the public quickly got the message that an unprecedented environmental disaster was unfolding. The Gulf event quickly engaged hundreds of environmental organizations from international to local in efforts to mitigate the emergency and intensified a continuing environmentalist campaign to reform radically American regulation of offshore energy exploration.

Before the wellhole was finally capped, an estimated 205 million gallons of crude oil and two million gallons of toxic dispersant intended to counteract the petroleum had spilled into the Gulf. The final magnitude of the environmental impact is still unresolved. The oil fouled 1,100 miles of beaches and marshes along the coasts of Louisiana, Mississippi, Alabama, and Mississippi together with 2,400 miles of levees. Despite a massive cleanup attempt involving at its peak more than 47,000 personnel, large patches of buried oil remain along Gulf beaches. The short-term damage to aquatic flora and fauna, especially to the ecology of coastal wetlands rimming the Gulf was severe; the long-term damage to the deep sea ecosystems, especially marine species, and the human health impact from exposure to the toxic dispersant Corexit are still under investigation. Estimates of the economic consequences of the oil spill also defy accurate calculation but will certainly exceed $8 billion, including a multiyear loss of employment and productivity to offshore fisheries, an especially severe problem for Louisiana, Texas, Alabama, and Mississippi because more than 87,000 square miles of commercial fishing grounds—about a third of the Gulf area—was closed for months, throwing thousands of workers out of employment.[3]

No corporation paid, and continues to pay, a greater price for the Deepwater incident than British Petroleum (BP). Corporate interests are inevitably stakeholders in every form of domestic energy production, but few petroleum producers had made a greater international effort than BP to cultivate a reassuring image of corporate environmental stewardship. The platform explosion made hash of BP's environmental image and depreciated its political clout. BP's subsequent frantic, frustrating efforts to cap the oil leak provoked international censure and anger from a growing legion of critics who held BP responsible for the catastrophe. The damaged corporate reputation was further diminished by the inept performance of the corporation's CEO, Tony Hayward, in a global interview following the event.

BP's economic damage continues to soar, the final cost unpredictable. By 2014, BP's own estimated expenses had exceeded $40 billion, including an initial $20 billion trust fund it has provided to satisfy the first public and private claims for damage, state and local response costs, and natural resource related expenses. Ongoing litigation, enough to employ a convention of lawyers, and large federal penalties for violation of the

Clean Water Act, have driven some estimates of BP's total expense close to $100 billion.

Federalism With Raw Edges

The Deepwater catastrophe from its inception was also a crisis of governance. Federal, state, and local governments are deeply implicated legally, economically, and politically in the production of every major source of American energy, and especially in the regulation of fossil fuel from exploration to consumption. Governmental collaboration in domestic energy management, while never ensured, has usually been cooperative. Here was an unprecedented regulatory disaster requiring an immediate federalized response—incisive, coordinated, and technologically sophisticated. Unfortunately, the Gulf explosion demonstrated that intergovernmental energy collaboration isn't ensured.

Since the Deepwater disaster was a federalized emergency, it quickly mobilized multiple governmental stakeholders. The peak of the response involved more than 45,000 individuals drawn from federal, state, local, and regional governmental agencies. What followed were weeks of difficult and often highly contentious efforts by the federal government to coordinate the rapidly multiplying array of other governmental stakeholders determined to protect their own interests.

The National Contingency Plan (NCP) existed to coordinate federal, state, and local governmental responses to such disasters. The governmental responses to the explosion, however, quickly degenerated into a persistent conflict between federal, state, local, and private interests about their respective roles and responsibilities as each attempted to intervene in some manner to stifle the oil leakage and to minimize their own anticipated risks from the impending environmental and economic damage.

The disaster plan called for the federal government, led by the US Coast Guard, to assume primary responsibility for controlling the spill and coordinating other governmental agency support. Other federal agencies quickly responding included the Department of the Interior, the Department of Homeland Security, the National Oceanographic and Atmospheric Administration, and the Department of Energy.

All the state and local governments within the Gulf, especially those closest to the spill from Louisiana, Texas, Mississippi, and Alabama, were aggressively involved and immediately dissatisfied with the federal response and soon created a "considerable confusion, delay and controversy that still prevails."[4] The contention early reached a level that persuaded the Coast Guard's Admiral Thad Allen, the very experienced and capable response Director, to warn his staff about the onrushing problems. "This isn't a sprint, or even a marathon," he cautioned, "this is a siege."[5] A final report on the Deepwater event noted the confusion:

> *During this spill . . . the Governors and other state political officials participated in the response in unprecedented ways, taking decisions out of the hands of career oil-spill responders. . . . Because the majority of the oil would come ashore in Louisiana, these issues of control mattered most there. Louisiana declined to empower the officials that it sent to work with federal responders within Unified Command, instead requiring most decisions to go through the Governor's office.*[6]

During the more than two months required to cap the stubborn oil leak, the local governments surrounding the Gulf also created their own, improvised responses to the spill without regard to whatever might have been prescribed by the National Contingency Plan. Louisiana's county governments (called "parishes"), for instance, attempted to assume as much independence in controlling the leaked petroleum as the state had asserted. Many parishes purchased their own equipment and created their own disaster management organization. Numerous private organizations, as well, rushed to share in disaster management often without regard for the managers and strategy of the National Contingency Plan.

"A Different Disaster": The Media Sends a Message

The omnipresent national media powerfully influenced the public's interpretation of the disaster and shaped profoundly much of the political repercussions. Once the national media had swiftly converged on the accident, they captured an enormous national audience for weeks while fashioning a narrative persuasively interpreting Deepwater's significance and shaping a public verdict concerning the responsibility for the disaster.

The Pew Research Center called Deepwater "a different kind of disaster" and observed that the spill "was a slow-motion disaster that exceeded the usual media attention span, commanding substantial media coverage week after week. From April 20 through July 28, the Gulf spill overwhelmed every other story in the mainstream media."[7] And the public was remarkably attentive. During three months following the explosion, an average of more than 54 percent on a major national poll reported that they were watching news of the catastrophe "very closely."[8] Media coverage, deliberately or not, also left most Americans convinced that BP was largely responsible for the tragedy—entirely responsible, according to many polls at the time.[9]

The Challenge of Policy Reform

For more than four decades preceding the Gulf event, a broad coalition of conservationists, environmentalists, and numerous allies had been waging a strenuous campaign to compel federal agencies to become more aggressive and rigorous in their regulation of domestic offshore energy exploration. Seven major Gulf oil spills had already occurred in the decade preceding the Deepwater incident.[10] For the critics, the Gulf had become a flagrant example of environmental risk and laggard regulatory oversight. But progress was slow and unsatisfactory, even though the Barack Obama administration had promised to deliver better regulatory management of offshore energy development.

Energy reformers were confronting a stubborn reality inherent in the design of the national governmental system: the powerful and pervasive tendency for national policy to change slowly and fitfully—an "incremental" policy style created by the American Constitution. But sudden bursts of rapid innovation and expansive policy reform do occur, albeit infrequently. This pattern of persistent incrementalism occasionally interrupted by bursts of accelerated change produces what has been called in policy studies a "punctuated equilibrium."[11] Just such a surge of policy transformation is what reformers might have expected from the Deepwater affair.

Critics had hoped the Gulf catastrophe would pack a political punch potent enough to drive Obama's relatively moderate offshore regulatory reforms in a much more aggressive and ambitious direction. The opportunity seemed obvious. The disaster, it was concluded in a later presidential investigation, had "undermined public faith in the energy industry, governmental regulators, and even our own capability as a nation to respond to crises" and thus seemed a compelling demonstration that something was dangerously deficient in current energy regulation.[12] Even while emergency workers were still fighting to control the underwater spill, the repercussions began to alter the Obama administration's regulatory reform agenda and unsettle the federal government's energy regulatory agencies. But, well into Obama's second presidency, the actual policy impact is disputed, and the sweeping reform of offshore energy regulation apparently so plausible in the wake of the crisis remains elusive.

"Only the First Step"

Some significant policy change was evident in the immediate wake of the Deepwater accident. A month before the accident, Obama had modified his original opposition to new oil exploration in the Gulf and had approved new drilling. The accident immediately compelled a White House reversal and a new drilling moratorium. Blaming the disaster on BP and on the federal Minerals Management Service (MMS) responsible for regulating offshore petroleum exploration, the administration initiated a sweeping investigation of BP's incompetent disaster management and the MMS's deficient regulatory oversight. And there was plenty of mismanagement and negligence to find.

The immediate results from this initial burst of investigations were new, numerous, federal indictments of BP for corporate violation of federal regulatory laws, the abolition of the discredited MMS and its replacement by a new federal regulatory agency with increased regulatory authority, and a wave of congressional hearings to accompany presidential investigations of the disaster and its aftermath. The Department of the Interior (DOI) initiated measures to improve coordination between federal and state governments in Gulf disaster management.

But these policy innovations, and others soon initiated, evolved slowly and contentiously while the public impact of the disaster—a critical consideration in producing an accelerated and comprehensive redesign of drilling policy—seemed to dissipate within weeks. Four months after the disaster, for instance, while the Gulf oil slick was still invading Gulf beaches, national polls reported that more than 50 percent of the public still approved of offshore oil exploration, and the disaster itself ceased to command major media attention.[13] Moreover, Louisiana and other Gulf states with economies enriched by royalties and employment flowing from Gulf energy exploration wanted no long-term interruption in these benefits—Deepwater explosion notwithstanding—and successfully applied pressure on the Obama administration, which reluctantly relaxed the new moratorium after only a few months.

Within months of the disaster, the federal courts—a certain venue in any important conflict about national energy regulation—were drawn into the conflict and will remain for years to come. The federal government sued BP to recover damages for criminal negligence and for violation of the federal Clean Water Act. Others with claims of injury against BP, including state and local governments, environmental groups, private parties, and other corporations, have initiated litigation.

More than three years after the disaster, both the presidential committee originally investigating the Deepwater explosion and a subsequent inquiry by the National Research Council concluded that the Obama administrative reforms were impeded by serious delays and but "a first step" toward a needed comprehensive reform and much more was required.[14] The Gulf disaster had receded so far from public consciousness as to virtually disappear, along with the momentary flicker of public interest in energy itself as a major public issue. Meanwhile, despite almost continuous congressional hearings since the event, by 2014 only two significant bills had been passed in response to the Obama administration's call for a much more comprehensive redesign of federal energy regulation. In short, after a brief burst of modest innovation and reform, policy was moving along incrementally.

MAKING ENERGY POLICY: A PRIMER

The slow and meandering pathway of policymaking unfolding in the aftermath of Deepwater Horizon is not unique to the Gulf tragedy nor to energy policy. The Gulf tragedy became a political stage throwing into sharp relief many elements common to the design of all domestic American policymaking, energy matters included. The influence of these policymaking fundamentals—along with some distinctive to energy policy—will be evident throughout later chapters as well, and merit a brief introduction.

The Constitution

The Constitution creates a master design for all US public policymaking. It is a document originally written by men deeply suspicious of a government armed with concentrated power and intended for a nation of farmers, shopkeepers, tradesmen, and merchants. What resulted was a government of countervailing forces with the power vested in each major institution limited by others and, in turn, limiting them.

This was not a government intended to "govern" energy production, or much else. The government that controls pollution and petroleum imports, licenses microwave ovens, regulates energy prices, fights oil spills, and oversees a thousand other programs now considered essential to energy management would have been unthinkable to the Framers. The Constitution has survived the enormous changes in American society and politics while preserving the political institutions it originally ordained. At the same time, the embedded cost is a continuing struggle to adapt constitutional institutions to the rapid and apparently accelerating pace of social, economic, and technological change nationally and globally.

Two of the Constitution's fundamental principles for dividing and limiting power—the elaborate checks and balances within the federal government and the division of power between the federal government and the states—fragment policymaking authority, exacerbate conflict between governmental institutions, and slow the pace of innovation. This dispersion of power often encourages deliberation and sensibility to a wide range of interests in policy issues, but at the constant risk of delay, conservatism, and unpredictability in making and implementing policy.

Checks and balances. The Constitution, as Richard E. Neustadt reminds us, creates a government of separated institutions sharing power.[15] This deliberate overlapping of authority, together with the

Constitution's vagueness in describing the nature of these powers and their proper division between governmental institutions, requires the institutions to collaborate if they are to govern and simultaneously incites rivalry between them. The checking and balancing of one institution by others, "ambition made to counteract ambition" in James Madison's words, overlays all policymaking within the federal government.

Institutional collaboration and conflict are most readily apparent at the national level in the relationship between the presidency and Congress. The Constitution invests each institution with unique powers, but it also compels them to share authority in legislating, taxing, and spending; oversight of the executive branch; and many other policymaking activities. Thus, the president may be responsible for ensuring that the Minerals Management Service enforces safety regulations on Gulf of Mexico oil drilling, but Congress writes the law the MMS implements. Without such collaboration, policymaking would be virtually impossible. The president and Congress, however, are divided by responsibility to different electorates, by institutional rivalries, by competing party loyalties, and by a constitutional obligation to check each other. Congress itself is a house divided into partisan factions, one congressional faction always committed to the electoral defeat of the White House incumbent.

Federalism. The Constitution also divides the government "vertically," granting some exclusively to Washington, some exclusively to the states, and some to be shared. This mixture of shared and separated authority encourages political rivalry as well as collaboration among the states and between the states and the federal government. Federalism gives a political form to state and regional interests, arms them with authority, and makes them influential participants in national policymaking. In the United States, policy is often the result of negotiation between a plurality of governmental entities—federal, regional, state, and local—whose distinctive interests are protected by federalism. One has only to observe the collaboration and collision between Washington and the Gulf States over management of the Deepwater explosion to confirm that federalism is alive and well today.

Incrementalism, "Punctuated Equilibrium," and Lurches

The governmental institutions created by the Constitution strongly encourage the incremental pace of policymaking, familiar to American government, in which "what is feasible is that which changes social states only by relatively small steps." Hence, decision makers, concerned with energy or otherwise, typically consider, among all the alternative policies that might be imagined to consider, only those relatively few alternatives that represent small or incremental changes from existing policies.[16]

But institutions and policymakers are sometimes shaken out of this deliberate pace by a potent fusion of sudden events and mobilized political interests that force rapid policy acceleration and innovation, producing what leading policy scholars Frank Baumgartner and Bryan Jones have characterized as a pattern of "punctuated equilibrium." In broad perspective, they note, "American political institutions were conservatively designed to resist many efforts at change and thus to make mobilizations necessary if established interests are to be overcome. The result over time has been institutionally reinforced stability interrupted by bursts of change. These bursts have kept the US government from becoming a gridlocked Leviathan despite its growth in size and complexity since World War II."[17] Thus, American policymaking is characterized by "long periods of relative stability or incrementalism interrupted by short bursts of dramatic change."[18]

These bursts of change, often called "shocks" and "lurches," have power but not always endurance. Perhaps the most powerful shocks to American energy policymaking since World War II were the "energy crises" of the 1970s, created by the sudden blockade of oil exports to America by Middle Eastern states. The resulting domestic petroleum shortfall badly disrupted the American economy, inspired consumer alarm, and rapidly elevated gasoline prices, compelling the federal government to hurriedly initiate new energy price controls, production regulations, and even some energy rationing. But few of these rapid policy lurches survived beyond the mid-1980s.

Governing Energy: Federal Institutions

The federal government dominates the institutional governance of energy. In addition to the White House, Congress, and the federal courts, at least eighteen other federal agencies are directly involved in more than 160 energy-related programs. These activities span the entire range of energy-related activities and often involve institutions that might seem unrelated to energy issues (such as the US Patent and Trademark Office, and the US Fish and Wildlife Service). The federal government in 2012 collected about $12 billion from energy-related programs including, especially, fees and royalties from development of federal energy resources and more than $35 billion in excise taxes on gasoline and other fuels.[19]

The White House. Since 1976, every president has included special advisors on energy and related policies within the White House staff. Beginning with George W. Bush in 2000, a rising sense of urgency about energy affairs has prompted the White House to initiate more aggressive efforts to coordinate energy policy within the executive branch with new White House staff arrangements. President Obama attempted the most ambitious of these innovations by initially creating, then abolishing, within the White House staff the White House Office of Energy and Climate Change Policy directed by an "Energy Czar," former EPA administrator Carol Browner, who reported directly to the President.[a]

Regardless of who is president and what priority may be given to energy policy, the president quickly discovers that, despite his lofty title as "chief executive," leading the large, persistently contentious, and extremely competitive federal energy departments and agencies, each preoccupied with its own mission and constituency, is a formidable and often frustrating task. The last comprehensive national energy plan, proposed by President George W. Bush in 2003, would have required coordination among twenty-nine different program activities, implemented by eleven different agencies—six agencies, for instance, were involved in programs relating to the impact of energy development and use of the environment.[20] Such coordination is always difficult and contentious.

---

[a] Browner's job was to promote "integration among different agencies; cooperation between federal, state, and local governments; and partnership with the private sector" in energy-related issues. In January 2011, however, Browner resigned as energy czarina, and the position was eliminated, suggesting that Obama, like his predecessors, had found energy planning too contentious politically to sustain a White House priority.

Congress. In formulating national energy policy, the president may propose and, within bounds usually dictated by Congress, may mandate energy programs, but ultimately, it is Congress that legislates energy policy, raises the revenue to underwrite, and oversees its implementation in the executive branch. The president's freedom to act independently of Congress on energy matters is always limited severely by law, custom, and political circumstance. Even when judges and administrators eventually formulate, interpret, and implement presidential directives, their policymaking is always constrained by congressional guidelines and oversight.

A multitude of committees. The most important centers of power within Congress are its numerous committees and subcommittees, the "little legislatures" inside the big one. The number of congressional committees and subcommittees with *energy* in their title or their jurisdiction is legion. In the 112th Congress (2011–2013), eleven House committees and four Senate committees exercised some authority over energy matters explicitly in their titles. However, numerous other committees, easily exceeding a dozen in each chamber, were also deeply implicated in energy policymaking by virtue of their comprehensive authority in related matters, such as the budget, foreign affairs, conservation, and environmental management.

The vigorous conflict over energy policy produced by each chamber's own squabbling, competitive committees is intensified by rivalries between House and Senate energy-related committees. Energy committees, within and between the chambers, often respond to different energy interests. This dispersion of authority among so many legislative entities can sometimes improve the quality of energy policy. But the bargaining and negotiating imposed by diverse congressional interests with leverage in the energy policy process often yields vague, complicated, and inconsistent legislation. Often, no legislative reconciliation of divergent interests is possible, producing the sort of deadlock that frustrated Obama's efforts in his first term to secure congressional approval of his climate warming proposals.

Five hundred and thirty-five ambassadors. The fragmentation of power in Congress is further advanced by the 535 geographical constituencies represented in both congressional chambers, a vast array of diverse parochial local interests with a powerful influence in the legislative process. Constituents regard their senators and representatives as ambassadors to Washington from their home districts, sent there to energetically promote and protect "the folks back home." It is hard for any member to resist pressures to act as local agents for their electorate.

With the advent of e-mail, cell phones, and mobile Internet access, legislators are now only a few keystrokes away from constituency voices. It's small wonder that many legislators consider their constituencies as an extension of their own personalities. Many congressional veterans can understand the late Alaskan Senator Ted Steven's angry warning to colleagues who voted against opening the Arctic National Wildlife Refuge to new energy exploration: "People who vote against this today are voting against me, and I will not forget it."[21]

Thus, when the Senate Committee on Energy and Natural Resources' Democratic majority proposed in 2009 a measure to expand the scope of offshore oil and gas exploration in the Gulf of Mexico, state loyalty trumped party for five of the committee's thirteen Democrats. Senator Mary Landrieu from Louisiana, for example, ordinarily a strong supporter of expansive drilling in the Gulf, opposed the measure because none of the potential federal royalties would come to Louisiana, while Senator Robert Menendez (D-N.J.) opposed the measure because it might encourage drilling off the New Jersey coast.[22]

The executive branch. The executive branch of the federal government is a constitutional fiction, even when organization charts confine the welter of administrative agencies called "the bureaucracy" within the boundary of the president's executive authority. Within the executive branch are thirteen cabinet departments, fifty-two independent agencies, five regulatory commissions, and numerous lesser entities. More than 2.7 million federal employees divide their loyalties among these institutions.

Congress and the courts often limit presidential authority. Political obstacles constantly confound White House designs for administrative management. The president must contend with agency self-interest, Congressional involvement in agency affairs, and the claims of an agency's own clientele. The president may be a poor administrator or bored with the job.

The impact of this bureaucratic pluralism is pervasive in energy policy. Congress and the White House personnel rarely formulate major policy without consulting with the affected energy agencies. Moreover, agencies have strong and conflicting preferences about energy management that often grow from their differing constituencies. For example, the Federal Energy Regulatory Commission (FERC), responsible under the 1935 Federal Power Act for promoting abundant, reliable energy supply, is more congenial to expansive energy production than the US Environmental Protection Agency (EPA) with its legislative mandate to control the environmental degradation from fossil fuel energy production.

Bureaucracy's influence in energy policymaking is rooted in the delegated authority and discretionary judgment inherent in the programs implemented by federal agencies. Congress must often grant to agencies very broad, general authority to implement programs, leaving administrators to decide when to apply the law in specific cases and how to interpret vague or inconsistent provisions. When the secretary of the interior decides that a segment of a national forest should qualify as wilderness to be forever free of mineral exploration and mining or when EPA's administrator determines that a coal-fired utility must install new pollution controls to meet air quality standards, policy is being made. Delegated and discretionary authority in energy policymaking also ensures that all major interests with a stake in federal energy programs will gravitate toward the agencies implementing those programs in an effort to sway the exercise of this authority.

Among the 16 federal departments and independent agencies most often concerned with some aspect of energy policy, four cabinet-level departments and four nondepartmental agencies assume particular importance because of their size, the scope of their energy-related authority, and the variety of programs that they implement.

The Department of Energy (DOE). Created in 1977 as a cabinet department, DOE's responsibilities now sprawl across the entire range of energy-related federal government activities.[23] In 2013, the DOE had a budget of $27.2 billion and about 16,000 employees. Currently, the DOE implements policies involving nuclear power, fossil fuels, and alternative energy resources, and it assumes responsibility for advancing the national, economic, and energy security of the United States, for supervising the national laboratories initially created for the development of nuclear weapons, and implementing the White House's National Energy Policy Development Group. DOE also inherited a double dose of hugely expensive and contentious nuclear regulatory responsibility: the agency administers the enormously costly, technically difficult, and politically volatile environmental cleanup of the nation's former nuclear weapons facilities and also assumes responsibility for the safe disposal of nuclear waste from the nation's commercial and military weapons facilities.[24]

From its inception, the DOE has had too much to do, too few friends, and too little authority. Much of the authority for domestic energy planning remains with the Nuclear Regulatory Commission, the EPA, the Department of Agriculture, and other agencies beyond DOE's statutory reach or political influence.

Notwithstanding these handicaps, the DOE has still improved energy management in significant ways. For the first time, all energy research and development (R&D) planning and implementation is organized through a single agency. The creation of the Energy Information Administration (EIA) within DOE has provided the federal government an increasingly large and richly diversified source of energy data independent of energy producers, the largest independent source of credible energy data within the United States, and the most commonly cited of all domestic energy information sources.

The Department of the Interior. The US Department of the Interior, is the nation's largest public land manager, the steward and trustee of America's vast public domain and all its energy resources. The secretary of the DOI heads a department that in 2012 employed 70,000 people, including expert scientists and resource-management professionals, in eight different bureaus and offices.[25]

Several of these bureaus and offices are especially important to federal energy management. The Bureau of Land Management (BLM) is responsible for leasing and oversight of energy exploration and production on more than 256 million acres of public domain, most of this land west of the Mississippi River, and 1.7 billion acres of the Outer Continental Shelf. These public lands are a primary source of current domestic energy production, a bountiful source of federal revenue, and a huge reserve for potential future energy development. The bureau has historically been the epicenter of controversy and competition between conservationists and energy developers over access to the energy reserves on these vast federal lands.

The public lands currently produce more than 30 percent of the nation's energy production, including 39 percent of natural gas, 35 percent of oil, 42 percent of coal, 17 percent of hydropower, and half the nation's geothermal energy.[26] In 2013, the Department of the Interior collected more than $11 billion from energy production on public lands and offshore areas.[27] Additionally, the federal lands provide rights of way for energy transmission lines, rail systems, pipelines, and other energy development infrastructure. Federal lands are also estimated to contain approximately 68 percent of all undiscovered US oil reserves and 74 percent of undiscovered natural gas.[28]

Rising concern over domestic energy supply now casts the public lands as an "energy frontier" where potentially vast new sources of renewable energy await development. The DOE estimates, for example, that federal lands can potentially generate 350,000 megawatts of electric power (a megawatt will produce enough energy to power as many as 900 average homes), provide 23 million acres for solar energy production, and produce significant new geothermal electric energy.[29] Currently, for example, almost three thousand wind turbines on California's public lands are producing electric power for 300,000 people.

The Office of Surface Mining Reclamation and Enforcement is responsible for implementing the Surface Mining Control and Reclamation Act (1977), the federal regulatory program to control the adverse environmental impacts of surface coal mining and to restore abandoned surface mine sites to ecological vitality. An estimated 5,200 abandoned mine sites, many extremely hazardous environmentally currently require remediation.[30] The Bureau of Ocean Energy Management, Regulation, and Enforcement (BOEMRE) regulates the development of energy resources, administers leasing of energy exploration, and enforces environmental protection laws related to energy production on the Outer Continental Shelf. The Deepwater Horizon accident underscored the growing importance of the BOEMRE and the Outer Continental Shelf, which is estimated to contain about 60 percent of oil and 40 percent of natural gas reserves still undeveloped in the United States.

Federal Energy Regulatory Commission. The Federal Energy Regulatory Commission (FERC) exercises its important energy development and regulatory authority, like BOEMRE, largely beyond the scope of public attention and interest. Nevertheless, the FERC, an independent regulatory agency composed of five commissioners appointed by the president, exercises critically important energy management authority, including jurisdiction over interstate electricity sales, wholesale electric rates, hydroelectric licensing, natural gas pricing, and oil pipeline rates. It also reviews and authorizes liquefied natural gas (LNG) terminals, pipelines, and nonfederal hydropower projects. The Energy Policy Act (2005) significantly enlarged FERC's authority by investing it with responsibility for tracking federal government progress on the act's mandated energy developments including liquefied natural gas projects, electric supply, the Alaska natural gas pipeline, requirements for new energy market transparency, pipeline land planning, and much else.

Nuclear Regulatory Commission. The Nuclear Regulatory Commission (NRC) is responsible for ensuring the safe use and environmental security of radioactive materials for nonmilitary purposes. The NRC, composed of five commissioners appointed by the president and confirmed by the Senate for five-year terms, is primarily responsible for regulating all nonmilitary reactors, nuclear materials, and the transportation, storage, and disposal of all nuclear waste.

These responsibilities produce a high political profile and predictably thrust the commission into public controversy over the management of the nation's commercial nuclear power sector, as chapter 5 illustrates. Critics of the nuclear power industry almost ritually indict the NRC for regulatory failures, and proponents of commercial nuclear power just as often complain that the NRC is insufficiently energetic in protecting and promoting the industry.

Environmental Protection Agency. The EPA, created by an executive order of President Nixon in 1970, is the largest federal regulatory agency in terms of budget and personnel. Its responsibilities embrace an extraordinarily large and technically complex array of programs ranging across the whole domain of energy-related environmental management. These programs include regulation of energy-related air and water pollutants, hazardous and toxic wastes, and chemical substances, including radioactive waste. The agency presently has about 18,000 employees and an annual budget exceeding $7 billion.

The agency, whose administrator is appointed by the president, consists of a Washington, DC, headquarters and ten regional offices, each headed by a regional administrator. Political controversy is the daily bread of the EPA's leadership. Almost all its significant energy-related regulatory decisions, such as rules for the disposal of coal ash from coal-fired electric power plants or limits of toxic air emissions from industrial boilers, are predestined to conflict, often enduring for years or decades, among regulators, the regulated, and their respective allies. Thus, EPA's mission is bound to create problems for the White House. "The White House—any White House—doesn't want to hear an awful lot from the E.P.A," observed former EPA Administrator William Reilly. "It's not an agency that ever makes friends for a president. In the cabinet room, many of the secretaries got along with each other, but they all had an argument with me. It's the nature of the job."[31] Nonetheless, the EPA is a major, inevitable participant in almost all the significant energy-related White House policymaking.

Governing Energy: The States

The States are important policymakers and stakeholders in US energy affairs. As policymakers, states share with Washington regulatory agencies the authority over energy production and distribution. Energy producing states, such as Oklahoma, Louisiana, and Texas, set the allowable rate for oil and gas production from existing wells, but the federal government, until recently, mandated the wellhead price of natural gas moving through interstate pipelines. The Energy Policy Act of 2005 requires that federal and state regulatory agencies share authority for the siting of interstate power transmission lines.[32] State regulatory authorities customarily set rates and other standards for investor-owned utilities—how much electricity, for instance, must be produced from renewable energy sources. Both federal and state governments regulate the siting of commercial nuclear power plants, tax energy production, such as coal production, and set health and safety standards for energy facilities. By 2014, federal-state collaboration in promoting energy conservation had emerged as an important aspect of national energy policy.[33] Most federal energy regulations are also enforced through the states.[b]

States are also stakeholders in the energy economy. The states well-endowed with fossil fuel or hydropower resources (sometimes called the "energy patch") are heavily dependent economically upon energy production, highly sensitive to changes in the supply, demand, and price for energy, and fiercely protective toward the political and economic interests of their energy producers. Any sharp decline in world petroleum prices, or significant increases in global petroleum production, can create sometimes severe, adverse impacts upon the energy states. Few states are more vulnerable to changes in the domestic petroleum supply and prices than Alaska, where all state enterprises have been subsidized by petroleum revenues. In 2013, Alaska's fossil fuel royalties were about $2.14 billion, or more than 90 percent of the state's total revenue income. (Every Alaska citizen also receives an annual share of this wealth, which has varied in recent years between $ 1,600 to $878 for each individual).[34] "Energy poor" states heavily dependent upon imported petroleum and natural gas, primarily in the Northeast, are vigilant to promote favorable regulation of national energy prices and energy transportation infrastructures essential to their economic growth.

Historically, the energy-producing states have been aggressive in creating regional energy alliances to protect or to expand their domestic and global energy markets and to limit petroleum production, if possible, when it seemed expedient to protect domestic petroleum prices. The energy producers, especially the coastal states, have also been ambiguous and vacillating about federal government efforts to promote more energy production within their jurisdictions. This has been a contentious matter for states with potential fossil fuel reserves on their Outer Continental Shelf (OCS) lands—especially California, Louisiana,

---

[b] During the energy crises of the 1970s, Congress authorized the states to enforce many other regulatory programs including the development of emergency preparedness plans, heating and cooling standards for buildings, weatherization programs for residential dwellings, and reform of electric utility pricing policies.

Oregon, Washington, Texas, Hawaii, Massachusetts, North Carolina, and Alaska—where fears of an environmental disaster, such as Deepwater Horizon, continually clash with the economic enticements of energy production.

There is no ambiguity, however, about the constant enthusiasm among almost all states to capture a portion of federal spending on energy-related activities, especially when the spending is generous. For example, after Congress enacted the American Recovery and Reinvestment Act (2009), providing $3.4 billion in federal support for innovative "clean coal" technology development, public officials in Texas, Illinois, and several other states immediately launched an extensive media and political campaign to convince Energy Secretary Steven Chu to invest in their competing clean-coal power plants, which would be among the most costly electric power plants ever proposed and a huge economic stimulus to the winning state.[35]

The states have also been energy "policy laboratories" where innovative energy policies have originated, sometimes becoming models for federal policy and often generating pressure on a reluctant Washington to act on energy issues. Recently, numerous states have enacted legislation or regulations creating Renewable Portfolio Standard (RPS), requiring utilities to generate a portion of their power from renewable energy sources. And, while Congress and the White House have debated and deadlocked since 2000 about creating a national regulatory policy to control climate-warming emissions (greenhouse gases, or GHG), a number of states have enacted various regional "cap-and-trade" regulatory strategies and other innovations to initiate their own regulatory regimes to cap their GHG emissions.[36]

POLICY DRIVERS

Energy policy is shaped in a political environment often subject to unpredicted and shifting public moods, to cultural and technological change, global military and economic affairs, contentious organized pressure groups, a legacy of inherited and possibly troublesome existing policy, and other realities—what have been called policy "drivers." These inevitable drivers make policymaking as much an art as a craft.

Public Opinion

Elective officials work in a culture saturated with sensibility about the public mood and dense with information about public attitudes. Most of the time, however, energy issues hover at the outer edge of public interest, neither compelling attention, nor lapsing into irrelevance to policymaking.[37] Between 2009 and 2013, for instance, most national opinion polls seldom, if ever, listed energy among any major issues concerning the public. Public understanding of energy issues confronts public officials with an especially formidable task. Energy management, observes public opinion expert Daniel Yankelovich, is a "unique challenge to policy makers: the combination of a fast-moving, complex problem and a comparatively slow-moving public trying to come to grips with it."[38] It usually requires an international crisis, a dramatic media event, or a powerful economic shock to the consumer's pocketbook to compel public attention to energy matters.

Gas pumps have become a national public warning system about energy affairs. The pump price of gasoline will most readily connect the public with energy policy. "When it comes to energy prices," writes economist Jon Krosnick, "voters are likely to think the same way—they are likely to blame the White House at least partly for gas prices across the country but not for their own personal pain at the pump. So a person's vote is likely to be influenced by perceptions of the nation's gas prices and efforts to reduce them. People will debate many questions 'Why exactly are gas prices as high as they are? Is it the speculators? Is it the supply? Is it the war in Iraq?' And the more they see the White House as having responsibility for current national conditions, the more people will vote accordingly."[39]

Even when Americans react with barometric sensitivity to short-term fluctuations in domestic petroleum prices, energy affairs are otherwise low on the scale of public issue concerns. In 2011, for example, at a time when retail gasoline prices were approaching $4.00 a gallon, "energy" ranked well below ten other issues in the public's issue priorities, and global climate change, perhaps the most constantly discussed energy issue by public media in the last five years, ranked next to last.[40]

The Economy

If energy seldom earns a mention among public issue concerns, the economy seldom fails to get attention—lots of it. Since 2009, opinion polls have shown that the public has almost always rated the economy the most important national issue.[41] In fact, energy and the economy are inseparably related. The nation's energy markets are deeply embedded in the larger setting of national and international economics. Energy markets respond, often rapidly, to macro- and microeconomic events and, in turn, constitute a powerful influence upon domestic and global economic affairs. This profound interdependence between energy markets and their broader national and international setting affects the domestic energy economy in several significant respects.

One characteristic of the domestic energy economy is the interdependence of market supply, price, and demand among major energy sources. Domestic energy prices, supply, and demand characteristically fluctuate as the market status of one or another source alters.

Another potent influence upon energy development is the availability of investment capital. The domestic commercial nuclear power industry has required large infusions of capital from both private business and federal government to evolve and survive. Renewable energy sources, such as wind, solar, geothermal, and biomass, have historically depended largely for their development upon federal subsidies, tax incentives, and R&D funding. Even so, wind farms, especially, require so much space for giant wind turbines that they often depend upon banks to finance 50 percent of the project cost. And corporate planning for future energy development is usually contingent upon the availability of new capital.[42]

Energy policy also reacts with acute sensitivity not only to changes in existing supply but also to estimates of future energy availability. While concern over future global crude oil reserves has haunted all national energy policy discourse for many decades, a more recent, if less widely publicized event has been the discovery of significant new domestic natural gas reserves. New estimates, based upon innovations in gas recovery technology, have fortified proponents of new natural-gas fueled electric power plants likely to emit less climate changing gasses than primarily coal-fired installations.

Energy prices are also a major component in the government's cost of living index and numerous other federal programs, such as entitlements, also indexed to consumer prices. Energy prices are considered by government policymakers to be a measure of consumer economic health and national economic vitality, thus, easily becoming a major cudgel to batter the political opposition or brandish in defense of existing policy in political debate.

Crisis

Crisis, especially when dramatic, media magnified, and ominous, is a potent driver of policy change, often *the* most powerful force. Over time, crises can release—at least temporarily—energy policy mired for years or decades in Washington political deadlock, creating the punctuated equilibrium characteristic of contemporary energy policymaking since the initial Organization of the Petroleum Exporting Countries (OPEC) oil embargo of 1972. The political force of crisis is not lost on policy practitioners and stakeholders, who often labor in policy venues to anoint a favored issue a "crisis" and thereby invest it with an urgency it might otherwise lack.

Political Partisanship

National energy issues since the 1970s have been characterized by a gradually increasing partisan cleavage over policy options between presidents, within Congress and among the public. Such vital energy issues as exploration for petroleum reserves in the Arctic National Wildlife Refuge (ANWR) and the Outer Continental Shelf (OCS), the pace of future fossil fuel mining, the relative priority for renewable and conventional energy, and the credibility of global climate warming now tend to divide Democrats and Republicans in Washington and among the electorate. Proclaiming an energy issue, or a proposed solution, to be a "Democratic" or "Republican" matter, moreover, arms policymakers with an evocative symbol that may attract to policy debate certain segments of the public with strong partisan sympathies who rally partisans behind a proposed solution.[43]

In general, Republicans in the White House and Congress have been more favorable than Democrats to relaxing environmental restraints on energy development, to accelerated petroleum and other fossil fuel exploration and utilization, to decreased taxation of energy production and, generally, to less governmental involvement in energy markets. Even before Obama's presidential commission investigating the Gulf disaster submitted its report to Congress in 2011, combative partisanship surfaced. In the House of Representatives, Republicans alleged, and Democrats denied, that the commission's secret agenda was to promote Democratic efforts to limit, if not prohibit, future offshore energy exploration.[44] When the commission subsequently submitted its recommendations to Congress, Democrats and Republicans on the House committee reviewing the report renewed that debate.

Partisanship has, in many instances, also polarized public opinions about the scientific and technical information supporting one energy policy option or another. This partisan politicization has been especially conspicuous in recent years over the credibility of global climate warming and its scientific basis. For example, Republican voters have been considerably more likely than Democrats to disbelieve in the existence of global climate warming, to attribute climate warming (if it occurred) to nonhuman sources, and to question the credibility of climate warming science and scientists.[45] When energy science becomes politicized, the resulting debate may be powerfully polarizing, placing scientists and other technical experts under intense pressure to shape their professional opinions in favor of one side or another and thus to compromise their scientific objectivity. The inherent tension between the objectivity essential to scientific inquiry and the partisanship deeply rooted in contemporary conflict over national energy policy now predictably invests conflict over policy options with assertions that one side or another has compromised the integrity of scientific information to its advantage.

Environmentalism

The environmental movement created a political fusion in which energy and environmental issues are now tightly and durably bonded. A political symmetry emerges: energy policy is now environmental policy; environmental policy is energy policy. The presence of environmentalism in all public discourse about energy policy has become an elemental force in shaping energy regulatory policies and public attitudes about energy regulation.

A recurrent theme in subsequent chapters on specific energy resources is their environmental implications. A few preliminary statistics can suggest the pervasive scope of environmental effects at every stage of energy use—extraction, refining, transportation, and consumption:

- Electric utilities produce about 66 percent of the sulfur oxides air emissions in the United States.[46]
- More than 33,000 abandoned hard rock mines, primarily associated with coal extraction, created serious environmental degradation in the twelve western states and Alaska.[47]
- Fossil fuel mining is a major source of surface and groundwater contamination by acid mine drainage; heavy metal contamination; and leaching, soil erosion, and sedimentation.

Environmental standards also influence the market price and competitiveness of different energy sources. Safety standards, for example, raise the capital cost of commercial nuclear power facilities and diminish the competitiveness of nuclear power in many markets where it competes with fossil fuels for electric power generation.

The compounding of environmentalism with energy production defines contemporary public debate about national energy management in several important respects. Current public discussion about energy policy is often framed as a "trade-off" between the various benefits of energy development and environmental protection—or, more fundamentally, as a debate about whether such a trade-off even exists. Public opinion polls, for example, frequently suggest that most of the public perceives, or can be persuaded to perceive, that energy and environmental protection are competing priorities.

Coupling environmental values with energy production has also become a defining framework in policy debate over the future of the public domain that constitutes one-fourth of America's continental land, the greatest natural inheritance still held by the federal government in trust for the American people. The western public lands are estimated to have a potential to generate wind and solar energy equal to almost three times current US electric generating capacity.[48] But much of this ecologically valuable land is fragile biosphere, inhabited by endangered species or valued culturally and esthetically by those who fear the degradation may come in the form of renewable energy technologies like solar and wind power.

Another increasingly significant instance of environmentalism's impact upon the course of national energy development is the association of conventional energy production with global climate warming. Environmental opponents of aggressive new fossil fuel development and proponents of increased fossil fuel production both recognize that public belief about the credibility of human-induced global climate change and its basis in fossil-fueled combustion can powerfully influence public preferences for future domestic energy production.

Interest Groups

So embedded in government are organized interests that it often seems to critics of interest-group power, such as political scholar and commentator George Will, that if "you want to understand your government, don't begin by reading the Constitution. Instead, read selected portions of the Washington telephone directory containing listings for all organizations with titles beginning with the word National."[49] Interest group access to the inner citadels of energy policymaking is treated with public ambivalence. It is the excesses, not the existence, of group claims to influence that invite censure. That privately organized interests should share in formulating public energy policy excites almost no one.

Energy-related interest groups have been among the largest contributors to congressional and presidential election campaigns, and, among the top spenders for lobbying among all national interest groups. In 2010, for instance, the nonpartisan Center for Responsive Politics, which monitors interest group political activities, reported that more than 1,600 individuals lobbied Congress and the White House on behalf of conventional and nuclear energy organizations.[50] Since 1990, most of the money spent on political campaigns by the energy sectors has gone to Republican candidates.[51] The energy sector is also among the largest of all interest groups contributing money to political campaigns and lobbying: in 2012–2013, this sector spent an estimated $144 million on such activity.[52] Fossil fuel and nuclear power interests dominate the energy sector in campaign spending, lobbying, and other political activities.

The rise of new issues on the governmental agenda often triggers the formation of new groups and, conversely, new issues on the agenda reflect the growing political influence of new interests. In recent decades, traditional energy sector groups have been increasingly challenged politically by a relatively small but growing array of energy-related environmental groups, state and regional interests, and new technology advocates, especially groups promoting renewable and nonconventional energy.

Energy administrators routinely consult, formally and informally, with representatives of affected organized interests who become "stakeholders." Congressional legislation frequently mandates that agencies responsible for implementing important legislation create advisory committees that include representatives of the programs affected by the legislation. If Congress fails to create an advisory committee, agencies often create their own. This ensures that these interests will be informed and solicited for their opinions during the program's implementation. In the Department of Energy (DOE), for example, the National Petroleum Council, consisting of almost 100 individuals representing major energy producers, research institutions, technology producers and related groups, is among the high-level DOE advisory groups, reporting directly to the secretary of DOE. The agency assuredly does not lack advisory help. DOE has at least 20 high-level program advisory groups and has terminated another 60 since its creation. However, compared with older federal departments, many of which have more than 100 advisory groups, DOE is hardly in the business.[53]

Administrative agencies also collaborate with organized groups by "working the clientele." Agencies turn to organized interests strongly supportive of their mission when help is needed. Thus, when DOE and the Environmental Protection Agency (EPA) struggle over congressional proposals to increase or relax pollution controls on public utilities, both sides mobilize their clientele to bring pressure on Congress. EPA appeals to environmentalists, DOE to utilities.

The Tyranny of the Electoral Cycle

Elections have an imperious hold on presidents, members of Congress, and their respective staffs. For elected officials, the clock segmenting the time during which decisions are made ticks away in four- and eight-year intervals. These are Washington's constitutionally appointed electoral cycles. Within these time frames, federal officials will continually sift policy decisions for their electoral implications. "Good" and "best" policy is often defined as much by electoral impact as by its substantive merit.

Elections affect energy policymakers in two particularly important ways. First, the short term dominates the long term. Presidents and legislators may talk about programs enduring for decades or defend the interest of unborn generations, but their eye is usually upon the program's impact on the next primary or general election. "Presidents and their staffs arrive at the White House charged up to produce results, to make good on the pledges of the campaign," observed presidential scholar Thomas Cronin. "The President and his staff think in terms of two- and four-year frames, at most. They strive to fulfill campaign pledges and related priorities with a sense of urgency, seeking ways to build a respectable image for the forthcoming electoral campaign."[54]

Members of Congress are similarly preoccupied with elections. The constituency is an unseen presence at any deliberation about public policy, the electoral impact on the folks back home a continual preoccupation. Any congressman or senator could probably sympathize with the two-term Democratic congressman caught between the dominant economic interests in his constituency and his own desire to support a decades-long regulatory program to reduce acid precipitation. "I feel," he lamented to a reporter, "as if I pitched my tent on an anthill, there are so many people crawling over me. . . . I can't win either way. This is how representatives get whipsawed. . . . I vote one way and the people say 'Aren't you supposed to represent the national interest? I vote the other way and people say, 'We sent you there to represent us.'"[55]

Globalization

The most potent impact of the domestic energy crises of the 1970s was the harsh message that the United States was increasingly vulnerable to the vicissitudes of global energy supply, politics, and economics. In the years since 1970, the United States has had to recognize, among other unwelcome realities, that it controls a significant but diminishing proportion of the remaining global petroleum reserves and may never achieve "energy independence." In this twenty-first-century world, the United

States competes increasingly with rapidly developing non-Western nations for available petroleum supply, still stakes much of its national security on insecure foreign petroleum and unstable national governments, and confronts potentially severe domestic environmental risks from global fossil fuel consumption it cannot control. Economically, the domestic energy markets are increasingly sensitive to global macroeconomic events such as fluctuations in international energy exploration and production. All these global interdependences are tethered to equally significant economic implications and political complexities.

Reserves and Resources: How Much Energy?

Succeeding chapters concerning specific energy sources begin with a brief assessment of the domestic energy supply, a fundamental consideration in all energy policymaking. However, disagreement over the available amount of a resource, especially fossil fuel energy, is a predictably contentious prelude to many discussions about how to manage the resource. Experts with respectable credentials frequently disagree about the precise amount of an energy resource physically available domestically or internationally.

One reason for this disagreement is different estimates concerning how much energy is recoverable under current economic and technological conditions (an *energy reserve*) and how much of the total energy source exists (an *energy resource*). A petroleum producer or a coal mining company, for instance, would define its reserves as the amount of petroleum or coal it is reasonably sure exists and can be located, extracted, and marketed under current conditions. Such companies would usually have a much larger energy resource. Additionally, experts may agree about the size of an energy resource or reserve, yet predictions of future availability may vary because of differing assumptions concerning future market demand. Chapter 3, concerning petroleum and natural gas, illustrates how predictions about a future natural gas "boom" depend, in good measure, upon whether the environmental impact of rapidly developing *fracking* technology that extracts natural gas from oil shale will be environmentally and economically acceptable.

Estimates of energy reserves and resources constantly change as new sources are discovered, older ones depleted, and economic or technological conditions alter. Consider the example of petroleum production. The rising price of domestic petroleum after 2000, for instance, made extraction of petroleum from the oil shale—previously considered too expensive to produce in quantity—now attractive to petroleum producers and refiners. Stated differently, with the right combination of technological innovation, market price, and anticipated demand, an energy resource can become a reserve.

National Security

It is a measure of the impact of domestic energy management upon national security that discussions of US energy policy are now commonly framed as "energy security." In the years since the energy shocks of the 1970s, national security has become increasingly vulnerable in all important senses—military, diplomatic, economic, political—to alterations in global energy markets. Slowly, very reluctantly, most American policymakers have accepted the reality that this vulnerability is likely to continue for decades, perhaps permanently.[56] Since 2010, however, the US boom in fossil fuel fracking, discussed in chapters 3 and 7, has prompted many experts to suggest that a new era of energy independence with its implied improvement in national security may be imminent. Others aren't so sure. In any case, *any* issue concerning US energy development will sooner or later involve a discussion of the national security implications.

In an effort to buffer the future impact of sudden imported petroleum shortfalls, the United States in 1975 created the Strategic Petroleum Reserve (SPR) located in salt domes along the Gulf of Mexico. The SPR, the world's largest emergency petroleum reserve, containing as much as 727 million barrels of crude oil, could provide, at best, several months of crude oil to meet a heavy domestic demand. Despite these and other measures to diminish the security risks posed to the United States by sudden adverse international energy events, the United States remains intricately embedded in the global energy system. Thus, exposed to the impact of global energy disturbances, practically all significant domestic energy policies, and their modification, compel domestic national policymakers to conceive the issues in the framework of national security.

WHAT FOLLOWS: AMERICAN ENERGY IN TRANSFORMATION

This chapter is a prelude to chapters that explore the unfolding transformations in the sources of American energy, together with the politics, and policy challenges emerging with this transformation. Institutions, actors, and themes inherent to energy policymaking, which constitute this prelude, will reappear in different combinations throughout these succeeding chapters.

The design of the succeeding chapters, each involving a different energy source, is similar. Each discussion includes these sections:

- The Energy Source: Its Significance and Changing Status
- Policy Prologue: Currently Important Resource Policies
- Contending Issues: The Flashpoints of Current Controversy
  - Policy Alternatives
  - The Play of Politics: Issue Activists
  - Venues: National, State, Global

In two of the following chapters, the discussion focuses upon the nation's primary sources of carbon fuels, petroleum, and natural gas (chapter 3) and coal (chapter 4). The subsequent narrative (chapter 5) concerns the continuing policy controversy over the future of domestic nuclear power. The final chapters concern electric power, renewables, and conservation (chapter 6) and the global policy arena (chapter 7).

MANAGING ENERGY
A Policy Primer

> "It was like gnawing on a rock."
> *Former president Jimmy Carter on his efforts*
> *to regulate the US energy economy*[1]

President John F. Kennedy liked to remind Americans that the essence of public policymaking is choice. Ultimately, he reflected, for the policymaker, the "responsibility is one of decision—for to govern is to choose." Governing the energy economy involves a multitude of policy options—always an array of competing and contentious alternatives creating the fabric of national energy management. This policy abundance, however, is created by variations on a relatively limited agenda of basic policy strategies that constitute the foundation of American energy governance. These policy fundamentals will appear in different variations throughout the succeeding chapters.

This chapter—a "policy primer"—concerns these policy fundamentals. It begins with a brief consideration of the defining decades that create the setting for twenty-first-century energy policymaking and then provides a short description of these policy foundations to American energy governance.

FROM ABUNDANCE TO INSECURITY

Americans have enjoyed throughout most of their history an abundance, if not an extravagance, of fossil fuel energy. Throughout most US history, energy policy, unencumbered by apprehension over the possibility of future energy shortages, seemed predicated upon the premise that the United States owned its energy future. Flush with this rich inheritance, after World War II the United States experienced an unparalleled economic prosperity resulting in decades of surging economic expansion and a ravenous appetite for energy. Protected by an apparently dependable, abundant reserve of domestically available coal, petroleum, and natural gas and fortified by secure sources of imported petroleum, particularly from the Middle East, South America, and Asia, American energy security seemed assured.[2]

Fossil Fuel Nation

America's energy economy is still sustained by fossil fuels. The proportion of different fossil fuels driving the American economy has varied since World War II, but a profile of energy production and consumption at the outset of the second Barack Obama administration illustrates the characteristic fossil fuel dominance. For example, Figures 2-1 and 2-2 illustrate that more than three-fourths of the nation's energy production and 81 percent of its energy consumption depended on fossil sources.

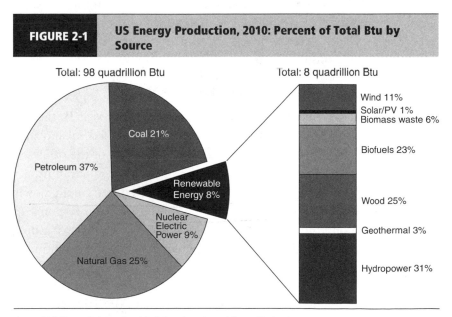

| FIGURE 2-1 | US Energy Production, 2010: Percent of Total Btu by Source |

Total: 98 quadrillion Btu

Total: 8 quadrillion Btu

Coal 21%

Petroleum 37%

Renewable Energy 8%

Nuclear Electric Power 9%

Natural Gas 25%

Wind 11%
Solar/PV 1%
Biomass waste 6%

Biofuels 23%

Wood 25%

Geothermal 3%

Hydropower 31%

Source: U.S. Energy Information Administration, *Annual Energy Review 2010.*

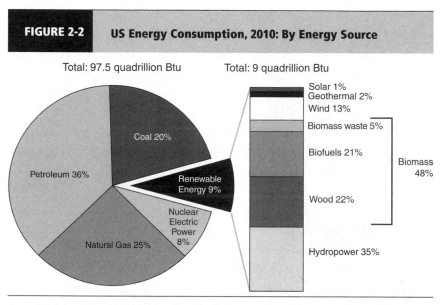

| FIGURE 2-2 | US Energy Consumption, 2010: By Energy Source |

Total: 97.5 quadrillion Btu   Total: 9 quadrillion Btu

Coal 20%

Petroleum 36%

Renewable Energy 9%

Natural Gas 25%

Nuclear Electric Power 8%

Solar 1%
Geothermal 2%
Wind 13%

Biomass waste 5%

Biofuels 21%

Biomass 48%

Wood 22%

Hydropower 35%

Source: U.S Energy Information Administration, *Monthly Energy Review,* Table 10.1 (March 2012), preliminary 2011 data.

As later chapters illustrate, the production and consumption of non-fossil fuels, presently constituting less than a fifth of the national energy profile, is expected to creep upward but remain the smallest of the energy sources for many future decades.

The Energy Boom Arrives and Departs: 1945–1988

Throughout the energy boom years following World War II, the domestic petroleum industry, with the willing assistance of federal and state governments, was concerned primarily with protection of the domestic oil market from foreign competition and control of production capacity to prevent price deflation. The flow of imported petroleum slowly enlarged, however, and domestic consumption increased in response to the continued outpouring of new automobiles, the rapidly expanding Interstate Highway System, suburbia's growing sprawl, and continued industrial expansion.

There had been warnings as early as the 1950s that national energy security might be fading. There were predictions that domestic petroleum

production would peak in the 1970s, a growing unease within the petroleum industry and government about the steadily increasing consumption of foreign petroleum, and debate among experts concerning the
amount of future petroleum reserves. Still, most governmental experts,
petroleum engineers, petroleum economists, and policymakers remained
confident about the adequacy of future petroleum reserves, the nation's
most strategic fossil fuel and the crucial energy capital expected to sustain
economic vitality. Then came the Energy Crises of the 1970s.

The Energy Crises of the 1970s. In October 1973, the Organization of
the Petroleum Exporting Countries (OPEC) cut the American jugular,
and it bled oil. Neither the nation's government nor its public was
prepared for that event or its consequences. The prelude was the
Yom Kippur War between Egypt and Israel beginning on October 6,
1973. Deeply resentful of Israel's long-standing treatment of its Arab
neighbors and angered by President Nixon's assurance of massive
emergency military assistance to Israel, OPEC voted in mid-October
to cut its oil production by 5 percent monthly until Israel changed its
Arab policies.

The economic blow immediately reverberated throughout Europe
and North America, and nowhere more traumatically than in the United
States. Moreover, the next day, the Saudis, OPEC's dominant oil producer, cut their oil exports by 10 percent and threatened to end all petroleum shipments to the United States until the Nixon administration
altered its pro-Israel policies. The sudden, short-term loss of two million
barrels daily in imported oil shocked the US economy. Within a few
months, the price of domestic refined petroleum and crude oil sharply
increased, and petroleum scarcities spread nationwide. Between 1970
and 1979, the price of a gallon of gas had risen by 152 percent, the cost
of imported crude oil by 800 percent a barrel.

Presidents Nixon and Ford initiated a multitude of unprecedented
measures to combat the sudden drop in imported petroleum supply.
Among many urgent policy decisions, the federal government assumed
authority to allocate and to price petroleum products, mandated year-
round daylight savings time, required a national fifty-five mile-per-hour
speed limit, created new federal agencies for comprehensive energy

management, funded new programs promoting solar energy research, and encouraged new commercial nuclear power development.

In 1976, newly inaugurated president Jimmy Carter declared energy supply a priority issue throughout his four-year administration and, supported by a reluctant Congress, declared that the national effort to overcome the energy crisis was "the moral equivalent of war." There followed an unprecedented outpouring of new presidential orders, congressional legislation, and administrative regulations rapidly expanding energy governance.[a] By the Carter administration's end, the president and Congress had created a new edifice of federal power raised on the foundation of an apparently continuing national vulnerability to petroleum shortages.[3]

Environmentalism arrives. Environmentalism arrived just slightly ahead of the energy crisis and permanently redefined the whole political setting of energy policymaking. The first Earth Day (1970) signaled the emergence of the environmental movement as a new and powerful presence in all future national politics and, most important, bonded environmentalism so firmly with energy in all future policy discourse that, in effect, energy and environmental policymaking became interdependent.

Among the cascade of federal environmental laws enacted during the 1970s that became the foundation of US environmental regulation, virtually all in one way or another changed the way Americans produced and consumed energy. The Clean Air Act (1970), for instance, mandated new air quality standards, compelling changes in the refining, sale, and combustion of petroleum, natural gas, and coal used in most industries using fossil fuels, such as automobile production, electric power generation, and chemical manufacturing. The Clean Water Act Amendments (1972) required new pollution controls on the disposal of virtually all

---

[a] These included a congressionally required National Energy Plan, creation of the new Department of Energy, new federal regulations concerning energy use in federal facilities, sharply rising federal funding for research and development of solar energy, "gas guzzler" taxes on energy inefficient autos, massive federal investment in the development of synthetic fuels to replace petroleum and natural gas and much more.

energy wastes. Other legislation compelled new, costly environmental conservation practices throughout the rapidly expanding surface coal mining industry. The environment-energy connection permeated the whole catalog of the decade's landmark environmental legislation, so all later energy policy now became almost inseparable from deliberation about the environmental consequences.

This fusion of energy and environmental policy has been further proliferated through America's governing institutions by the states, which have created their own array of similarly bonded laws and regulations concerning energy governance. Often, the states have been the initiators and innovators with environmentally relevant energy legislation when the federal policymakers were gridlocked or distracted with other matters. One example is the several regional agreements negotiated by the states during the G. W. Bush presidency to control state climate warming carbon dioxide (CO_2) emissions while Congress remained deadlocked on the climate issue.

A new reality: neither crisis nor security. By 1980, the energy crisis was fading. Carter had gambled most of his political capital on national energy planning and lost. Political support for the avalanche of earlier federal energy crisis measures had badly disintegrated. Carter's energy policies were burdened with political mismanagement and economic liabilities, including a nasty combination of recession and inflation, excessive haste in formulation and complexity in design, and feeble public appeal (energy regulation and rationing have never been popular for long, even during World War II). Congress, always reluctant partners in Carter's ambitious energy policies, was fractured by partisan battles and state competition over energy regulations and markets. Ronald Reagan's rout of Carter in the 1980 presidential campaign effectively ended a decade of the nation's most ambitious but fleeting initiative in national energy governance. Later, a disappointed Carter lamented about his energy regulations: "It sapped away a substantial portion of my domestic influence to harp on this unpleasant subject for four solid years."[4]

Ronald Reagan, in contrast, inherited a fortunate improvement in national and international energy supply. By 1980, OPEC couldn't sustain its global boycott, and petroleum imports from non-OPEC countries gradually enlarged US access to alternative foreign petroleum. Domestic petroleum supply increased, prices for crude and refined petroleum rapidly dropped. All this was splendidly timed, for Reagan's road to the White House had been paved with promises to reduce drastically federal economic and environmental regulation. Immediately after his inauguration, Reagan took dead aim on the federal government's recently acquired panoply of regulations and regulators, much to the approval of a new Republican senate majority.[5]

Within three years, the Reagan administration had dismantled most of the energy governance created in response to the 1970s petroleum shocks. Federal spending on research and development of renewable energy technologies and energy conservation plummeted. Energy production received more White House and congressional attention, the adverse environmental impact of energy production much less. Public concern about the nation's energy issues withered to insignificance. As the economy continued a vigorous revival, the 1970s Energy Crises and their politics rapidly receded into the twilight of public near invisibility.

Still, memory of the 1970s energy shocks lingered and stalked US policymakers throughout the 1980s. Washington and the states could no longer be confident about future energy security—another nastier, more dangerous future energy crisis now was plausible, especially considering the relentlessly growing US dependence upon imported foreign oil. Thus, energy *in*security increasingly haunted discussions about US energy governance. It seemed obvious that the United States needed to create—at least to attempt—comprehensive national energy planning to avoid a repeat of the 1970s. But a sense of urgency was lacking.

From Insecurity to Renewed Planning: 1988–2008

The 1990s, recalled Paul L. Joskow, director of the MIT Center for Energy and Environmental Policy Research, were characterized by "abundant supplies of energy, stable or falling real energy prices, and relatively little public or political interest in national energy policy issues. Energy demand continued to grow steadily, but supply was sufficient without major increases in prices until the end of the decade. Energy prices were stable or falling, no serious supply disruptions occurred, little public interest in energy issues prevailed, major new energy policy initiatives never rose very high on the policy agendas of either the Clinton administration or Congress during the 1990s."[6] Thus, the presidencies of George Bush (1988–1992) and Bill Clinton (1992–2000) were largely years of energy policy inertia.

Despite the stability of the 1990s energy economy, events were steadily eroding any enduring sense of national energy security. Domestic petroleum production and consumption continued to move in opposite directions, petroleum imports climbed relentlessly, federal and state concern about energy conservation and renewable energy was fitful, and the future of commercial nuclear power precarious. Production of renewable energy, always the stepchild of American energy policy, seemed frozen at less than 10 percent of total domestic energy production. In 1990, the *First Assessment Report* appeared, written by the Intergovernmental Panel on Climate Change (IPCC) and created by the United Nations and the World Meteorological Society to examine the probability of global climate warming being precipitated by worldwide emissions of carbon dioxide (CO_2) and other greenhouse gas (GHG) emissions. The report, the first of three assessments during the decade (1990, 1992, and 1995), predicted with growing assertiveness the probability of potentially calamitous alterations in global atmospheric chemistry without imminent worldwide efforts at mitigation. By decade's end, the IPCC reports were the ominous underside to a now persistent national political and economic unease about energy security and the environmental cost of traditional energy production.

Planning revives in two acts. In 2000, George W. Bush entered the White House on a cascading tide of events compelling a renewed national attention at all governmental levels to the energy future. Energy prices were rising. The United States was now competing with rapidly industrializing China and India for world petroleum supply, a situation further exacerbated by reductions in OPEC petroleum exports. There were rolling electric power blackouts in California precipitated by flawed state and federal energy regulations, political instability among major global petroleum producers, and shortages of specialty gas blends resulting from environmental regulations and refinery shortfalls of crude oil. Gas soon cost an unprecedented $2.00 at the pump and would go higher.

The World Trade Center bombing on September 11, 2001, compelled national awareness of proliferating energy insecurities and the menace posed by the politically volatile Middle East to US energy and military security. Thus began a newly invigorated national debate over energy policy and the gradual emergence of new White House and Congressional initiatives intended to restore priority to a national energy plan.[7]

George W. Bush left the White House in 2008 having initiated two major national energy acts that accomplished significant changes in federal energy policy. These were preceded by Bush's National Energy Policy (NEP) in 2001, the creation of a White House special energy policy planning committee. The NEP contained over 100 recommendations emphasizing increased fossil fuel and commercial nuclear power production blended with modest innovations in energy conservation, renewable energy development, and energy research. Many of these recommendations were subsequently contained in two later, ambitious legislative energy programs.

The Energy Policy Act (EPAct) of 2005 (Pub. L. 109–58) was the most comprehensive national energy legislation in more than two decades, an omnibus measure that became the centerpiece of the Bush administration's energy policies. The act was a mélange of ambitious renewable energy policy innovations and proposals for greater energy conservation, all coupled with a solid reliance upon fossil fuel technologies, atomic energy, and aggressive new fossil fuel exploration and mining to secure America's near-term energy future. The EPAct rejected any aggressive federal action to regulate GHG emissions. The EPAct is further explored in later chapters.

Overall, the EPAct was an important innovation, creating significant reforms when compared to then current energy policies. Among the major provisions were new incentives for energy conservation and renewable energy production, a substantial increase in the amount of ethanol that refiners must add to gasoline, new incentives for construction of more commercial nuclear power plants, and increased federal government assistance in exploration and production of offshore energy, and a one-month extension of daylight saving time beginning in 2007.[8]

The Energy Independence and Security Act of 2007 (Pub. L. 110–140), the second major Bush administration energy initiative, was a massive 822-page document focused primarily on domestic energy conservation and renewable energy technology development. Its important provisions included increased mileage standards of passenger automobiles and light trucks, incentives for accelerated production of electric hybrid autos, further requirements for biofuels production and consumption, new incentives for energy efficiency in government and public institutions, and support for modernization of the national electric power production and distribution through new "smart grids."[9]

Imagining the "Clean Energy Superhighway": The Obama Administration

On the eve of Obama's accession to the presidency, the *Wall Street Journal* echoed a complaint common among practically all the nation's major stakeholders in national energy issues, who agreed on little else. "History isn't tilted in Mr. Obama's favor. Presidents all the way back to Richard Nixon . . . were thwarted by short attention spans, other urgent problems and gyrations in the energy market."[10] Obama proposed to move in a different direction.

An ambitious and embattled first term. Unlike George W. Bush and most previous presidents, Obama avoided ambitious proposals to achieve "energy independence" and finessed the issue instead. Obama did give significant attention to promoting more—and more environmentally safe—domestic fossil fuel production. But the Obama energy agenda's greatest appeal was to environmentalists and renewable energy advocates who had early and often promoted his candidacy. The agenda was a trinity of themes that he asserted would lead gradually to greater national energy security: clean energy, energy efficiency, and energy conservation, pathways he predicted on Earth Day 2009 would become "the clean energy superhighway." During the campaign, Obama pledged to spend $150 billion during the coming decade to promote alternative energy technologies, such as wind and solar. (To demonstrate its credibility, the White

House produced low-energy and low-carbon inaugural balls, where attendees were "encouraged to carpool or ride public transit, even in evening gowns and tuxedos" and "to use a hybrid vehicle or purchase carbon offsets.")[11]

The most significant departure from George W. Bush's energy agenda was Obama's commitment to immediate, decisive action nationally and internationally to mitigate global climate change—a potent but risky commitment. It rallied environmentalists and energy conservationists to his campaign but launched his administration on a collision course with congressional Republicans, with a substantial portion of the public dubious about the credibility of climate warming science, and with influential segments of the fossil fuel and transportation sectors, such as coal mining, electric utilities, and automobile manufacturers. After a long, bitter, exhausting, and fruitless congressional struggle over his proposals to mitigate climate warming, Obama reluctantly abandoned the battle in 2010. It was the administration's most conspicuous energy policy failure.

The administration was considerably more successful with its "clean energy" agenda. At the end of Obama's first term, his administration had initiated a number of clean energy programs:

- The American Recovery and Reinvestment Act included more than $80 billion in the generation of renewable energy sources, expanding manufacturing capacity for clean energy technology, thus, advancing vehicle and fuel technologies.
- More stringent energy efficiency standards were mandated for commercial and residential appliances, including microwaves, kitchen ranges, dishwashers, light bulbs, and other common appliances.
- An executive order committed the federal government to reducing greenhouse gas emissions by 28 percent by 2020, increasing energy efficiency, and reducing fleet petroleum consumption.
- New efficiency and emissions standards were set for medium- and heavy-duty cars and trucks.
- An executive order to the Environmental Protection Agency initiated regulation of domestic GHG emissions through the Clean Air Act and initiated inventory of national GHG emissions.

But Obama had also arrived at the White House amid the most severe economic recession since the Great Depression. The national economic malaise compelled the administration to give urgent attention to economic recovery, a task progressively dominating the administration's domestic policy and political concerns to which the "green agenda" had to yield priority. Moreover, the 2010 midterm congressional elections returned a Republican majority to the House of Representatives that was committed to a legislative agenda quite incompatible with most of Obama's energy policies.

As Obama's first term proceeded, the administration's energy initiatives seemed progressively diminished and frequently irresolute, the once ambitious climate change agenda stalemated. The president continued to promote new measures for energy efficiency, the development of new renewable energy technologies, and reduced GHG emissions in his State of the Union messages and annual budgets. But the 2012 presidential election forced the administration's attention away from "green energy superhighways" and toward the reelection campaign and the still faltering economy.

The "clean energy superhighway" returns. Energy issues seldom received major attention in Obama's second presidential campaign—that distinction went to the economy and foreign affairs—but it was quickly apparent from the president's 2013 State of the Union and onward that Obama intended to revive and intensify his earlier clean energy and energy conservation initiatives. The agenda looked a lot like the first term: more development of renewable energy, more federal support for energy conservation in the electric power and automobile industries, more federal money for clean energy research, and a vigorous renewal of federal initiatives to control domestic emissions of climate warming gases. At the same time, Obama again faced the challenge in finding a politically successful but always precarious balance between his clean energy initiatives, his equally forthright commitment to increasing domestic fossil fuel production, and energy security.

Many priority issues on the Obama administration's contemporary energy agenda appear in all the following chapters and illustrate the constant problem in finding that elusive and successful policy balance between energy production, energy conservation, and energy security. Among these issues are the following:

- Controversy over natural gas "fracking," the proposed new Keystone XL oil shale pipeline from Canada through the United States, and more Outer Continental Shelf (OCS) petroleum production (chapter 3)
- Prohibiting "Mountain Top Removal" in strip mining for coal, and control of CO_2 emissions from electric utilities (chapter 4)
- Disposal of nuclear waste from commercial nuclear power plants and the fading of the nuclear power "renaissance" (chapter 5)
- The economic and environmental risks associated with wind and solar power and the requirement for ethanol in current gasoline formulations (chapter 6)
- The impact on US security from the growing global competition for petroleum and natural gas (chapter 7)

These issues, like virtually all energy issues since the crisis-ridden energy politics of the 1970s, have challenged the Obama White House, as well as Congress, and multiple federal administrative agencies, not only by their formidable complexity. The solutions are also loaded with alternatives that always mean contentious choices between alternatives armed with different political and economic costs, rewards and benefits. These alternatives, however, are usually compounded from a relatively few policy instruments, which appear in many variations and combinations in American energy governance.

GOVERNING AND CHOICE: ENERGY POLICY OPTIONS

In one way or another, most existing US energy policies and most proposals about future ones are likely to fall somewhere between two ideological poles. These poles are the extremes of a profound and unrelenting disagreement, one of the Great Holy Wars in American policymaking, concerning whether resource development should be largely free, or, substantially influenced by governmental involvement—a variation on the historic controversy about whether Americans are best served economically and politically by a governmental regulation or an unregulated economy. Every proposal to create new governmental intervention in energy development or to remove an older one—for instance, to subsidize solar power arrays or to end federal financial support for commercial nuclear power—revives these battles.[12]

Except for implacable purists, however, who denounce *any* governmental involvement in the energy marketplace, conflict over contemporary energy governance is mostly over *how much* governmental involvement is desirable. The contention over how much usually involves three issues: Which energy resource requires governmental involvement in its development? If government intervenes, what policies should be chosen? When should governmental intervention end—if ever? All basic energy policy instruments are an answer to one or more of these questions.

Governance and Regulation

Whenever government is involved in determining how energy is produced, marketed, and consumed—whenever this is not left to an economic marketplace free of governmental interventions—it is energy governance. Much of this governance assumes the form of "regulation" involving decisions specifically by federal and state regulatory agencies with authority to issue rules for the economic management of energy.[b]

Most of these regulations carry out legislative enactments or presidential directives—for example, the US Department of Energy determines when mineral resources on public lands can be leased for exploration by energy companies, according to broad guidelines in congressional legislation. Energy regulations are usually issued by federal, state, or local regulatory agencies headed by appointed boards or administrators, such as the US Environmental Protection Agency or numerous state utility commissions, which are presumed to be politically independent

---

[b] Economists usually distinguish between "economic regulation" and "social regulation." Economic regulation involves "rules that limit who can enter a business (entry controls) and what prices they may charge (price controls)." Social regulation includes "rules governing how any business or individual carries out its activities, with a view to correcting one or more 'market failures.'" "A classic way in which the market fails is when firms (or individuals) do not take account of the costs their activities may impose on third parties (externalities)." Robert Latin, *A Concise Encyclopedia of Economics: Regulation,* accessed June 20, 2013, www.econlib.org/library/Enc/Regulation.html.

from pressure and manipulation from Congress or the White House. However, regulations may also come from federal executive agencies, such as the Department of Energy or the Occupational Safety and Health Administration (OSHA), among many others.[13]

In reality, most common types of contemporary energy policy—whether they are called "legislation," "executive orders," or "administrative agency decisions"—amount to some kind of energy regulation because they impose rules upon private firms or other governmental entities, concerning some economic or social aspect of energy development.[c] Ronald Reagan, no friend of big government, frequently complained that "governments tend not to solve problems but to rearrange them," and federal regulations were his favorite example. As a practical matter, while governmental regulations are often deservedly criticized, energy governance, by regulation or otherwise, is now inseparable—and considered essential—to the modern American economy.

Federal regulation. The federal government possesses considerable freedom in deciding why energy regulation is necessary, what form it should assume, and when it should occur.[14] Washington regulates the energy economy for many important reasons, of which the most common examples include the following:

- *Protecting Public Health and Safety.* This includes controls on air and water pollution from energy production and combustion; safety requirements for energy production and transportation facilities, such as oil and natural gas pipelines, petroleum refineries, and coal mines; guidelines for formulation of gasoline; and specifications for the composition of products manufactured from fossil fuel stocks, such as Styrofoam and plastic containers.
- *Preventing "Market Failure."* Such failures occur when energy monopolies, cartels, and other arrangements intended to control or dominate energy markets engage in "unfair competition" that produces excessive

---

[c] Technically, a "regulation" is issued by a regulatory agency, but many governmental acts, such as legislation, executive orders, and administrative agency decisions have the effect of regulation.

profit—or what government deems excessive profits. These economic measures include regulation of consumer prices charged by public utilities and other public services that are "natural monopolies" and ceiling prices on wholesale and retail prices for most fossil fuels during energy shortages, national emergencies, and other economic crises.

- *Controlling the Interstate Production and Consumption of Energy.* These controls are used to avoid conflicting or competing state standards and to intervene when necessary to protect public safety when states are unable or unwilling to act. For example, regulations are issued by the Federal Energy Regulatory Commission (FERC), which protects the reliability of the high voltage interstate transmission system through mandatory reliability standards.

- *Achieving Economic Efficiency in Energy Production and Consumption.* Common examples include the federal government's fuel economy standards (corporate average fuel economy, or "CAFE standards") requiring manufacturers of automobiles and light trucks to attain progressively higher average miles per gallon, eventually 35 miles per gallon by 2020 for car and light truck fleets; and state regulations promoting economic efficiency in electric power consumption by requiring local utilities to offer their consumers important energy efficiency programs.

These and other related measures constitute a very substantial portion of more than 2,500 major new regulations, and 80,000 pages describing them, produced annually by the federal government.[15]

Regulatory federalism. While some forms of energy regulation are reserved for the federal government, state governments collaborate with Washington in many forms of energy governance and also possess regulatory authority independent of Washington. The federal government, for instance, has a constitutionally mandated, exclusive authority to regulate interstate commerce, including interstate energy transportation. The states and Washington share regulatory authority over construction and operation of commercial nuclear power and hydroelectric power facilities, over regulation of energy-related air and water pollution, and over the permitting and siting of energy generators and electric transmission lines. States usually have exclusive authority to set electric utility rates and terms of service for utilities within their jurisdictions.

Energy issues often dwell in a regulatory "Twilight Zone" where the respective authority of Washington and the states is vague and variable. Then, collaboration between Washington and the states over energy regulation can be a complicated and contentious affair (as the Deepwater Horizon disaster introducing chapter 1 illustrates). Where, for instance, does federal power end and state authority begin in the siting of future wind towers transmitting electric power across state lines? Or when safety standards are to be created for nuclear waste transported across state lines? Often, neither resorting to the Constitution, nor to existing legislation, nor to existing federal court decisions will clarify to the satisfaction of one party or another how to divide some disputed territory in energy governance. Almost inevitably, these disputes over regulatory federalism arrive—and perhaps end finally—in the federal courts.

Energy Taxes

Taxing energy production, transportation, marketing, and consumption can serve many purposes and will dependably produce contention whether a tax is proposed for adoption or abolition. Washington can use energy taxes—or tax combinations—to create revenue for specific purposes: to discourage or prohibit various forms of energy development at any stage; to limit export or import of energy sources, such as petroleum and natural gas; to discourage environmental pollution; to create incentives for states' collaboration in energy development (energy "royalties"); to create a market advantage or disadvantage for an energy source or production process, and much else.

Federal taxes on gasoline, that invisible hand from Washington reaching into every driver's wallet from the pump, have been collected since 1932. In 2013, these federal taxes amounted to 18.4 cents per gallon on gasoline and 24.4 cents per gallon for diesel fuel. Much of the revenue generated by these federal taxes has for more than sixty years financed the massive US Interstate Highway System. Each state adds its own additional fuel tax for its own purposes. Figure 2–3 illustrates these state taxes in 2013:

FIGURE 2-3

State Gasoline Tax Rates (Cents Per Gallon), Ranked Highest to Lowest, 2013

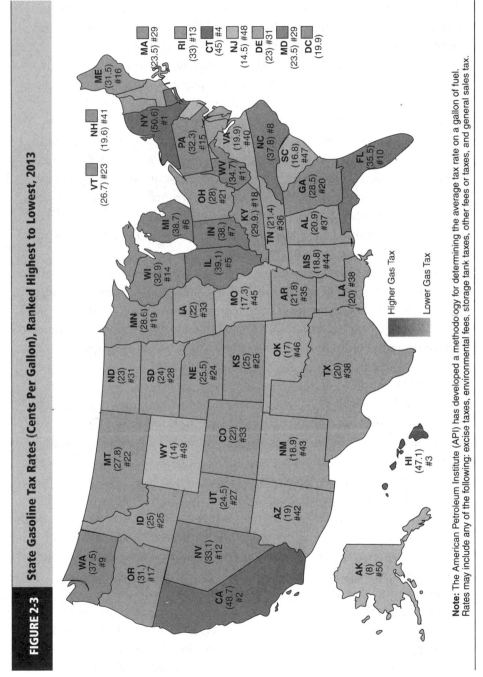

Note: The American Petroleum Institute (API) has developed a methodology for determining the average tax rate on a gallon of fuel. Rates may include any of the following: excise taxes, environmental fees, storage tank taxes, other fees or taxes, and general sales tax.

Source: Tax Foundation, "Weekly Maps: State Gasoline Tax Rate," http://taxfoundation.org/blog/weekly-map-state-gasoline-tax-rates.

US energy producers also pay federal and state income taxes, royalties from energy extraction to Washington and the states, and fees for leasing governmental resources among other forms of taxation.

The power to tax is also the power to discourage or eliminate energy practices declared incompatible with the public welfare. For example, the prolonged and indecisive congressional battle over legislation requiring controls on domestic CO_2 emissions has been incited, among other provocations, by proposals to tax emissions (a "carbon tax") both to raise revenue for renewable energy development and to discourage use of high CO_2 emission fuels, such as coal. In contrast, tax credits can be promoted by federal, state, and local governments to encourage desirable energy management practices. These credits are being adopted to encourage consumer installation of solar home heating and to practice "green" principles in home construction.

Virtually any energy tax or new tax proposal is likely to inspire heated contention about who are, or will be, the financial winners and losers. The policy struggle often resolves into a contest over which side can create the most politically persuasive (not necessarily the most accurate) definition of winners and losers for the public and policymakers.

Subsidies

A subsidy is any governmental action that "provides a substantial financial benefit associated with the use or production of a fossil or renewable fuel. Potential beneficiaries may include manufacturers, supply chains, workers, and consumers within the fuel sector."[16] Subsidies can assume many forms, and the federal government is by far the most abundant wellspring of energy subsidies which flow in excess of $40 billion through the whole domain of energy management.[17] Estimates indicate that Washington supports more than sixty different energy subsidies intended to increase energy production, underwrite energy consumption, or increase energy efficiency.[18]

Fossil fuels, and particularly oil and natural gas, have historically received by far the largest share of federal energy subsidies as Figure 2–4 suggests. However, beginning with the G. W. Bush administration in 2000, both federal support for renewable energy production and renewables' share of the total federal energy subsidies escalated rapidly and further enlarged during the Obama administration (see Figure 2–5). By 2013, renewable subsidies are estimated to account for almost 40 percent of all federal energy subsidies.[19]

Distinctions between a subsidy and a tax policy instrument can be confusing since the same policy instrument can serve several purposes. A tax, for example, can both discourage some form of energy use and at the same time promote (subsidize) the manufacture of another. Such a scheme has been proposed to limit US CO_2 emissions by a carbon tax which simultaneously discourages industrial combustion of coal and provides a subsidy for more renewable energy production and marketing. Vehement debate often erupts among policy stakeholders, concerning whether a federal energy policy is actually a subsidy, even when it is called something else.

In addition to fossil fuel producers, the commercial nuclear power industry has been a significant and intensely controversial beneficiary of federal subsidies. This flow of federal largesse and its implications for commercial nuclear power are explored in chapter 5. Suffice it to note here that the commercial nuclear power industry could not have been

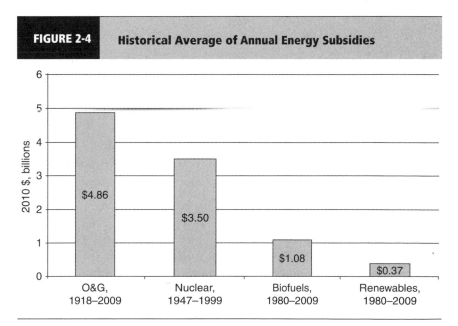

FIGURE 2-4 **Historical Average of Annual Energy Subsidies**

Source: Nancy Pfund and Ben Healey, *What Would Jefferson Do?: The Historical Role of Federal Subsidies in Shaping America's Energy Future* (Washington, DC: DBL Investors, 2011), 29.

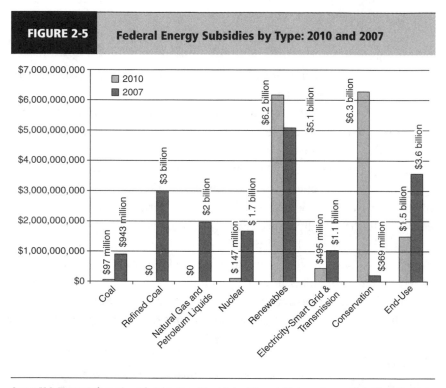

FIGURE 2-5 Federal Energy Subsidies by Type: 2010 and 2007

Source: U.S. Energy Information Administration, *Direct Federal Financial Interventions and Subsidies in Energy in Fiscal 2010.*

created, nor could it have economically survived, without a lavish diversity of subsidies since the early 1950s. The total amount of the industry's subsidies since the 1950s defies easy calculation. For instance, some estimates range from a conservative $73 billion to more than $200 billion, depending on who is counting and what is considered a subsidy.[20]

Research and Development (R&D)

The federal government provides considerable financial support directly to the private sector to encourage the creation and implementation of new energy technologies, primarily through the Department of Energy. Energy R&D represented only about 9 percent ($13 billion) of the federal government's total $142 billion R&D budget in 2013 (most federal R&D funding goes to the Defense Department). However, competition for energy R&D funding is intense. Energy R&D funding has become especially important during the Obama administration because it has become a primary source—often the *only* source—of funding for the development of many innovative renewable energy technologies with potentially significant economic and environmental benefits but too experimental to attract private investment.

Energy R&D can be crucial to the whole national energy economy because it can support energy development at many different stages. The most significant forms of support include the following:

- Encouraging energy efficiency by redesign of existing energy technologies (such as electric power generation and transmission) or by creation or modification of newer technologies, such as hybrid auto and truck motors
- Creating new renewable energy technologies
- Subsidizing manufacture of renewable energy technologies, such as solar cells and wind towers to improve their competitive market status
- Developing new green materials for home, commercial, and industrial facility construction
- Testing the market competitiveness of new energy technologies

Federal R&D funding can yield significant economic, environmental, and political benefits for public and private sectors. It can ensure survival, and frequently economic success, for important energy technologies and management strategies. But R&D is still a gamble with the future that may become a bad bet or worse. The Obama administration's unwise R&D investment of $535 million in Solyndra—a California manufacturer of materials for solar cells that went bankrupt in 2011—turned into a dismal trinity of economic failure, political controversy, and public scandal stalking Obama well into his second term. Solyndra remains a cautionary tale about the risks the federal government inherits along with the potential rewards from energy R&D for any future White House.[21]

Rationing

Energy rationing is exceptional, drastic, and unpopular, usually the strategy of last resort adopted by reluctant governments to force energy conservation during periods of crisis and emergency when less severe measures seem inadequate. Rationing may be the only means, however imperfect, to achieve rapid management over energy production and consumption and to sustain for long periods of time if necessary.

Americans have not experienced sustained national energy rationing since World War II, but less severe energy emergencies in the intervening years have caused the federal government, and many states, to acquire emergency authority to mandate many kinds of discretionary energy rationing—and the authority has been used.

During the energy crises of the 1970s, the federal government, and many states, sought to combat sharply rising energy prices, diminishing wholesale petroleum supplies, and long lines of automobiles competing for gasoline at the retail pump with a variety of strategies to control both petroleum supply and demand. The federal policies included limiting consumer gasoline purchases according to an odd-even license plate system, creating a 55-mile-per-hour speed limit, new requirements for auto fuel efficiency, new requirements for energy efficiency in public buildings, extended daylight savings time, and numerous new legislative and executive measures to equip Washington with additional emergency energy management authority when needed in the future.

Energy rationing has been involved occasionally since the 1970s when emergencies appeared to require it. In the aftermath of Hurricane Sandy's devastation along the East Coast in October 2012, gasoline scarcity created miles of automobiles waiting hours at retail pumps, panic buying, hoarding of fuel for home electric generators, and other problems. In response, both New Jersey and New York governments mandated an odd-even license plate system of gas rationing until the supply crisis had passed.

Price Controls, Quotas, and Tariffs

A quota creates governmentally mandated limits on the amount of energy that can be produced, sold, imported, or exported in an energy market. Price controls set governmental restrictions on the wholesale and retail price of energy. At various times, both the federal and state governments have attempted to limit the supplies of domestic and imported petroleum by various interventions in the energy marketplace and by controlling domestic energy prices.

During the 1930s, major domestic oil producers convinced the federal government to pass legislation that allowed the states to set quotas on oil production within their jurisdictions.[22] This restricted domestic competition among the major producers, limited the US petroleum supply, and raised US petroleum prices as the major producers wished. After World War II, the major domestic petroleum producers convinced Congress to pass additional legislation authorizing the president to limit imported (and lower cost) foreign oil, thus, using new quotas to protect domestic petroleum producers from foreign competition. These quotas on imported petroleum lasted until 1973.

Early in the 1970s, in the wake of the first economic shocks from the decade's energy crises, the federal government limited domestic petroleum prices to diminish the sudden rise in US petroleum prices in the aftermath of the OPEC oil embargo. Later in the 1970s, still struggling with the economic tribulations from the decade's energy crises, Congress passed additional legislation further restricting domestic petroleum prices. Congress and the White House continued to produce further price controls and quotas on domestic and imported petroleum resulting in considerable economic confusion and controversial results. Nonetheless, the federal government retained considerable authority to impose market interventions again in the future if circumstances warranted them.

The federal government also created the Strategic Petroleum Reserve (SPR) in 1975 to provide a buffer against a future rapid increase in domestic petroleum prices similar to what occurred several times during imported oil embargoes in the 1970s. In the event of a new imported embargo or other emergency creating a rapid shortfall in the domestic petroleum supply, the federal government can release petroleum from the SPR to stabilize the domestic market against severe price inflation and panic buying. The SP Reserve, located in underground salt domes at four locations along the Gulf of Mexico, has a capacity in excess of 720 million barrels, enough to provide about a month's domestic consumption at current petroleum prices.[23]

A *tariff* (sometimes called a "duty") is a tax by another name imposed on imports or exports of energy between states or between the United States and the global energy market. Such a tariff may be intended to raise revenue, but often it is used to limit imports or exports. Tariffs can be governmentally imposed on any form of energy, and at any level. Thus, federal, state, and even local governments can often impose tariffs on electric power generation and consumption, and states or regional regulators may sometimes impose tariffs on energy importing and exporting between states.

National Energy Planning

The United States lacks a single, comprehensive, long-term energy management strategy. To the extent that the national government has attempted to create a long-term, consistent strategy for its energy development, the result has been a series of episodic "national plans," usually prompted by crises and packed with sensible and foresighted proposals but usually dependent upon uncertain, often highly controversial congressional or White House initiatives for implementation. The most recent such proposals were initiated by the White House in 1992, 2005, and 2007. Additionally, a multitude of other federal executive agency plans regularly appear and focus upon specific energy sources or issues of current importance, such as energy efficiency or energy security.

The most recent White House proposal for a comprehensive, long-term energy development plan was the National Energy Policy (NEP) created in 2001 by a special presidential commission appointed by president George-W. Bush and headed by Vice President Dick Cheney. The NEP plan was highly controversial from its inception. Critics charged that the commission was packed in favor of advocates for aggressive new fossil fuel and commercial nuclear energy production and deficient in advocates for energy conservation and efficiency. Much of the plan never materialized in White House or congressional policies.

Many ambitious and sweeping energy development proposals, often anointed "plans," have originated in Congress or the White House. The Bush administration did succeed in collaborating with Congress in the creation of two major, sweeping legislative enactments that constitute the most important energy legislation since 1990—the Energy Policy Act of 2005 and the Energy Independence and Security Act of 2007. Not quite government-wide, coordinated strategies proposing implementation with the breadth and depth required of a true national energy plan, the two Energy Acts, which are discussed in later chapters, nonetheless dramatically set major energy development priorities with considerable attention not only to fossil fuels but also to energy conservation, the development of innovative and efficient energy technologies, energy resource planning, and much else.

Despite these and other significant initiatives, innumerable public and private organizations and experts continue to call for national energy planning on a scale that would create a coherence, coordination, and breadth of national impact still lacking. In particular, a recurrent theme is the need for a national governmental entity, empowered with White House authority, to create, review, and update periodically an ongoing national energy strategy throughout the entire executive branch of the federal government.[24]

CONCLUSION: THE GOVERNED ENERGY MARKETPLACE

Governance, the presence of government in one form or another, pervades the American energy economy so thoroughly that virtually no aspect of energy exploration, production, and consumption is now unaffected by public policymaking. In each of the following chapters, it will become apparent that future energy development will be influenced in crucial ways depending on how many of these policy options are interpreted and applied.

First, as energy governance at all levels focuses more on renewable energy, sustainable energy, and energy conservation, so sustained federal subsidies, R&D, and tax incentives have become increasingly important for ensuring that innovative technologies are continually created and their commercialization enhanced. It is apparent that active federal funding and promotion of renewable energy and energy conservation are now a bipartisan enterprise—though important differences continue about how much federal investment should be involved and for how long. In short, the future of energy security, to the extent it depends upon an expanding and innovative renewable energy sector, depends upon active governmental interventions in the energy economy.

Second, federal energy regulations and regulatory agencies, particularly those associated with environmental protection and energy transportation, are certain to enlarge with an anticipated boom in petroleum and natural gas fracking and enactment of further regulatory limits of domestic climate warming emissions. Regulatory issues will also become significant in the uncertain economic future of the coal industry, which confronts not only a diminishing domestic market but also the likely enactment of new environmental regulations on surface mining.

Finally, the substantial federal subsidies, R&D funding, and tax incentives to encourage continuing commercial nuclear power development will be increasingly contested as the safety and commercial viability of the industry seems increasingly dubious. The survival of nuclear power is likely to be settled on the policy battlegrounds of nuclear waste disposal and reactor safety.

CHAPTER 3

CARBON POLICY
Petroleum and Natural Gas

On February 2, 2012, one of the most significant events in sixty-four years of American energy history was virtually ignored by the media, the public, and all but a small cadre of energy experts and policymakers. The Department of Energy reported that not since 1949 had the United States exported more refined energy products—gasoline, heating oil, and diesel fuel—than it had imported.[1] And this, moreover, occurred in a remarkable year when US petroleum exports exceeded imports for the first time since 1989.[2] These and similar data seemed prophetic to many energy experts, policymakers, and stakeholders: a gateway on the road to a new American "energy independence" had been passed. Others weren't so sure.

AN ERA OF TRANSFORMATION

Few eras in US energy history since 1970 have been more surprising or unexpected than the remarkable transformation in the status of US petroleum and natural gas supplies that began shortly before Barack Obama's presidency and is now predicted to prevail well beyond 2030. The primary responsibility for these transformations cannot be claimed by the White House, Congress, nor the major political parties. Rather, these transformations result from a mix of technological innovation, increasing energy efficiency, changes in the domestic and global energy economies, and increased petroleum imports from Canada. Riding this wave of change in the domestic energy economy are increasing predictions of a growing energy independence that will fortify future national security.

Predictions about future energy conditions and their security implications, however, always depend upon assumptions about the future of the domestic and global energy economies, about frequently uncertain environmental and political events, and about the reliability of emerging technologies. Despite encouraging energy data and optimistic predictions of many experts, the future impact of recent transformations in domestic petroleum and natural gas status remains uncertain in many respects. Even as the new era of petroleum and natural gas development was apparently arriving, for example, a former high official in the Obama administration was warning about America's continuing vulnerability to a global energy economy in which the United States is only one participant. "We have allowed ourselves to be worked slowly into a very delicate position with this international oil market controlled largely by countries who are at best neutral toward the United States, at worst antagonistic," he said. "It's all so delicate that one little quiver here can shake the whole thing."[3] In short, the United States never completely controls its own energy destiny.

PETROLEUM

Virtually all the petroleum, produced domestically or imported, ends in the gas tank of a light vehicle, bus, or truck. As Figure 3-1 indicates, about 70 percent of domestic petroleum consumption is created by the transportation sector. At the same time, domestic production of petroleum continues to grow with the boom in "fracking" technology, which is discussed later in the context of natural gas. By mid-2013, US oil production reached the highest level since January 1992, encouraging energy experts to expect more increases in the future.[4]

Growing Exports, Decreasing Imports

How recent has been the transformation in the US petroleum economy is evident in the changing status of petroleum imports and exports since 2000. In Figure 3-2, which illustrates the long-term trend in US petroleum imports and exports since 1990, the most important lines are

| FIGURE 3-1 | United States Petroleum Consumption by Sector, 2012 |

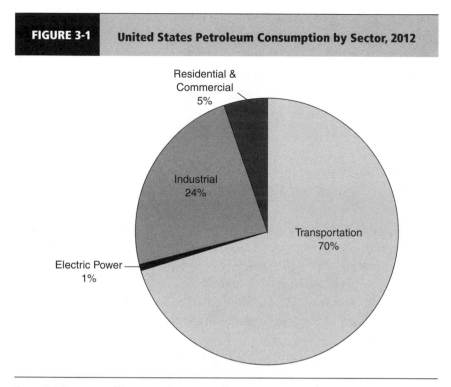

Source: U.S. Department of Energy, *Total Energy: Monthly Energy Review,* Tables 3.7a, b, and c (March 28, 2012).

the sharply rising size of exports beginning about 2006 and the intersection of imports and exports in 2011, marking the first time since 1990 that the United States became a net exporter of petroleum products (which include other petroleum fuels besides gasoline).

A second important indicator of the rapidly changing petroleum economy, and a closely watched statistic for energy policymakers, is Figure 3-3 that reports the percentage of US petroleum consumption dependent on imported oil. The proportion of imported oil has been rapidly decreasing. In 2005, the nation imported 60.3 percent of its oil. In 2011, that figure was 40 percent and will likely drop further as domestic production continues to grow.[5]

Many factors have contributed to these changes. Since 2008, Americans have been driving less while auto energy efficiency has been increasing.

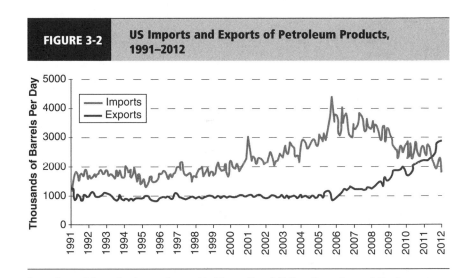

FIGURE 3-2   **US Imports and Exports of Petroleum Products, 1991–2012**

Source: Energy Information Agency. Presented by Morgan Housel, "3 Huge Recent Economic Developments You May Have Missed," *The Motley Fool*, January 20, 2012, at www.fool.com/investing/general/2012/01/20/ 3-huge-recent-economic-developments-you-may-have-.aspx.

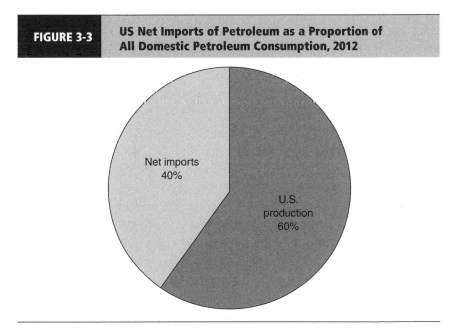

FIGURE 3-3   **US Net Imports of Petroleum as a Proportion of All Domestic Petroleum Consumption, 2012**

Source: U.S. Energy Information Administration, *Monthly Energy Review* (April 2013).

Ethanol, now required as an additive, has enlarged the domestic gasoline supply at a time when foreign demand for exported American gasoline has grown. Increased use of biofuels, ethanol, and diesel fuels continues. The severe recession beginning in 2008 has inhibited domestic petroleum consumption in most economic sectors. And fracking technology, soon to be discussed, is creating a surge in both petroleum and natural gas production.

The growing size of US domestic petroleum production has prompted the federal Energy Information Administration (EIA) to predict that by 2017, the United States will become the largest global petroleum producer, replacing both Saudi Arabia and Russia.[6]

Risks As Well As Rewards

Predictions about growing US energy independence sustained by a continually rising petroleum and natural gas production are safest when forecasters are nearsighted and fix their vision on an energy horizon confined to a decade or less. As predictions reach increasingly into the future, risks increase. Economic models commonly used to predict future domestic and global energy markets depend upon numerous assumptions concerning future domestic energy policy, technological change, global politics, and much else that may prove unpredictable. In 2000, for example, most energy experts were predicting a continuing decline in domestic petroleum production and increasing national security risks by heavy US dependence on imported Middle Eastern oil. Moreover, future political events can surprise all policymakers.

The US Energy Information Administration, among the most reliable and competent of America's important sources for energy information and energy modeling, has suggested a number of uncertainties that arise in making its current long-term energy forecasts. First, major global energy producers, such as Saudi Arabia and Russia, will continue to have significant influence in setting global petroleum prices, which can affect future demand for US petroleum abroad and the price of domestic oil. Additionally, domestic economic trends, such as a continuing recession, or sudden economic shocks from an unexpected source, such as international conflicts, can upset future energy scenarios. Federal energy policies can also change. Finally, important current and anticipated future energy technologies may not develop as anticipated.[7]

The Politics

The federal government continues to exert its most potent influence on the domestic petroleum industry through taxes, tax subsidies, regulation of worker safety, and environmental impacts involved in energy production and consumption. Tax subsidies have been by far the most politically contested of all federal and state energy policies for more than five decades. The petroleum industry is among the most heavily subsidized of all domestic industries. Tax breaks at almost every stage of petroleum production have resulted in an effective tax rate estimated to be lower than virtually any other industry.[8]

Petroleum tax subsidies have been a favorite target of criticism by the Obama administration. The petroleum industry continues to fight fiercely and successfully to protect its presently generous tax subsidies. The Obama White House, moreover, has had to accept what every Democratic president has experienced since World War II: When it comes to petroleum subsidies, state loyalty trumps party loyalty among congressional Democrats. Oil-state Democrats seldom vote against the industry when subsidies are at stake.

The traditionally close ties between oil-state Democrats and the industry is testimony to the importance the oil producing states assume in America's energy governance. Petroleum and natural gas exploration has created geographically large and politically influential petroleum royalty dependencies throughout the American West, the Gulf of Mexico, the Atlantic coast, and Alaska. At the outset of the Obama administration, "Alabama, Louisiana, Mississippi, and Texas receive [d] 37.5 percent of the revenues collected by the federal government for offshore energy production," reported the Southeast Energy Alliance, and onshore states "such as Colorado, Montana, New Mexico, and Wyoming receive 50 percent of the royalties collected for energy development on federal lands."[9] The Alliance asserted that North Carolina, ambitious for a share in potential OCS energy production, could receive as much as $577 million annually. Energy industry visions of future state income from new energy production are frequently exaggerated, but there is doubtless enough potential income to whet the appetite of income-strapped state and local governments.

Much of the responsibility for regulating the petroleum industry's workplace safety, environmental impacts, and infrastructure management is shared by the federal government with the states. Historically, states with significant petroleum or natural gas resources have given the responsible regulatory agencies duel and potentially contradictory mandates both to regulate and to promote petroleum or natural gas exploration and production. "Wyoming regulators," as noted in a survey of these state regulatory agencies,

> *are expected to "serve" the industry. Pennsylvania's Bureau of Oil and Gas says its goal is to "facilitate" development. And nearly every other oil and gas agency has a mandate or mission statement establishing increased development as a goal. "We're there to regulate and promote, if you will," Wyoming Oil and Gas Supervisor Tom Doll explained. "Protecting the environment—that's part of the task."[10]*

The Deepwater Horizon tragedy discussed in chapter 1 is a reminder of how deeply the energy states are committed to petroleum production. The West is equally ambitious about its petroleum resources. The White House and the Department of the Interior (DOI) are continually pressed by western state political leaders, including particularly congressional Republicans representing Utah, Colorado, Wyoming, and Montana, to facilitate greater development and further expansion of federal petroleum and natural gas exploration leases.

The political weight of petroleum-dependent geographic constituencies is powerfully amplified by trade associations representing the petroleum and natural gas industry and the hundreds of satellite advocacy organizations for industries and trade groups dependent upon petroleum and its by-products. Petroleum dependent industries, moreover, are a very substantial constituent of the much larger and politically powerful "energy lobby," a broad coalition representing all current conventional energy producers who are estimated to collectively employ more than 1,500 registered lobbyists to look after their interests in Washington.

GOVERNING PETROLEUM: SEEKING A POLICY FUTURE

The energy crises of the 1970s set in motion a variety of federal government interventions in the national and international petroleum markets intended to relieve the short-term, adverse political and economic impacts of domestic shortfalls in petroleum supply. The history of subsequent US petroleum policy is a complex skein of federal attempts to protect national security and to stabilize the domestic petroleum market. The mélange of policies included efforts to control domestic petroleum prices, to buffer the US economy from the shock of future restrictions on oil imports while encouraging more domestic petroleum production, to guarantee domestic reserves sufficient to protect short-term national security, to create an equitable allocation of existing supplies in case of further import shortfalls, and to prevent domestic petroleum producers from harvesting "unfair" profits from sudden escalations in domestic retail gas prices, among other measures.

The substance and impact of these policy experiments have been exhaustively studied and continue to be debated. Energy policy analyst Peter van Doren's conclusion seems reasonable:

> America's experience with oil regulations from the 1930s through the 1970s has been much studied, and an academic consensus is that those regulations had large negative effects on both oil producers and consumers. Congress has typically responded to petroleum-market problems with inappropriate legislation that has damaged markets and prompted further rounds of legislation and regulatory action.[11]

By the early 1990s, in any case, most federal efforts to regulate the domestic petroleum market ended, or transformed into emergency measures, as a result of improving domestic petroleum supply, general price stability, and the absence of effective blockades of imported petroleum.

As the United States heads into the second decade of a new century, numerous policy options continue to be debated to ensure greater security and economic stability of petroleum supply in the future. Equally important, plausible policy options—those politically feasible and potentially effective economically—will often depend to a considerable extent on whether the policy horizon is short term (a few decades) or longer. As a practical matter, noted in chapter 2, short-term policy alternatives are likely to receive greater attention from the White House and Congress and consequently to define the energy policy debate in the political marketplace. Among these policy options, several assume continuing prominence.

Federal Subsidies and Related Petroleum Production Incentives

In July 2011, during the impassioned partisan battle in Congress over extending the limit on the national debt and thereby avoiding a rapidly impending national crisis, contention broke out anew over federal energy subsidies. Apparently, there is seldom a time too troubled for Congress to deny itself an opportunity to debate about energy subsidies. Controversy over the scale and apportionment of federal energy subsidies is a perennial congressional event, beginning with dispute over how the allocations are measured and to which energy sector's advantage. There is no uncertainty, however, that federal subsidies for petroleum exploration and production are generous and fiercely defended by the petroleum industry and its partisans. The EIA has estimated, conservatively, that federal support for the US petroleum and natural gas sector equaled at least $2.8 billion in 2011. Equally important, and unlike support for most unconventional energy resources, particularly solar and wind energy, federal subsidies for petroleum and natural gas, like other fossil fuels, is written into the US Tax Code and is not time limited.[12]

Partisan dispute over the extent of these petroleum subsidies has intensified in recent congressional sessions, with Republicans generally defending existing subsidies against Democratic initiatives to reduce their scope and duration or, alternatively, to increase the tax burden, particularly on petroleum. This partisan polarization is complicated, as we earlier noted, by the political stakes in petroleum production held by states dependent upon energy royalties, or hoping to become so. Disagreements about the magnitude of federal support for petroleum are often grounded, as well, on embedded disputes over how much federal support should be invested in renewable energy and over the comparative proportion of the federal budget allocated to the two energy sectors. Equally important, the economic, political, and national security stakes involved in new petroleum policies are increased because policies intended to significantly influence the future of domestic petroleum production and consumption must necessarily be framed in terms of policy impacts over many future decades.[13]

Environmentalists have been consistently critical of the scale and duration of federal petroleum and natural gas subsidies. They have often been joined by partisans with other, sometimes different policy priorities and professional perspectives, such as national security experts, physical and biological scientists, who nonetheless share a concern with reducing US dependency upon petroleum, domestic or imported. When it comes to policy strategies, discussion almost always focuses upon reducing subsidies, or increasing corporate taxes, or some combination of both. As usual, the devil in the details becomes a divisive influence, even among allies of restrained petroleum production, and thus further complicates an already tangled array of policy options for future petroleum subsidies.

Accelerated Domestic Exploration and Production

Proponents of increased domestic petroleum supply customarily look mostly to a combination of four options: OCS lands, onshore federal lands, Canadian reserves, and oil sands or shale. All these options involve environmental risks whose magnitude is a major source of controversy between partisans and opponents of increased domestic petroleum supply.

OCS lands. The Deepwater Horizon disaster in 2010 again forced upon national attention the contentious political and environmental controversy inseparable from energy development on the Outer Continental Shelf (OCS lands). The controversy is compounded by federalism issues, as well. Jurisdiction over OCS lands is divided between the coastal states, whose authority extends three miles from their ocean borders (except for Texas and the west coast of Florida where state jurisdiction extends to nine nautical miles), and the federal government, which controls OCS lands for 200 miles beyond the state three-mile limit.

Altogether, production from existing state and federal energy leases accounts for about 30 percent of domestic petroleum production and 25 percent of natural gas. The Energy Policy Act (2005), which passed during the G. W. Bush administration and was intended to encourage more domestic production, also increased federal subsidies for OCS energy production. Estimates of the remaining OCS petroleum and natural gas reserves vary considerably, but most suggest very substantial known and potential reserves. The DOI, for instance, estimated in 2006 that reserves of 8.5 billion barrels of oil and 29.3 trillion cubic feet (tcf) of natural gas exist (the United States consumes about 19 million barrels of petroleum and 1.6 million tcf of natural gas daily).[14]

Regulation of energy exploration on the vast federal OCS is vested in the Department of the Interior and, until recently, primarily in the DOI's Minerals Management Service (MMS). The DOI has historically strong ties to petroleum, natural gas, and other fossil fuel interests because DOI's historic, and inconsistent mission, has been to both encourage and regulate exploration and production of resources on the public domain. The Deepwater Horizon oil spill thrust the MMS into unwelcome national attention and dramatized the agency's failure to enforce federal environmental regulations upon petroleum corporations drilling in the Gulf of Mexico. The MMS became a classic example of the problem created when federal agencies are responsible for both regulating and promoting the same industry.

Investigation by the DOI's own inspector general, a bipartisan congressional committee, and numerous other official and unofficial entities between 2007 and 2011 revealed the MMS's close identification with regulated petroleum corporations and the congenial collaboration that resulted even before Deepwater Horizon. "Federal officials who oversaw drilling in the Gulf of Mexico," the inspector general reported in 2008, "accepted gifts from oil companies, viewed pornography at work, and even considered themselves part of the industry." A Louisiana MMS district manager was unapologetic about his agency's regulatory soft touch. "Obviously, we're all oil industry," he said.[15] He continued,

> *Almost all of our inspectors have worked for oil companies out on these same platforms. They grew up in the same towns. Some of these people, they've been friends with all their life. They've been with these people since they were kids. They've hunted together. They fish together. They skeet shoot together . . . They do this all the time.*

In the aftermath of more investigations following the 2010 Gulf oil spill, the Obama administration radically reorganized the MMS to end this intimate and pernicious collaboration between regulators and the regulated.

The White House and Congress continue to share a keen and, increasingly, partisan interest in the future of the OCS lands. While congressional Republicans have pressed for accelerated OCS energy development and Democrats have usually advocated restraint, political and economic cross pressures often blur partisan differences, particularly concerning the OCS lands under state jurisdiction. Thus, for example, Florida's Senate and House delegations of both parties are usually together in opposing any OCS development likely to create environmental damage to the state's coast. President Obama initially appeared to favor restrained energy development on OCS lands but, even in the aftermath of Deepwater Horizon, was compelled in the presence of the country's persistently deep economic recession to modify his stance and to advocate "safe and responsible" oil production. He went so far as to declare that his administration officials were working to speed up the leasing process for exploration in the already developed National Petroleum Reserve-Alaska (ANPR), "while also giving oil companies better financial incentives to use and extend certain existing leases in the Gulf of Mexico and elsewhere."[16] The president also indicated his support for accelerated testing of areas off the East Coast for possible future drilling.

ANWR. In addition to the Gulf of Mexico, another continuing flashpoint of OCS controversy has been the waters close to the Arctic National Wildlife Refuge (ANWR). The ANWR constitutes 16.6 million acres of prime polar bear wilderness in the remote northeastern coast of Alaska, among the wildest and most inaccessible of US public lands. Like most public lands owned by the federal government, ANWR's size and purpose are defined by Congress, and the responsibility for its oversight is vested in the DOI.

Much of ANWR has been opened to oil and natural gas exploration. The Trans-Alaskan pipeline, created in 1971, has been producing almost one million barrels of petroleum daily from Prudhoe Bay on Alaska's North Slope, and 90 percent of the adjacent coastal lands remain open for gas and oil leasing. However, about 1.5 million acres of the coastal plain, considered to be the most biologically rich and vulnerable within the ANWR, has been restricted from energy exploration unless such activity is specifically authorized by Congress. This region is the epicenter of the political conflict over the ANWR.

The ecological riches of this area, known as "1002 Area," are undisputed. This natural endowment includes 160 bird species; the most important onshore denning area in the United States for polar bears; the principal calving ground for 130,000 migratory porcupine caribou; habitat for grizzly bears, arctic foxes, wolves, wolverine, and numerous whales; and many endangered plant and animal species. Ruggedly beautiful wilderness and vast Arctic panoramas invite recreation and tourism. Alaska's natural endowment resonates powerfully among environmentalists who believe much would be sacrificed to produce exaggerated quantities of petroleum unlikely to alleviate significantly the nation's energy problems.[17]

Some of the stakeholders in the ANWR conflict are highly visible: Congress, the White House, the DOI, environmental advocates, energy industries, labor unions representing workers employed in related energy production, and foreign governments, including Japan and China, that might become large consumers of the petroleum produced from the 1002 Area, and Alaska. Alaska's situation is unique. Royalties from energy production are the state's economic foundation. Every Alaskan resident—man, woman, and child—is reminded about this economic dependence by an annual check representing his or her share of more than $660 million in annual dividends from state oil royalties.[18] Alaskans largely support energy exploration in ANWR and resent what they consider interference by Washington, DC, and other interests, especially environmentalists, in what should be Alaska's own affair. Many of Alaska's Native Americans, however, are unlikely to cheer. The Inupiat Eskimos and the Gwich'in Indians, an indigenous subsistence culture, are among the native tribes heavily dependent on the 1002 Area's continued ecological vitality for food and fuel. The state's commercial fishing interests were also disturbed by the possible degradation of their offshore stocks.

Proponents of energy exploration in the 1002 Area speak primarily about national security, energy supply, and coexistence between energy production and environmental protection. They assert, for instance, that drilling in the area could produce petroleum equal to thirty years of oil imports from Saudi Arabia. They also contend that newer, more efficient energy production technologies will limit the amount of land that would be disturbed by energy production to a few thousand acres and, in any case, that the ecological disruption involved is vastly exaggerated by environmental opponents. Most important, proponents of further energy production argue that the reserves now untapped under the 1002 Area will improve US security by decreasing dependence on imported oil.[19]

Since 1980, the DOI has been ready to sell energy exploration leases on the 1002 Area, but, because Congress must first agree, the political battle over exploration has been waged largely within Congress and the White House. Since 1996, legislation permitting the leases has been approved in the House of Representatives twelve times and then defeated, usually in the Senate.[20] Generally, the ANWR issue has been a partisan affair, dividing pro-development Republicans from Democratic opponents and leaving Congress deadlocked over the ANWR issue throughout the Obama administration.

Obama declared his opposition to ANWR development, during his first presidential campaign. However, the Obama administration has become increasingly irresolute on the issue. Generally, the Obama administration has repeatedly declared that the Alaska refuge "is a very special place" that must be protected but energy exploration has not been precluded if it can be proved environmentally safe. Public opposition to OCS development, including the ANWR, appeared to grow in the immediate aftermath of the Deepwater Horizon oil spill. However, with the passage of time and the persistent increase in retail gasoline prices through much of 2012, public approval for new OCS development appeared to increase significantly while opposition to ANWR exploration seemed to diminish, thus, leaving the ANWR insecure and destined for continual contention among a multitude of political and economic interests.

Oil shale and the Keystone XL pipeline. The price of global crude petroleum has risen almost continually since 2000, providing petroleum producers with incentive to seek or to expand once unprofitable alternative petroleum sources and to develop technologies for their exploitation. "Oil shale" has become the prime candidate for accelerated development to supplement traditional petroleum reserves.

Oil shale, sometimes called "oil sands" or "tar sands" is primarily three different petroleum products: oil shale (rock that releases petroleum-like liquids when heated in a special chemical process); tar sands (heavy, thick, black oil mixed with sand, clay, and water); and heavy crude oil (thicker and slower flowing than conventional oil). Significant quantities of petroleum are usually mixed with these materials "like an egg in cake batter," requiring a much more complicated and expensive technology for extraction and refinement than traditional petroleum reserves. Global oil shale contains an enormous volume of potentially extractable crude petroleum, often called "bitumen."

> *The most extensive deposits . . . are in North and South America. A region covering parts of Colorado, Utah, and Wyoming contains oil shale totaling about three times the proven oil reserves of Saudi Arabia. About two-thirds of the world's supply of tar sands (estimated at 5 trillion barrels, though not all of it recoverable) is found in Canada and Venezuela. Venezuela also has the largest known reserves of heavy crude oil, estimated at 235 billion barrels.[21]*

Canada and oil shale. Canadian oil shale has been especially attractive to American energy policymakers because it is a large and secure oil and natural gas source. The Canadian deposits, mined since 1967, cover an area approximately the size of England, primarily in Alberta province, and contain an estimated 170 billion barrels of oil. The Keystone XL project would double the amount of Canadian petroleum presently imported into the United States and would itself provide 5 percent of current US petroleum consumption and represent 9 percent of US petroleum imports.[22]

Three existing portions of the pipeline now extend from Alberta Province to Oklahoma. The fourth component, the proposed Keystone XL, would add several additional segments to the existing line to create a new route from Alberta Province to the Gulf of Mexico. This new route would extend the pipeline for the first time through Montana, Nebraska, and Oklahoma to the Gulf Coast. The 485-mile southern leg of the new pipeline is virtually complete. After initially opposing the southern segment, Obama approved it in March 2012 after the developers made sufficient changes to satisfy the White House. What remains in dispute is the so-called Northern leg, a 1,179-mile northern line yet to be built between Hardisty, Alberta, and Steele City, Oklahoma.

The "fracking" controversy. The fracking technology rapidly spreading across the United States and Canada for oil shale drilling has been environmentally controversial, as the later discussion about natural gas further illustrates. What is undisputed is that oil shale mining requires extensive surface and subsurface geological disruption with potentially adverse environmental impacts. A National Academy of Sciences report notes that oil shale mining "is much more costly, energy intensive, and environmentally damaging than drilling for conventional oil. The processes by which we mine and refine oil shale and tar sands to produce usable oil, for example, involve significant disturbance of the land, extensive use of water (a particular concern in dry regions where oil shale is often found), and potential emissions of pollutants to the air and groundwater. In addition, more energy goes into these processes than into extracting and refining conventional oil, and more CO_2 is emitted."[23] Canada's Alberta oil shale production has removed thousands of acres of Boreal forest, requiring the displacement of 100 tons of surface soil for every barrel of refined petroleum eventually produced. Surface water is often polluted with potentially harmful levels of heavy metals—including cadmium, copper, lead, mercury, nickel, silver, and zinc.[24] However, evidence of fracking's adverse environmental impact has been fragmentary and inconclusive. The US EPA is expected to issue an important report on the environmental aspects of fracking in late 2013 or 2014.

Because the proposed XL line crosses international borders, responsibility for its environmental assessment and eventual permitting rests with the US Department of State (USDOS). The State Department's required environmental review of XL, completed in 2011, declared the project would have "no significant impact" on the environment, a decision quickly renewing an already heated controversy over the pipeline.

The pipeline issue creates an unusual mix of partisans and opponents. On the supporting side are business groups, oil companies, labor unions (plumbers, pipefitters, operating engineers, construction unions), the Canadian government, numerous congressional Republicans and construction equipment manufacturers, and congressional representatives of Utah, Colorado, and Wyoming who contended that the Obama administration was "locking up" their own states' large oil shale reserves.[25]

On the other side are environmentalists, ranchers, and farmers in Nebraska and other states designated potential pipeline sites; political conservatives who "don't like the idea that TransCanada [the pipeline builders] might say that their land had to be used for this pipeline"; proponents of renewable energy development; and many congressional Democrats and conservationists, among others.[26] There was no doubt that many environmental organizations, normally dependable Democratic presidential supporters, had been prepared to penalize Obama in the 2012 election if he permitted Keystone XL.[27]

No final decision about Keystone XL. In November 2011, the State Department, with the President's endorsement, announced that it would delay an XL decision because "it was concerned about the Nebraska part of the route and . . . finding and reviewing an alternate path could take until 2013," apparently leaving a prickly political legacy for the next White House occupant.[28] Then, in January 2012, the president postponed a decision about the northern segment of the Keystone, arguing that more time should be given to study that portion after the 2012 presidential election. Later in 2012, Obama approved the southern XL extension, still leaving the fate of the northern segment unresolved. So the issue remained into 2013 when it appeared that a final White House decision might not appear until 2014.

Regardless of the pipeline's eventual fate, many petroleum industry spokesmen, policy analysts, and political representatives from states with significant oil shale deposits are predicting a vigorous "boom" in domestic petroleum production driven by the new shale fracking technology. One group of experts has predicted that at least twenty US shale formations can yield significant new crude oil. But other energy industry experts, wary of the economic uncertainties in future petroleum markets and the durability of the newer mining technologies, are less certain about the long-term implications of accelerated oil shale mining. Once again, predictions about long-term petroleum use, like predictions about the future of other energy sources, rest uneasily on a shifting foundation of assumptions about future economic, political, and social conditions. The increasing development of oil shale drilling and the generally benign regulation it currently experiences from federal and state governments suggest a high probability that it will account for an increasing proportion of domestic crude oil production, perhaps accounting for as much as 10 percent of total annual domestic crude oil production within a decade.[29]

Creating More by Using Less: Petroleum Conservation and Substitution

Increased conservation of petroleum usage remains an important and feasible strategy for diminishing the rate of growth in domestic petroleum production and consumption. Usage conservation can displace otherwise consumed petroleum and thereby extend the future supply of petroleum. Most experts believe presently available technologies, together with existing and proposed future federal, state, and local legislation, could reduce annual domestic petroleum consumption by 10 to 15 percent.

Since energy policies are always related, many policies not targeted primarily at reducing domestic petroleum consumption may directly, or indirectly, encourage greater petroleum conservation. Federal air pollution standards, for instance, encourage the use of cleaner burning auto fuels and greater fuel efficiency. State policies intended to reduce emission of climate warming gases, such as CO_2, may also encourage industrial and commercial installations to substitute biofuels, such as ethanol or natural gas for petroleum.

Federal and state governments have already enacted numerous laws explicitly promoting petroleum conservation. These include the following:

- Auto and truck fuel efficiency standards—federal law currently requires that all new automobiles and light trucks purchased in the United States achieve an average fuel efficiency of 35 miles per gallon by 2020

- Labeling, which provides consumers comparative information on fuel efficiency
- Incentives, both financial and nonfinancial, which target manufacturers and consumers to encourage market front-runners to develop and purchase more efficient vehicles
- Technical assistance, which assists the public and private sectors in adopting fuel-efficient technologies and implementing policies to reduce fuel consumption
- Urban planning and behavior change, including zoning, traffic design, and idle reduction rules to reduce fuel consumption
- Research and development (R&D) support to encourage development and testing of more energy efficient technologies—for example, incentives to increase efficiency and market competitiveness of hybrid and alternative fuel engines
- Replacement of petroleum in the transportation sector with biofuels, or blended petroleum and biofuel[30]

Alternative fuels for petroleum became one of the most significant energy conservation issues crowding the Washington policy agenda at the end of Obama's initial term when the federal government's continuing promotion of ethanol—the nation's most important transportation fuel additive—was entangled in congressional controversy over reducing the national debt.

Ethanol

In 2011, at a time when the virtues of "renewable energy" had become virtually a cliché in American political discourse, ethanol fuel producers and blenders faced a paradox. For the first time in more than three decades, they confronted a fierce political battle to protect their privileged status in federal and state law.

Most Americans may know little about ethanol, but they use lots of it. Ethanol is as close to the average American as the nearest gas pump. Virtually all gasoline now sold in the United States contains ethanol, a "biofuel" distilled from corn. Producers and marketers of gasoline customarily blend ethanol and gas in the cargo tanks of gasoline delivery trucks before the mixture is transported to energy markets. Most gasoline consumed in the United States is blended in a mixture of 10 percent ethanol and 90 percent gasoline (often called E10), the legal limit of ethanol additive permitted by federal law until 2010.

Domestic corn ethanol is an example right out of Government 101, exemplifying how energy resources, like numerous other commodities in the American energy economy, are politically promoted, protected, and defended through the institutional, legal, and economic structures of the American policy process. In this respect, as subsequent chapters will illustrate, there is nothing unique to corn ethanol, which joins other energy resources like coal, petroleum, and nuclear power in acquiring economic advantages through public law and which, once attained, are formidably difficult to diminish and powerfully defended by the beneficiaries.

A financially privileged biofuel. In the aftermath of the energy shocks during the 1970s, the federal government passed the Energy Policy Act (1978), creating a subsidy for blenders, and created a tariff to protect domestic producers from imported ethanol. Ethanol gained additional federal patronage as a result of two major congressional acts passed during the G. W. Bush administration. The Energy Policy Act of 2005 required an increasing volume of ethanol and biodiesel to be blended with the US fuel supply between 2006 and 2012. The Energy Independence and Security Act of 2007 mandated a progressive increase in domestic renewable fuel use to 36 billion gallons annually by 2022. These combined incentives created an increasingly strong ethanol market growing from two million gallons in 1981 to about thirteen billion gallons in 2010. By 2011, combined federal ethanol subsidies exceeded $6 billion annually.[31]

Most experts believe that the two Bush-era programs practically ensure a continually growing market for ethanol fuel. Moreover, the EPA ruled in October 2010 that cars and light trucks in model year 2007 and thereafter can also use a richer blend of 15 percent ethanol and 85 percent gasoline ("E15"). The newer blend requires a *flex fuel vehicle* that is expected to become more common as environmental regulations and increasing gasoline prices increase ethanol's market appeal.[32] Producers and blenders of ethanol fuel, having successfully defended this federal largesse for more than three decades, now confront increasing opposition to continuing federal subsidies and import tariffs in the aftermath of the severe economic recession beginning in 2008 and the resulting federal budget crises.

End to subsidized ethanol? The federal subsidy for ethanol producers and blenders created in 2005 was mandated to expire at the end of 2011. The mandate was renewed for five additional years in 2011, however, despite considerable opposition from an unusual alliance of environmentalists, fiscal conservatives, producers of competing biofuels, and many congressmen in both parties. Fiscal conservatives and a substantial bipartisan congressional coalition believe that federal law now ensures a growing future demand for fuel ethanol that precludes the need for continuing subsidies, especially when federal budget deficits have created an economic crisis requiring severe reductions in federal expenditures. The battle against the mandate has continued well into Obama's second term.

Many environmentalists assert that ethanol has been unwisely exempted by Congress from a provision of the 2007 Energy Independence and Security Act requiring all other, potentially competitive biofuels to reduce greenhouse gas (GHG) emissions by 20 percent compared to gasoline, thereby, giving ethanol a competitive advantage over alternative, and more environmentally beneficial, biofuels. (Corn-based ethanol creates more GHG emissions than alternative biofuels, such as cellulosic and sugar cane.) Additionally, they argue that federal subsidies have encouraged the increasing conversion and environmental degradation of farm land—about 40 percent of all corn cultivated domestically is used for ethanol production—that could be used for more environmentally beneficial crops. Additionally, corn ethanol production is asserted to be more energy intensive than potentially competitive biofuels.[33] Moreover, the critics add, the subsidies aren't needed to ensure corn ethanol an attractive market. Ending federal subsidies, remarked a spokesperson for the influential Environmental Working Group, "is definitely overdue. We think of it . . . as a 50-year old that needs to move out of their parent's basement."[34]

Ethanol growers are concerned that the end of federal subsidies will also be accompanied by termination of the tariff on imported ethanol that has protected domestic producers from global competitors,

Natural gas
• where is it found
• uses
• what is it
• price ceiling

CARBON POLICY: PETROLEUM AND NATURAL GAS   8

particularly Brazil, the second largest global producer of corn etha-nol and an aggressive marketer internationally. Competitive ethanol imports, argue corn ethanol proponents, also will cost Americans jobs and income. "Ethanol is America's fuel: It's made here in the United States, it creates US jobs, and it contributes to America's national and economic security," asserted retired Gen. Wesley Clark, cochairman of Growth Energy, a major ethanol industry interest group.[35] And, striking a note intended to resonate with environmental advocates, corn ethanol proponents have warned that opening the domestic market to imported Brazilian ethanol will accelerate further destruction of the already badly reduced Brazilian rain forest ecosystem.

NATURAL GAS: A MIX OF REWARDS AND RISKS

Natural gas in its several different forms is, in many respects, the most attractive of all the fossil fuels in the nation's near future. Natural gas is commercially produced primarily from oil fields and natural gas fields, although the industry is now aggressively extracting natural gas from unconventional sources such as shale gas and coal bed methane. Traditional *casinghead*, or "associated" gas, principally methane mixed with numerous impurities, is refined into ethane, propane, butanes, pentanes, and other commercial forms, which for convenience are often collectively called "natural gas." While the largest proven natural gas reserves are located in Russia, Iran, and the Arabian Gulf states, US proven reserves are significant and, as new extraction technolo-gies develop, steadily increasing. To many US energy sectors, natural gas is increasingly attractive, economically and environmentally, as an alternative to petroleum and coal *if* its entailed risks prove acceptable. And, like all projections about future domestic energy use, predictions depend upon numerous assumptions or "scenarios"—such as con-tinued economic growth and absence of major political crises—that caution against treating predictions as if they are destiny.

Domestic Resources: Increasing Supply and Demand

Proven reserves of domestic onshore and offshore natural gas have grown annually since 1999 as a result of improved technologies and the development of economically practical extraction from shale with fracking technology.[36] According to the EIA, the United States possesses 2,543 trillion cubic feet (tcf) of potential natural gas resources. At the 2010 rate of US consumption, this is enough natural gas to supply over one hundred years of domestic use. More than 90 percent of current domestic natural gas originates from onshore sources, the rest primarily from the Gulf of Mexico. Nineteen states are estimated to possess significant natural gas reserves.[37] Domestic production of natural gas is expected to increase significantly in the future, but so is total US energy demand; the EIA has predicted that by 2030 natural gas will provide about 25 percent of domestic energy consumption—about the proportion of current consumption. However, the predicted changes in how natural gas is produced and consumed are important.

A Versatile Fuel

Natural gas is the most versatile of domestic fossil fuels. As Figure 3-4 indicates, it provides a significant portion of energy to several important US economic sectors. The anticipated growth in natural gas supply into a widely predicted boom is the result of increased profit margins for gas extracted from shale, and especially from the technological improvements in horizontal hydraulic fracturing, or fracking. The potential productivity of fracking has also incited increased pressure upon Washington from many states to accelerate gas exploration on federal lands within their borders. The environmental controversy is certain to magnify as expectations for future gas production from hydraulic fracturing increases: the DOE has estimated that fracking may provide as much as 20 percent of the nation's total natural gas supply by 2020.

Much of the expected change in future natural gas production and consumption is expected to result not only from increased fracking but also from changes in fossil fuel consumption by the electric power and industrial sections, which together consume almost two-thirds of current natural gas production. Both economic sectors have responded to tougher air pollution regulations and the increasing economic attractions of natural gas by substituting gas for coal-fired facilities in existing or planned installations. Progress Energy, for example, one of the nation's largest electric utilities, has announced plans to shut down eleven North Carolina coal plants by 2017 and to substitute natural gas in two of them.[38]

FIGURE 3-4	US Natural Gas End Use, 2012

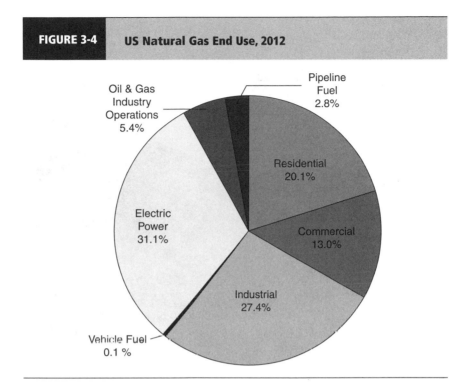

Source: Center for Climate and Energy Solutions, "U.S. Natural Gas Overview of Markets and Use, 2011," at http://www.c2es.org/publications/natural-gas-markets-use-overview. Based upon U.S. Energy Information Administration, *Natural Gas Annual*, 2012 (Washington, DC: Energy Information Administration, 2012), Table 1, p. 1.

"Almost a Miracle" or an Environmental Menace?

In 2000, the future domestic supply and economic competitiveness of natural gas seemed problematic, an important concern because natural gas has many environmentally attractive qualities. It releases fewer emissions of regulated air pollutants and CO_2 per Btu than coal or petroleum, a major reason electric utilities consider it an attractive substitute for more environmentally polluting coal. Thus, the prospect for an unanticipated growth in future gas reserves sufficient to enhance its economic competitiveness with other fossil fuels has been potentially good news for natural gas consumers and, especially, for the industry itself.

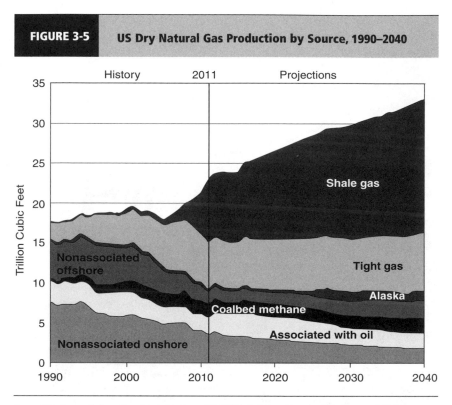

FIGURE 3-5   **US Dry Natural Gas Production by Source, 1990–2040**

Source: U.S. Energy Information Administration, *AEO2013 Early Release Overview* (Washington, DC: Energy Information, 2013), 2.

The fracking boom. Enormous deposits of oil shale underlie the United States, as illustrated in Figure 3-6. The natural gas industry is riding a rising tide of optimism sustained by fracking technology. At the outset of the Obama administration, the new drilling boom incited by fracking seemed to many industry leaders a certain path toward a bright future. "It's almost divine intervention," burbled Aubrey K. McClendon, chairman and chief executive of the Chesapeake Energy Corporation, one of the nation's largest natural gas producers. "Right at the time oil prices are skyrocketing, we're struggling with the economy, we're concerned about global warming, and national security threats remain intense, we wake

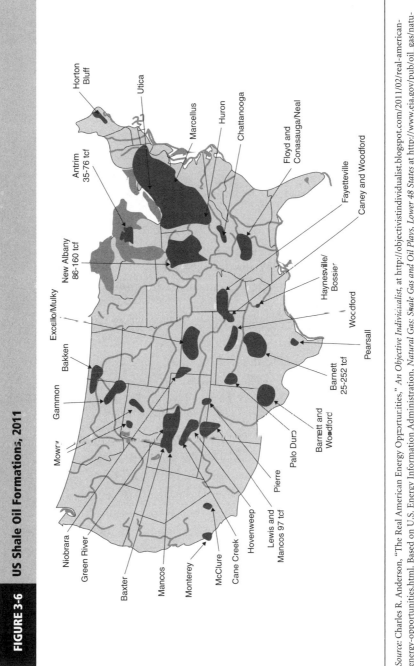

FIGURE 3-6   **US Shale Oil Formations, 2011**

Horton
Bluff

Utica

Marcellus

Antrim
35-76 tcf

Huron

Chattanooga

Floyd and
Conasauga/Neal

New Albany
86-160 tcf

Fayetteville

Caney and Woodford

Excello/Mulky

Haynesville/
Bossier

Woodford

Bakken

Gammon

Pearsall

Mowry

Barnett
25-252 tcf

Niobrara

Barnett and
Woodford

Green River

Palo Duro

Baxter

Pierre

Mancos

Hovenweep

Monterey

Lewis and
Mancos 97 tcf

McClure

Cane Creek

Source: Charles R. Anderson, "The Real American Energy Opportunities," *An Objective Individualist*, at http://objectivistindividualist.blogspot.com/2011/02/real-american-energy-opportunities.html. Based on U.S. Energy Information Administration, *Natural Gas: Shale Gas and Oil Plays, Lower 48 States* at http://www.eia.gov/pub/oil_gas/natural_gas/analysis_publications/maps/maps.htm.

up and we've got this abundance of natural gas around us."[39] Not all industry experts share this confidence. Still, steadily increasing gas production throughout the Obama administration's first term encouraged most energy experts and financial markets to view the industry's future with cautious optimism.

A disputed environmental impact. The issue that most conspicuously threatens to dissipate optimism about a coming boom in natural gas production is the environmental risks entailed with fracking technology.

Hydrologic fracturing "involves pumping liquids under high pressure into a well to fracture the rock and allow gas to escape from tiny pockets in the rock." Millions of gallons of chemically treated water called "brine" mixed with sand is blasted down a drilling hole to shatter petroleum shale and release the embedded gas. The return water, called "flowback," is a cocktail of water, chemical toxins, and carcinogens; other chemical wastes sometimes including radioactive components; and inert substances that must be purified before the flowback is suitable for other uses. Most of the return water, however, is pumped back underground into shale sites for containment. Almost all natural gas exploration and production from leases on federal lands, most west of the Mississippi River or in the Gulf of Mexico, use fracking technology regulated by the Department of the Interior. The largest private fracking operations are sited on the Barnett Shale formation near Fort Worth and on the vast Marcellus Shale underlying portions of Pennsylvania, New York, West Virginia, and Ohio. Pennsylvania alone has more than 57,000 gas producing wells. These nonfederal sites are presently regulated by the states.

Environmentalists and many residents in communities near fracking operations regard hydrologic fracturing ambivalently. They recognize fracking's economic appeal, especially amid a severe economic recession, but they also contend that fracking disrupts surface and ground water and eventually can infiltrate community water supplies with a variety of environmentally hazardous chemicals, such as dissolved or ambient methane, and inert materials.[40] Because many existing and planned fracking operations are located near sources of drinking water for large population centers, such as Chicago, Philadelphia, and New York, state and local officials have become increasingly insistent that federal EPA and state environmental regulators investigate the environmental risks associated with the technology. Federal law does not now require drilling companies to disclose the ingredients for their mining water.[41] Under considerable political pressure from oil shale states, environmentalists, Congress, and communities near fracking operations, the EPA has initiated studies to characterize the content and dispersion of flowback. The final report is scheduled in 2014.

Many gas production companies contend their brine formula is a trade secret and refuse to disclose its composition. Also, they contend that their brine is environmentally safe because it is injected thousands of feet below drinking water aquifers, sufficiently deep to avoid groundwater contamination, and that the flowback not returned deep underground is purified before it's released for other purposes. Moreover, drillers assert that proven technologies are available for distilling an environmentally safe liquid from flowback when needed. (The CEO of Halliburton Co., a major energy consulting firm, was so convinced of the safety that he invited an associate to drink some of it during a meeting of the Colorado Oil and Gas Association, and the media reported that his associate consumed a "bit of the liquid.")[42]

Many states overlying large oil shale deposits are not waiting upon EPA's final determination about fracking and have initiated their own investigations with a view toward possibly regulating fracking themselves. New York is among the earliest to impose constraints on hydrologic fracturing until more is known about its environmental consequences. Environmentalists and many residents of communities near fracking operations maintain that the flowback has already created surface and groundwater contamination, air pollution, and residual solid wastes from brine processing including heavy metals and other chemicals toxic to humans and ecologically dangerous.

Governance: Future Policy Options

The future of domestic natural gas policy is a fabric bound together with "ifs" and "buts." With no economically and technologically viable short-term substitute, further domestic exploration and production of natural gas seems inevitable. The Obama administration continued a long-standing federal policy of encouraging domestic natural gas exploration and production on both public and private lands, while simultaneously assuring it would vigilantly regulate the adverse impacts if fracking proves an environmental hazard, thus, leaving the future unsettled. Washington is also under considerable pressure from natural gas producers, the economic sectors dependent upon natural gas—especially the electric power industry—and some states to open additional public and private land overlying gas shale to further exploration and natural gas production. Since the Energy Policy Act (2005) currently exempts fracking operations from federal regulation and a final EPA determination of fracking's environmental impacts, an essential requisite for any future federal regulation is several years in the future; thus, the short-term regulatory initiative has been assumed by the states—unless an environmental disaster on the scale of the Deepwater Horizon crisis compels rapid federal attention to hydrologic fracturing.

At the same time that natural gas is expected to constitute at least a quarter of domestic energy consumption over the next several decades, federal and state governments also have the ability to create additional incentives to fortify the electric power industry's already strong desire to increase its consumption of natural gas as a primary fuel. These incentives might include federal or state tax subsidies for increased production, state regulatory commission requirements that utilities use an increasing proportion of natural gas for power generation, or federal and state regulations that encourage greater utility and industrial reliance on natural gas to replace fossil fuels with higher CO_2 emissions for energy units, and much else. Major policy studies concerned with future domestic energy consumption show that natural gas is, at the very least, an environmentally attractive alternative to other fossil fuels in creating a "bridge" to greater reliance on renewable energy and all the more attractive because it is a secure domestic resource.

Environmentalists have been divided and tentative about the role of natural gas in the nation's energy future. They recognize that continued reliance on natural gas perpetuates the importance of fossil fuels, with all their recognized environmental liabilities, in future energy production. The emergence of fracking as an important production technology awakens apprehension about the long-term environmental risks involved in future natural gas consumption but, at the same time, the availability of natural gas as a less air polluting substitute for coal, especially in electric power production, may enhance its appeal.

Several states overlying large gas shale deposits, such as New York and Pennsylvania, have either adopted, or are considering adopting, short-term moratoriums on new fracking operations until federal or state environmental agencies can make a reliable assessment of the environmental risks entailed in the technology. States may also have an option to control some aspects of fracking by regulating CO_2 emissions, thus, creating a strategy for encouraging greater natural gas consumption as a substitute or alternative for coal consumed in industrial and commercial sectors. Some communities near fracking sites are also contemplating regulation, and in a few instances, they have already initiated efforts to characterize the environmental impact of the process. The three-layer deep governmental concern about fracking regulation also creates a classic federalism issue involving uncertainty and potential conflict over regulatory powers and responsibility for drilling oversight.

CONCLUSION: THE FOUNDATION OF ENERGY POLICY

Petroleum and natural gas remain the foundation fuels of the American energy economy. Since World War II, petroleum has provided almost exclusively the energy powering domestic transportation and will continue to be the primary source of transportation for many future decades. Beginning in 2005, new and unconventional technologies associated with fracking have vastly increased the potential supply of natural gas and petroleum, leading many experts to predict a surge in domestic petroleum that within a few decades will vastly improve national energy security now hostage to imported petroleum. Fracking technology, additionally, is widely predicted to create a boom in future petroleum and natural gas supplies. The policy implications of a fracking boom might be profound. A growing future supply and diminishing cost of natural gas, already a significant fuel source of electric power, could accelerate the substitution of gas for coal as the primary fuel for power generation. Since natural gas also creates significantly lower emissions of air pollutants and climate warming chemicals than coal combustion, the collateral value of natural gas in future environmental regulation could also be important.

Petroleum and natural gas also pose significant policy challenges for national policymakers. The long-running conflict over federal government subsidies and tax concessions for petroleum producers remains. Controversy prevails about access to domestic petroleum and natural gas reserves; about the priorities to be accorded renewable energy, nuclear power, and energy conservation; and about governmental subsidies for alternative energy from biofuels, such as ethanol. Environmentalists and their allies continue to press Washington and the states for more vigorous environmental regulation of the production and consumption of carbon fuels and, especially, for an aggressive national regulatory program for climate changing emissions from carbon combustion. Domestic petroleum producers have urged the White House and Congress to accelerate their access to domestic petroleum reserves on interior public lands and the OCS. These controversies have been intensified by a growing polarization between Republicans and Democrats in Congress and the White House across almost all domains of energy policy.

In many respects, the resolution of these essential policy issues will also depend upon often problematic, contested estimates of domestic and foreign energy reserves and upon the accuracy of the economic and scientific models upon which policymakers often rely when attempting to anticipate future energy supply and demand. Additionally, the optimistic glow attending many predictions of future energy supply associated with new fracking technology cannot conceal the dark uncertainties about fracking's potential environmental risks yet to be accurately characterized.

CARBON POLICY
Coal

> "The men who work in surface mining are terrified they will lose
> their jobs. I am terrified that my granddaughter will not
> have clean drinking water when she is of child-bearing
> age if we don't stop this."[1]
>
> *Resident, Coal River Mountain, West Virginia*

> "Coal has been an energy that's basically domestic, that's affordable and
> reliable and dependable. Until we find the next clean fuel of the
> future that does everything that coal does 24/7, let's not
> destroy what has brought us to where we are."[2]
>
> *Democratic Gov. Joe Manchin of West Virginia*

The year 2008 was a vintage year for financial failures. It was the year of
the great housing market collapse, the Wall Street panic, the $7 billion
bailout of federal government mortgage agencies Fannie Mae and
Freddie Mac. By the end of the year, the stock market had collapsed by
34 percent, and America plunged into the worst economic recession
in history.

So saturated was the year with grim financial news from Washington
that the national media virtually ignored a comparatively minor federal
failure when Washington decided to write off perhaps $100 million in

preliminary costs and to cancel further development of Future Gen, thus, ending construction of the world's first, and most widely advertised, unconventional coal-fired power utility intended to capture 90 percent of its CO_2 emissions and store them safely underground. The modest cost of Future Gen's cancellation, however, was deceptive. For proponents of coal energy, Future Gen marked a major setback for "clean coal," and continues to blight the vision of an American future built on the one fossil fuel abundantly and securely American.

THE TROUBLED FUTURE OF FUTURE GEN

The Bush administration had announced in 2003 its intention to construct a near zero-emission, coal-fired power plant called Future Gen to demonstrate to the electric power industry the economic and technical feasibility of electric power production with clean coal. Future Gen was to be the "marquee" example of the new technology's economic and technical feasibility.[3] The coal industry and other proponents of clean coal anticipated the creation of a facility that would simultaneously gasify coal to separate out its pollutants from hydrogen then use the hydrogen to drive electric power generators while pumping CO_2 emissions securely underground. The demonstration facility with the capacity to power 70,000 homes was to be constructed by a partnership between the federal government, private investors, the electric power industry, and international partners, such as China and Russia, near Mattoon Township, Coles County, Illinois. The project was vigorously promoted in Congress and at the Department of Energy (DOE) by more than a dozen coal companies and utilities from around the world. If Future Gen lived up to expectations, it was predicted to initiate a new global era of clean coal-fired electric utilities.

The economic and political stakeholders had fought hard to get Future Gen to Mattoon Township. Like many federal government projects initially supported with R&D money from DOE, Future Gen had significant economic attractions. The state of Illinois, local government business and political leaders, coal industry interests, and electric power labor unions, among others, expected clean coal to generate jobs—lots of them. State and local interests predicted that Future Gen might create 1,300 construction jobs and 150 high-skilled staff positions. Moreover, proponents of Future Gen were very much aware that DOE planned to spend more than $1.1 billion on future clean energy projects. Perhaps a successful Future Gen would invite further federal investment in project development.

By mid-2008, however, a Future Gen near Mattoon Township was an illusion. DOE estimated the costs would soar unacceptably to $1.8 billion, cancelled the project, and later announced that a Future Gen 2.0 based upon a different technology would be built in another Illinois county. Moreover, as if to season disappointment with insult, DOE also planned to convert the Mattoon project into a facility to store underground CO_2 emissions from a new Future Gen 2.0 built elsewhere, when and *if* Future Gen 2.0 materialized. By the end of the first Barack Obama administration, Future Gen had faded into a future ripe with formidable economic and political uncertainties. For proponents of clean coal technology, it was a major setback. Disillusioned state and local leaders withdrew their invitation to build a DOE demonstration facility in Coles County. [4]

In the long perspective of national coal history, Future Gen 1.0 has become a metaphor for the promise and perils inherent to any policy designed for the future of domestic coal consumption. As Future Gen illustrates, coal policy is simultaneously embedded in a complex matrix of political, technological, environmental, and economic issues not easily or quickly resolved into a coherent policy framework. The substance of all coal policy, however, begins with the geography and economics of coal mining and combustion.

THE RESOURCE: "A SAUDI ARABIA OF COAL"

Every American president from Richard Nixon through George W. Bush has tried, in one way or another, to dam the flow of imported oil with a wall of coal—understandably, for nature was not merely generous but extravagant with the coal resources inherited by the United States. Coal is America's most abundant fossil fuel resource, capable of sustaining current domestic consumption for at least several more centuries if Americans were willing to ignore the environmental risks inseparable from coal development.

Once America's "Great Black Hope"

The 1970s energy shocks inspired the coal industry to claim that coal was "the great Black Hope of America" and, one way or another, coal consumption since the 1970s has been equated with American security in all energy policy discourse. Coal represents about 90 percent of America's remaining hydrocarbon reserves. This coal rests in three great geologic reserves: Appalachia's wooded hills and hollows sprawling across seven southeastern states, the Midwestern plains, and the western plains and grasslands. As Figure 4-1 illustrates, five states produce most of America's currently consumed coal.

Coal produces about 22 percent of America's total energy consumption. More than 90 percent of this coal is presently consumed by the electric power industry, which, in turn, produces about half of its power from coal combustion. Thus, coal and electric power policy are inextricably linked technologically, economically, and politically.

Until the end of World War II, most domestic coal was produced from Appalachian deep shaft mines (Figure 4-2). Since 1960, however, an increasing proportion of US coal production has been surface mined. Currently, surface mines produce about two-thirds of the all-domestic coal consumption. The shift to surface mining has profoundly transformed coal's economic and environmental impact.

For most major coal companies, surface mining is less labor intensive, more efficient, and more economically attractive than deep-shaft mining. Surface mining has also elevated by several orders of magnitude the long-term environmental risks entailed in coal production, especially west of the Mississippi River where most large surface mines currently operate.

A Troubled Future

Historically, the coal industry has been economically fragile, plagued by recurrent cycles of boom and bust, repeated labor and safety problems, and gradually increasing competition from competing fuels to generate electric power. Since 2003, coal consumption by the electric power industry has steadily diminished from 50 percent to less than 40 percent in 2012, primarily the result of the emerging boom in natural gas production.

FIGURE 4-1 Top Coal Producing States, 2011

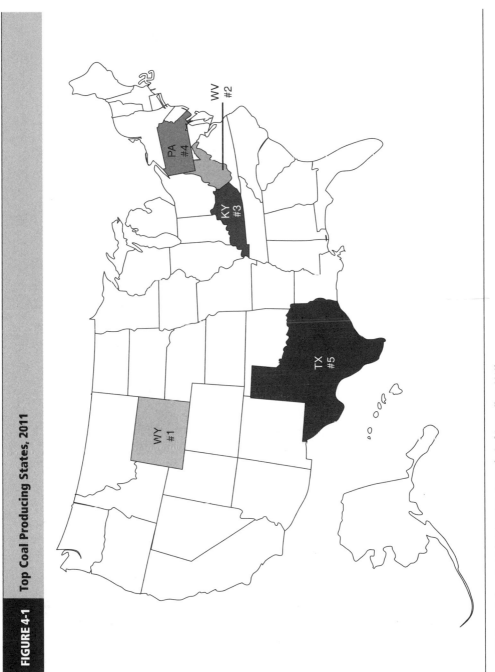

Source: U.S. Energy Information Administration, *Quarterly Coal Report* (June 2012).

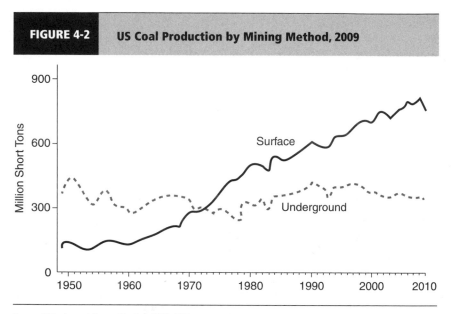

| FIGURE 4-2 | US Coal Production by Mining Method, 2009 |

Source: EIA, *Annual Energy Outlook*, 2009, 297.

As the price of natural gas has decreased, it has become increasingly attractive as a primary fuel for electric utilities that find it cheaper and more environmentally clean than coal for current and future facilities.[5]

Currently facing an economically risky future, the industry's most formidable challenges are to discover technologies that can reduce its air pollution emissions so that it can remain competitive with natural gas in the domestic electric power industry, and to find new overseas markets, especially in China and India, which would compensate for its falling US consumption.

When "Clean Coal" Isn't Clean: The Environmental Impact of Coal

No issue stalks discussion of national coal policy more relentlessly and disruptively than the environmental impact of coal mining, transport, and combustion. The coal industry has waged an expensive campaign for more than twenty-five years to cultivate a public perception that coal is clean energy. While coal may be clean energy when consumed in the form of electric power, it presents a multitude of environmental problems in all other respects. Every stage in the coal utilization cycle entails significant environmental and human health risks unless properly managed and regulated. These hazards range across practically all major environmental domains:

- *Air pollution.* Coal combustion is a leading cause of smog, acid rain, the carbon dioxide associated with global warming, and air toxins. More than 850 electric power plants, release numerous pollutants regulated nationally by the Clean Air Act. "Electricity generation is the dominant industrial source of air emissions in the United States today," reported the US Environmental Protection Agency (EPA). "Fossil fuel-fired power plants are responsible for 67 percent of the nation's sulfur dioxide emissions, 23 percent of nitrogen oxide emissions, and 40 percent of man-made carbon dioxide emissions."[6] A large proportion of all regulated air toxins originate from electric power plant emissions.[7]

- *Surface and ground water pollution.* Wastewater created by "scrubbers" utilized to control air pollution from electric power plants contains pollutants, such as chlorine and heavy metals, that often contaminate ground and surface water.[a] Acid mine drainage from underground and surface coal mining is an additionally significant source of water pollutants in mining states.[8] A growing concern is the toxic runoff from solid waste dumps created by electric power companies for disposal of solid and semisolid wastes produced by scrubbers.

- *Solid waste.* A large, coal-fired power plant can produce more than 125,000 tons of ash and 193,000 tons from a smokestack. "More than 75 percent of this waste has been deposited in unlined, unmonitored onsite landfills and surface impoundments," notes the Union of Concerned Scientists.[9] Another study identifies thirty-nine additional coal-ash dump sites in twenty-one states that pollute drinking water with arsenic, lead, and other heavy metals.[10]

---

[a] Typically, power plants also add chlorine or other toxic chemicals to their cooling water to decrease algae growth.

- *Cooling water discharge.* The water used by coal-fired electric utilities to create steam needed to drive turbines is customarily taken from nearby ocean, lake, stream, or groundwater sources. A large coal-fired plant draws about 2.2 billion gallons of water from adjacent water bodies annually. When this water is returned to its source without sufficient cooling, it can create "thermal shock," changes in the dissolved oxygen and redistribution of organisms in the recipient water sources.
- *Climate warming.* Growing international concern about global climate warming has transformed the scientific, economic, and political context for all policy discourse about coal. Coal combustion is the single greatest source of climate warming gases. It accounts for 25 percent of global CO_2 emissions and 80 percent of US emissions. Electric power generation, the major domestic source, produces about 41 percent of annual CO_2 emissions.[11]

THE POLITICS OF COAL POLICY

Between the end of the Civil War and the Great Depression, coal rapidly displaced other fuels to become the major energy source for heavy industry and electric power generation. Domestic coal production peaked in 1918. During the rest of the century, petroleum gradually replaced coal as America's primary energy source.

Throughout much of its history, the coal industry has produced a highly competitive fuel, and coal producers turned to government primarily to gain market advantage. When coal producers confronted an excess capacity between 1930 and the 1970s, coal policy commonly involved conflicts between high-cost and low-cost coal producers pursuing market leverage through various governmental policy interventions and bitter contention between the United Mine Workers, the industry's most important union, and mining companies over working conditions, wages, and related workplace issues. Federal and state governance involved primarily regulation of wages and workplace safety, coal transportation costs, and intermittent wage and price controls. Beginning in the 1960s, the federal government gradually withdrew from economic regulation of coal production, combustion, and markets.

By the mid-1980s, coal politics had been profoundly transformed. The simultaneous impact of the energy crises and the political ascendency of environmentalism substantially redefined the politics of coal policy. Washington's policymakers were strongly interested in coal as a strategic energy resource capable of diminishing, or displacing, demand for imported petroleum. The environmental movement created a vast, new domain of issues and interest conflict focused on the regulation of mining's environmental impacts. Since the 1970s, the politics of coal policy has been dominated by the large coal producers and their trade associations, the coal producing states, environmental interest groups, the federal agencies concerned with energy development and regulation—especially the Department of the Interior, the Department of Energy, and the EPA—and the United Mine Workers, the union voice of working miners.

The Coal Industry

The coal market is currently dominated economically and politically by six corporations, all part of larger energy conglomerates, which collectively produce more than half the nation's annual mined coal: Peabody Energy Corporation, Arch Coal, Cloud Peak Energy, Alpha Natural Resources, CONSOL Energy, Inc., and Massey Energy Co.[12] The coal producers and their economic allies are represented nationally by the National Mining Association (NMA), which describes itself as "the voice of the American mining industry in Washington." The NMA includes "more than 325 corporations involved in all aspects of the mining industry" (see NMA.org), and its membership constitutes a virtual inventory of coal mining's economic and political constituencies: coal, metal and industrial mineral producers, mineral processors, equipment manufacturers, state associations, bulk transporters, engineering firms, consultants, financial institutions, and other companies that supply goods and services to the mining industry.[13]

The NMA, the coal mining corporations, and their various organized policy advocacy groups, such as the American Coalition for Clean Coal Energy, are also among the biggest spenders in the energy sector for legislative lobbying and for state and federal office candidates. In 2008, a presidential election year, mining companies and their trade associations spent more than $31 million on Washington lobbying. During the 2008 elections, coal companies and their employees spent an additional $13 million to support congressional candidates, mostly Republicans.[14]

No states have been more active politically in promoting and defending the coal industry than West Virginia and Kentucky, which produce most of Appalachia's deep-shaft and surface coal. In West Virginia, especially, coal is king, virtually the sole source of economic vitality for the state.[15] Most state residents consider mining's environmental risks a necessary price for good jobs and a steady income. "You couldn't survive in Boone County," observed a local businessman, "without coal. You've got McDonalds. But it would be gone, too, without the miners to eat there."[16] Throughout Appalachia, the Obama administration's advocacy of new environmental regulations for surface mining has become a political liability for Democratic state and federal office candidates and a major reason John McCain won the 2008 presidential election in West Virginia and Kentucky.[17]

Electric Power and Coal

The electric power industry's historic association with coal production creates a community of interest with coal mine operators. Power companies have been concerned through most of their history with ensuring that coal at an acceptable price would be available in sufficient quantity. Electric power companies are among the most regulated industries by both state governments and Washington thus creating a very strong and durable industry engagement in the politics and policy of coal regulation. The National Academy of Sciences has estimated that electric power generation is the single most significant source of adverse environmental impact from coal use in the United States as well as the largest single national source of climate related CO_2 emissions.[18]

With the ascendency of climate warming on the national and state policy agenda, electric power companies have been increasingly concerned with the development of new technologies to control utility CO_2 and other greenhouse gas emissions (GHG), and with evolving federal and state climate warming regulatory programs. Electric power companies have strongly supported federal R&D funding for the development and commercial scale up of experimental designs for new, more energy efficient and low-GHG emission facilities, such as the aborted Future Gen 1.0 plant and its possible Future Gen 2.0 successor.

The United Mine Workers

The histories of American coal mining and the United Mine Workers (UMW), the most important union representing coal miners, are inseparable. Beginning shortly before the Great Depression, the UMW waged a fierce, prolonged, often extremely violent, battle with coal mine owners to organize mine workers that ended only when the Roosevelt administration and union organizers succeeded in compelling the mining corporations to recognize the UMW's right to bargain with management concerning pay, working conditions, and worker safety. In recent decades, the UMW has occupied an uneasy middle ground in conflict over federal and state coal mine regulation, at times allied with the company management in opposing state and federal regulations perceived to inhibit the industry's economic development, at other times supporting stronger governmental oversight of mine safety and working conditions. The UMW remains a major participant in coal field politics and policymaking, but it is not the force it was once. The UMW, reaching a membership exceeding 400,000 during the 1930s and 1940s, was responsible for vastly improved mine safety, worker pay, and working hours. UMW membership and political power steadily diminished with the decline of deep-shaft mining, the growing mechanization and spread of surface mining, and the employment of nonunion workers. By 2010, it diminished to 70,000.

Environmentalism and Coal

The rise of American environmentalism transformed the politics of coal production. Environmental organizations have been intensely concerned with the development and implementation of tough coal regulation policy at every stage of coal production, and at every governmental level from federal to local. While environmentalists and coal mine owners share a common interest in many aspects of coal utilization, including the development of clean coal technologies and planning future infrastructure of electric power generation and transmission, the relationship has more often been bitterly adversarial. "From climate change to mountaintop removal," observed a West Virginia coal trade association with but slight overstatement, "environmentalists and coal producers are usually at each other's throats."[19] The flashpoints of greatest contention between environmental advocacy organizations and the coal mining industry during the Obama administration, as later discussion will amplify, have been mountaintop removal mining, the regulation of toxic coal ash created by electric power generation, and the regulation of GHG emissions from electric utilities and other major combustion sources. Regardless of the specific coal issue, however, the EPA's responsibility for federal air and water pollution regulation, and the Department of the Interior's mandate

for oversight and development of domestic coal resources, almost predes-
tines these two federal agencies to join the White House as the habitual
combat zones between coal and environmentalist policy advocates.

GOVERNANCE: COAL POLICY AND THE FUTURE

The energy shocks of the 1970s persuaded Washington that vastly accelerated domestic coal use could displace considerable future petroleum
consumption and buffer the disruptions of a future imported oil embargo. For a while, the coal industry capitalized on anointing itself the
great Black Hope for American energy independence. From presidents
Nixon to George W. Bush, the White House and federal energy plan-
ners were committed to policy initiatives involving some mix of federal
support for the development of clean coal technologies, coal-based
synthetic fuel substitutes for petroleum, promotion of new coal-fired
electric power generation, increased coal production on federal land,
and other policies intended to ensure continued growth of the coal industry. Energy conservation, however, had been more often praised than
enthusiastically promoted by the White House from Ronald Reagan's
presidency until the end of the second Clinton administration.

The Energy Policy Act (EPAct) of 2005, the most significant White
House coal related legislation in several decades and vigorously promoted by George W. Bush, attempted to create a balance between
increased domestic coal production, environmental quality, and development of renewable energy and energy conservation. The EPAct
encouraged increased fossil fuel exploration and production on federal
lands, a new surge of coal-fired electric utility construction, and modest, but significant, support for energy conservation and development of
renewable energy technologies.[b]

---

[b] EPAct created many new programs with evident appeal to environmentalists and
renewable energy proponents. These included more than \$14 billion in various
tax incentives over the next three decades for increased energy conservation and
efficiency, substantial support for research on biofuels, such as ethanol, various research and development incentives for the creation of a "hydrogen economy" based
on hydrogen fuel cells, and other proposals for increased energy efficiency. EPAct
temporarily put to rest the administration's controversial plan to expand energy
exploration in the Arctic National Wildlife Refuge (ANWR).

Obama, Coal, and a "New Energy Future"

Obama's election marked the most politically and economically comprehensive White House commitment to energy conservation, renewable energy technologies, and moderated fossil fuel development since 1970. The Obama administration, in contrast to the Bush White House, placed a much higher priority on renewable energy and energy efficiency that would pave the way to what Obama called "a new energy future." In this future, coal would continue as an important resource, but the great Black Hope no longer appeared in White House discussions about the foundations for future energy security or energy independence.

Much to the delight of environmentalists and their allies, Obama endorsed early and often energy policies that "will curb our dependence on fossil fuels and make America energy independent" and new air pollution measures "after decades of inaction." Obama also promised his pathway toward a "new energy future" would include "addressing the global climate crisis."[20] The White House-sponsored measures included proposals for tougher air pollution emission standards for coal-burning industries, renewed efforts to pass a comprehensive regulatory program to control domestic GHG emissions, new controls on mountaintop surface mining, restraint on leases for fossil fuel exploration on federal Outer Continental Shelf (OCS) land, and much more. This agenda clearly targeted coal production and combustion as a priority for new environmental regulation, and this mobilized the coal industry and its economic infrastructure, the electric power industry, environmentalists, and advocates of energy conservation for the regulatory battles that flared throughout Obama's first term.

This agenda was loaded with more than ordinary political risks. Opponents of new fossil fuel regulations, including a new Republican majority elected to the House of Representatives in 2010, charged that these initiatives stifled economic growth and further endangered a fragile national recovery from the recession—a potent political indictment in grim economic times. By the end of Obama's first term, the president's struggle to reconcile an ambitious coal agenda with the need to stimulate economic recovery, like the rest of his ambitious energy program, increasingly led to compromise and policy revisions, provoking anger and disappointment among environmentalists and their collaborators. Four coal policy issues assumed great importance during Obama's first term and continue contentiously into his second term: increased regulation of coal surface mining, disposal of electric utility waste, the continuing search for a clean coal technology, and climate warming emissions.

Surface Mining and Mountaintop Removal

Until the 1970s, except for federal mine safety and labor laws, the coal industry experienced a generally benign regulatory oversight primarily by state governments that—especially in coal rich regions of Appalachia and the western plains—were concerned with protecting and promoting industry than with regulating its adverse environmental impacts. The rise of environmentalism brought new federal regulatory regimes converging upon the coal industry: the Surface Mining Control and Reclamation Act (SMCRA), the Clean Air Act (CAA), and the Clean Water Act (CWA). These laws have created a formidable array of contentious regulatory issues that the Obama administration inherited and that remain an unsettled legacy.

Surface mining. Virtually all coal mined west of the Mississippi River and half the coal produced in Appalachia is surface mined. Surface mining has rapidly replaced underground mining because it is more efficient, more profitable, and less labor intensive. Unless rigorously regulated, however, surface mining is environmentally catastrophic. More than 1.5 million acres of American land have been disturbed by coal surface mining; more than a million of these acres remain wrecked and ravaged wastelands, long abandoned by their destroyers. More than one thousand additional acres are disturbed each week by surface mining, and more than thirty states have been scarred by unreclaimed surface mines.

In Appalachia, surface miners had roamed the hills virtually uncontrolled for decades. The evidence is written in the thousands of sterile acres, acidified streams and rivers, decapitated hills, and slopes scarred by abandoned mine highwalls. In the western prairies and grasslands, unregulated surface mining left thousands of barren, furrowed acres buried under spoiled banks so hostile to revegetation that they seem like moonscapes to observers. The difficult struggle to create federal regulation of coal surface mining ended in 1977 when President Jimmy Carter signed into law the Surface Mining Control and Reclamation Act.

Considerable dissatisfaction smoldered among the several Appalachian states, however, where public officials now became reluctant enforcers of tougher federal laws. To these states were added newer western ones where rapidly expanding surface mining created more stakeholders in federal regulation. Thus, controversy has been the regulator's lot wherever the federal law has been implemented.

The Surface Mining Control and Reclamation Act (1977). The legislation signed by President Jimmy Carter created federal standards for the creation, operation, and restoration of surface mined land and invested mining states with responsibility for implementation and oversight of the federal mandate. The act's major features included the following:

- Requirements for environmental standards governing removal, storage, and redistribution of topsoil; siting and erosion control; drainage and protection of water quality; and many other matters affecting environmental quality
- Requirements that mined land be returned, insofar as possible, to its original contours and to a use equal or superior to that before mining commenced
- Special performance and reclamation standards for mining on alluvial valley floors in arid and semiarid areas, on prime farmland, and on steep slopes
- Enforcement of the act through a mining permit program administered jointly by the federal government and the states, according to federal regulations
- Protection of land unsuitable for mining from any mine activity
- Creation of an agency, currently the Office of Surface Mining Reclamation and Enforcement (OSMRE) within the DOI, to enforce the act[21]

From its inception, the OSMRE's responsibility for exercising oversight over state enforcement of federal surface mine regulations has been embattled, politically troubled, underfunded, and assailed frequently by state regulators who are dissatisfied at what they perceive to be heavy-handed, arbitrary, and expensive federal interventions. In addition to shared responsibility for oversight of active surface mines, OSMRE and the states confront a hugely expensive and complex problem in protecting public health and safety on America's abandoned surface coal mine lands. Estimates suggest the total cost of restoring these ravaged and deserted acres is $8.6 billion.[22]

A succession of directors continues through the OSMRE's revolving door, and the amount of improvement in program administration remains problematic. OSMRE struggles to improve its public image (perhaps in desperation, its website includes a children's link where young viewers can download a workbook of word games, a crossword puzzle, cartoons, and a coloring page about mining's "off site impacts").[23] Environmentalists have been extremely protective toward the embattled OSMRE, which they perceive continually at risk of capture by regulated coal mining interests.[24]

After almost four decades of regulation, it seems apparent that OSMRE cannot or will not exercise dependably vigorous oversight of state enforcement programs. Still, some observers believe that the controversies surrounding SMCRA have had constructive results, including greater sensitivity in Washington to the needs of the states and greater economic efficiency through more flexibility in program regulations. Proponents of tough federal surface mine regulation remain hopeful, but not confident, that OSMRE can still fulfill its regulatory mission.

Mountaintop removal (MTR). Mountaintop removal by surface mining has enlarged into a bitterly contentious issue as the practice spreads primarily through Appalachia and the Midwest. Science writer David Biello concisely describes MTR's impact:

> *The litany of problems—both to the environment and human health—caused by a practice that involves blasting the top off a mountain to get at the coal beneath it more easily [includes] heavy metals, sulfuric acid and other mine contaminants in waterways and drinking-water wells; deformed fish carrying toxic levels of selenium found in 73 of 78 streams affected by mountaintop mining; entire streams filled in by blasted mountain rock; and forests cleared to get at the mountaintop beneath them. Add to that the fact that this form of mining has increased exponentially in the past 30 years, supplying roughly 10 percent*

of US coal, and you have a recipe for much of the environmental devastation visible across northern Appalachia.[25]

MTR, currently accounting for more than 20 percent of coal production in central Appalachia, produces much of the fuel for the nation's largest electric utilities, such as Duke Power, and figures prominently in their anticipated future coalfield development.

MTR is also one of many environmental activities regulated by multiple federal laws and agencies. The Army Corps of Engineers possesses the initial authority to permit surface mining while SMCRA regulates the operation, closing, and environmental restoration of surface mined lands. The CWA, however, grants EPA a veto (rarely used) over the Corps mining permits if EPA determines the mining will pollute surface or groundwater in violation of the CWA. Under the Obama administration, the EPA, with White House support, made an unusual decision in 2011 by threatening to veto a proposed MTR by Arch Coal Inc. at Spruce Mine No. 1 in West Virginia, a 3,113-acre project that would bury more than seven miles of streams. Environmentalists have fought the project since the latter 1990s. The Spruce Mine has become symbol and centerpiece of the angry battle over MTR and Obama's commitment to control MTR, pitting coal miners and owners, West Virginia's political leadership, and opponents of increased federal environmental regulation against environmentalists, energy conservationists, and their allies.

Mining companies argue that MTR is the only way to get at many coal deposits. "Coal in these areas is found in very narrow seams, and the surrounding rock geology is less stable than in areas of layer seams," explained Carol Raulston, senior vice president of the National Mining Association. "It creates flat terrain on what was the top of the mountain but the mountain is still there."[26] Critics, however, say that the land is devastated, that people, property, and the environment endure severe collateral damage. Arch Coal, like other large coal mine owners, is determined to protect mountaintop removal. "The Spruce permit is the most scrutinized and fully considered permit in West Virginia's history," asserted a company spokesman. "The 13-year permitting process included the preparation of a full environmental impact statement, the only permit in the eastern coal fields to ever undergo such review . . . We are evaluating all possible options for relief from the government's actions and intend to vigorously defend the Spruce permit by all legal means."[27]

MTR can also inflame angry community divisions between miners and business, which depend on MTR for employment and income, and environmentalists, who are joined by others protective of local history and culture. The mountaintop issue seems destined to stalk the White House, EPA, and OSMRE for many years, remaining politically volatile well after the 2012 presidential election.

The restoration gamble. One ultimately important test of surface mine regulations is whether they result in an environmentally safer mining industry and a significant restoration of the many thousand orphan mine sites across the United States. The answer is elusive, partly because the restoration of surface mine sites is difficult under the best of circumstances and public resources to underwrite much of the restoration cost remain unpredictable. Thus, a critical issue arose in the future of surface mining: Is restoration of mined lands in the manner contemplated by the act achievable? Technical studies suggest that the capacity of mining companies to restore mined land to conditions equal or superior to their original condition is likely to be site specific, that is, dependent on the particular biological and geological character of each mining site. Western mining sites are often ecologically fragile; relatively limited varieties of sustainable vegetation and scarce rainfall make the ecological regeneration of the land difficult.

The prospects for restoration are less forbidding in Appalachia, where an abundance of precipitation, richer soil, and a greater diversity of native flora and fauna are available. Nonetheless, many experts believe that the disruption of subsurface hydrology and the drainage of acids and salts from the mines' spoil heaps may not be controlled easily even when surface revegetation is achieved. Restoration remains a gamble with nature. After decades of experience with SMCRA, evidence of successful restoration has been limited, the uncertainties persistent.[28]

Coal and Clean Water: Coal Ash

The Clean Water Act (CWA) authorizes EPA and states implementing the act to regulate most activities involving environmental pollution created by discharges into surface and groundwater or by obstructing or impounding these waters. An important component of coal utilization, coal ash, has become a major regulatory issue as a result of the CWA.

The regulation of coal-burning emissions, mostly from electric power generation, annually creates 125–130 million tons of toxic ash and sludge, enough to fill a million railcars; more than half this volume resides in ponds and pits, primarily on electric utility property. This waste was virtually invisible politically until December 22, 2008, when an earthen dam containing a billion gallons of ash waste from the Tennessee Valley Authority (TVA) Kingston Fossil power plant, near Kingston, Tennessee, failed. The released slurry erupted through the containment "like a volcano," reported one resident, flooding three-hundred acres, including Kingston and the nearby Emery River with sludge containing elevated levels of toxic metals (including arsenic, copper, barium, cadmium, chromium, lead, mercury, nickel, and thallium) and other pollutants.[29] Kingston residents claim the residue continues to create serious health problems.

Subsequent investigation by the TVA's own inspector general revealed that coal ash has contaminated the groundwater at nine Tennessee Valley Authority power plants, some at levels high enough to make it a health hazard. "The levels of beryllium, cadmium, and nickel," noted the report, "are above drinking water standards at the utility's Gallatin plant, as are the levels of arsenic, selenium, and vanadium at its Cumberland plant. The report also found that for more than 10 years, the utility has been finding arsenic in the groundwater at its Allen coal facility."[30] "A rapid EPA national survey disclosed 431 facilities similar to the Kingston site, of which 49 were considered 'high hazard' because their failure could endanger human life. These containments are a portion of more than 1,300 sludge and ash pits estimated to exist nationally, most of them unregulated and unmonitored."[31]

Coal ash becomes an especially nettlesome problem because it resides in a regulatory twilight. Depending on where it appears and what it contains, it can be considered a solid waste, water pollutant, toxic waste, groundwater contaminant, or even an air pollutant, and it is therefore subject to various federal and state regulations—or perhaps to no specific regulation or to conflicting laws. Consequently, although most states regulate some aspect of coal ash deposition, there is little consistency and considerable ambiguity about how environmental controls are applied and if the most effective management prevails. The EPA has proposed new comprehensive ash pit regulations, but the EPA and officials in the White House budget office do not agree on how to proceed. The coal ash pits constitute a major regulatory challenge for the Obama administration that will be closely watched by environmentalists, many critical of what they believe is an irresolute and tardy White House response—in effect, this issue is becoming a test of the administration's political credibility with environmental advocates.

The Uncertain Search for "Clean Coal"

One of the most unsettled aspects of future CO_2 regulation is the availability of a control technology for the large electrical utilities creating most of domestic GHG emissions. The EPA's anticipated GHG regulations are expected to require that new coal-fired plants must use the "best available control technology," although no such commercial technology currently exists for CO_2 emissions. Thus, the coal and electric power industries have been strongly motivated to discover a clean coal technique to reduce their air pollution emissions.

In an effort to encourage development of clean coal technologies, the Obama administration's massive $775 billion American Recovery and Reinvestment Act (2009) included $3.4 billion in the federal support for carbon capture and sequestration (CCS) development. Without the prospect of this substantial federal R&D support, public and private electric power companies were unlikely to invest alone in the estimated $1 billion required to create an operational electric power facility equipped with a new and largely unproven CCS technology.[c]

The coal industry's major hope for commercially viable CO_2 emission control still rests precariously with the experimental CCS technology. In CCS operations, "CO_2 is separated from the fuel and captured

---

[c] In 2009, for example, Summit Power Company's contemplated Odessa power plant with CCS would have cost an estimated $1.6 billion, or about ten times as much as a modern gas-fired power plant. Rebecca Smith, "U.S. News: States Vie for Share of Clean-Coal Cash," *Wall Street Journal* (Eastern edition, New York), March 23, 2009, A3.

either before or after the combustion of coal. It is then compressed to a super critical liquid, transported by pipeline to an injection well and then pumped underground to depths sufficient to maintain critical temperatures and pressures." If the technology works, "The CO_2 seeps into the pore spaces in the surrounding rock and its escape to the surface is blocked by a caprock, or overlaying impermeable layer . . . Underground storage capacity in the United States is believed to be ample and widespread, and long-term leakage . . . is expected to be negligible."[32]

In 2010, with considerable R&D funding by the DOE, the American Electric Power Co. began site experiments at its Mountaineer power plant near New Haven, West Virginia, with the earliest pilot CCS project.[33] An enormous weight of political and economic expectations had been loaded onto the Mountaineer project, and the company's decision to cancel Mountaineer less than a year later was a severe setback to the coal and electric power industries. Even though DOE was willing to invest more than $300 million in Mountaineer, American Power was reluctant to invest further until the murky future of national CO_2 emissions regulation is clarified.[34]

The fate of the Future Gen and Mountaineer projects suggests that formidable challenges crowd the future of CCS. CCS itself remains a primitive technology. Assuming an optimistic scenario, the time required from initiation of a successful pilot project to the construction of a commercially viable facility is estimated to require perhaps two decades and an investment of several billion dollars. If federal CO_2 regulations are enacted, a significant reduction in electric power emissions will require CCS installation or retrofitting in perhaps hundreds of facilities; many electric power industry experts believe the federal government must commit much more to CCS development than the present $3.4 billion available from the American Recovery and Reinvestment Act. In an obituary for the failed Future Gen, the principle research engineer for MIT's CCS program warned about government failure to understand the magnitude of the CCS challenge. "How can we do hundreds of these plants by 2050—and that's what we'll need," he commented, "if we can't even do one?"[35]

Environmentalists have largely opposed any version of CCS because they assert CCS power plants will be too costly to build and maintain in comparison to their economic or environmental benefits, and they will divert investment from more productive, renewable energy technologies. Additionally, they cite substantial and often unknown environmental risks inherent to underground CO_2 itself and the collateral environmental damage of the surface mining to supply future coal.

The electric power industry has become extremely wary about investing in experimental CCS and other clean coal technologies without a much greater and more predictable future commitment of federal R&D funding by DOE. One source of this industry reluctance continues to be unfamiliarity with the technology. Moreover a CCS power plant would be hugely expensive, beyond the cost of any current electric utility.[36]

The industry is divided and tentative about the future of coal combustion. Utilities currently depending primarily upon natural gas or planning future gas-fired facilities frequently support new CO_2 regulation because this may give them a significant advantage over coal-burning competitors. Conversely, coal dependent power companies usually assert that new CO_2 regulations will impose unacceptable future costs upon themselves and their consumers and stifle national recovery from an already severe recession. Many utilities confronting the large uncertainties about the substance and timing of new federal CO_2 regulations, and experiencing a decline in electric power demand created by the recession, have adopted a wait-and-see attitude.

COAL, CLIMATE WARMING, DEADLOCK, AND IMPROVISATION

Climate regulation is a huge question mark hovering over future coal policy. Perhaps no policy issue is ultimately more important to the future of the coal industry, or its impact more confounding to predict, than the ongoing, unsettled, and fiercely contested controversy over federal climate warming legislation. The coal industry, its consumers, and the national economic infrastructure built upon coal are reluctant captives to federal irresolution about the ultimate plan for the long-term regulation of CO_2 and related greenhouse emissions. And the future of climate warming regulations already implemented by many state governments, or plans now being debated by others, will be profoundly affected when—and if—a long-term federal policy is settled.

The Clean Air Act and CO_2

Since Obama's reelection in 2013, the Clean Air Act has become the principal setting for the unresolved national conflict over future GHG regulation. But the CAA may not be the ultimate source, or the only source, for a regulatory strategy.

Following the 2008 presidential election in which Obama declared climate legislation a major priority, Obama vigorously championed legislation creating a comprehensive domestic GHG regulatory regime. Congress ponderously struggled with numerous climate bills, and in 2009, the House enacted a massive legislative proposal and sent it to the Senate, where it perished amid more urgent issues and irreconcilable partisan conflict. Then, the 2011 election of a Republican majority in the House and the persistent economic recession drove the GHG issue from both White House and congressional agendas.

Meanwhile, a coalition of states, impatient at the glacial pace of federal GHG regulatory action, sued the EPA in 2007, asserting that the CAA compelled the EPA to determine if CO_2 could potentially endanger human health or the environment and, if so, required the EPA to write appropriate domestic CO_2 regulations. The Supreme Court agreed with the states, and in a landmark decision, *Massachusetts v. Environmental Protection Agency* (2007)—known as the "endangerment finding"—the Court instructed the EPA to determine whether CO_2 was a pollutant requiring regulation according to the CAA and, if so, the Court ordered the EPA to create appropriate rules under the Clean Air Act. As expected, the agency made its investigation, declared in 2010 that CO_2 should be regulated under the CAA, and proceeded in 2011 to produce an initial proposal for national CO_2 emission controls. The proposal, however, was launched into a morass of political, legal, and legislative infighting that delayed any final EPA regulations until 2013.

In June 2013, the president, using his executive authority and the CAA, created a new climate initiative. This fresh initiative, called The President's Climate Action Plan, demonstrated the high priority he placed on CO_2 regulation in his second term. Obama ordered the EPA to proceed with drafting its final regulations, now intended to control emissions from both old and new power plants and to reduce total emissions by 17 percent in 2020 when compared with 2005. The Climate Action Plan also called for the federal government to establish emission level goals for each state based upon their past emission levels.[37]

The action plan is politically risky for Obama. Congressional Republicans have joined numerous other critics of the complex proposal, including segments of the coal and electric power industries, in contending that the CAA is neither legally appropriate nor economically efficient for GHG regulation. Opponents of the EPA's regulations have promised to fight the new rules politically and legally, virtually ensuring a protracted excursion through the federal courts, congressional deliberation, and electoral debate before the regulatory future of CO_2 emissions becomes evident. Whether the new, and necessarily complex, EPA regulations will survive the predictable federal court reviews is unpredictable. The new regulations' impact upon the economy and the regulated coal and electric power industries is equally problematic.

Cap and Trade

The ongoing controversy over using the CAA to regulate CO_2 emissions has been accompanied by a second, equally vehement, debate over whether the best strategy for regulation should include some type of "cap-and-trade" scheme for emission controls. The EPA could choose cap-and-trade as a major emission control strategy in its final regulations to implement Obama's Climate Action Plan. Or cap-and-trade might evolve separately as congressional legislation—always a possibility but likely to be near miraculous in light of past congressional deadlock on the issue.

Numerous versions of cap-and-trade, wherever and whenever proposed, share some common features. The government "determines which facilities or emissions are covered by the program and sets an overall emission target, or 'cap,' for covered entities," explains the Pew Center. "This cap is the sum of all allowed emissions from all included facilities. Once the cap has been set and covered entities specified, tradable emission allowances (rights to emit) are distributed (either auctioned, or freely allocated, of[or] some combination of these. Each allowance

> *authorizes the release of a specified amount of greenhouse gas emissions, generally one ton of carbon dioxide equivalent (CO_2e). The total number of allowances is equivalent to the overall emissions cap (e.g., if a cap of one million tons of emissions is set, one million one-ton allowances will be issued).*

Covered entities must submit allowances equivalent to the level of emissions for which they are responsible at the end of each of the program's compliance periods.[38]

Then, allowance trading occurs among regulated facilities. "For some emitters, implementing new, low-emitting technologies may be relatively inexpensive. Those firms will either buy fewer allowances or sell their surplus allowances to firms that face higher emission control costs . . . By giving firms a financial incentive to control emissions and the flexibility to determine how and when emissions will be reduced, the capped level of emissions is achieved in a manner that minimizes overall program costs.[39]

Proponents of cap-and-trade assert that it has numerous advantages as a GHG regulatory regime:

- It provides a continuing incentive for firms to create new methods of emissions control because such innovation can significantly reduce regulatory compliance costs.
- It allows regulated firms to "bank" excess emissions credits to be later used or sold on the emissions market to other firms needing emission credits.
- It creates strict limits on emissions that can produce large pollution reductions.
- It promotes high compliance levels, transparency, and accountability.
- It is estimated to provide more benefits at less cost to regulated firms.[40]

Critics of cap-and-trade assert that, among many other problems, the regulations will inhibit economic recovery from the severe recession, impose excessive cost upon regulated firms that can better control GHG emissions with alternative fuel combinations and new clean coal technologies, and will prove too unenforceable. Moreover, the European experience with cap-and-trade has so far failed technically and economically to meet expectations.

Meanwhile, the States Take the Initiative

Sixteen states have adopted their own GHG emissions reduction targets, thirty-nine states have joined the multistate Climate Registry to monitor and report their GHG emissions, and state partnerships have formed three regional cap-and-trade programs: the eastern Regional Greenhouse Gas Initiative (RGGI), the Western Climate Initiative, and the Midwestern Climate Initiative.[41] In addition, California had enacted a regulatory program that exceeded federal standards for GHG emissions from the transportation sector, and twelve other states proposed the adoption of the standards as well. The state programs involve a mix of different provisions, which usually include the following:[42]

- *State climate change commissions.* Executive or legislative commissions examine the possible consequences of climate change for a state and the costs and benefits associated with addressing them and then develop recommendations for appropriate policies.
- *Climate action plans.* State-designed climate action plans are established to meet individual state conditions.
- *GHG reporting.* Mandatory or voluntary reporting of GHG emissions from major sources is required in many states, such as California, Wisconsin, West Virginia, and Hawaii. Most of these states also joined the national Climate Registry, a nonprofit organization measuring and publicly reporting GHG emissions.
- *Economy-wide GHG reductions.* Emissions goals (usually voluntary) are established for all major emission sources within the state.
- *GHG performance standards for electric power.* Electric power generated within the state must meet a common standard for GHG emissions.
- *GHG performance standards for vehicles.* Federal law requires states to follow federal emissions standards for cars and light trucks or to follow California's higher standard. Eleven states had adopted, or planned to adopt, the California standard.

CONCLUSION: COAL AT THE CROSSROADS

The contemporary coal industry confronts policymakers with issues whose resolution may well redefine the final status of coal in the future American energy economy. Moreover, the electric power and coal industries share an intricate political and economic interdependence, ensuring that future coal policy will significantly, and perhaps profoundly, shape the future development of the electric power industry as well. While coal remains the most abundant American fossil fuel and the primary fuel for domestic electric power generation, the recent commercial success of "fracking" technology and new regulatory pressures upon coal-fired electric utilities may be hastening the decline of coal and the ascendance of natural gas as America's primary source of electric power. These pressures are likely to persist, and probably intensify, as regulatory controls of climate warming emissions from coal-fired industry and electric power plants become increasingly important. These new developments compound the economic and political challenges already confronting the coal industry from continually tightening environmental regulation of coal surface mining.

The coal industry has reacted vigorously to these pressures economically, politically, and technologically. The industry's greatest gamble appears to be its commitment to creating an economically viable "clean coal" technology capable of reducing climate warming gases and other air pollution emissions. This has so far been an unsuccessful initiative whose future success, if it occurs, will depend upon substantial, long-term financial support from the federal government in addition to the industry's own resources. At the same time, the nation's major coal companies stubbornly resist increased environmental regulation, particularly new efforts to ban "mountaintop removal" and coal ash dumping.

And uncertainties—great uncertainties—persist to confound any confident predictions about the future of the coal industry. Two issues, in particular, are likely to shape decisively the development of the coal industry through midcentury. Fracking has yet to prove its economic and technological viability despite its great potential. And policymakers must resolve the continuing conflict over the substance of regulations to control climate warming emissions from coal-fired industries. Until policymakers resolve—if they can—these confounding issues, predictions about the domestic coal industry remain precarious. This chapter also provides a useful introduction to the following chapter that explores the present status and prospects for the commercial nuclear power industry, whose future is intimately bound to the political and economic fate of the coal industry. Because the commercial nuclear power industry has increasingly promoted itself as the alternative technology of choice to fossil fuels for electric power generation, it has once again climbed high on the agenda of current energy policy discourse, continuing its roller-coaster ride up and down the national energy agenda for more than a half-century.

NUCLEAR ENERGY

> Misfortunes come on horseback, and go away on foot.
>
> *French proverb*

The catastrophic tsunami that ravaged Japan's northeast coast on March 11, 2011, left in its wake a disastrous succession of unprecedented emergency equipment failures, several reactor meltdowns, and significant radioactive emissions. It also devastated far more than the Fukushima Daiichi commercial nuclear facility. It may have shattered the American nuclear industry's cherished vision of a "nuclear renaissance." The Japanese disaster became the latest episode in the contentious development of the American commercial nuclear power industry, another chapter in the crisis-driven history of the domestic nuclear power policy.

A RISING AND FADING "RENAISSANCE"

After decades of economic stagnation, the domestic nuclear power industry seemed in 2010 about to revive. In 2000, statistics about commercial nuclear power read like the industry's obituary. Since 1980, the Nuclear Dream—the vision of almost unlimited, cheap electricity generated by hundreds of nuclear reactors—had been dying. The commercial nuclear power industry was failing under a burden of economic and technological misfortunes, an increasingly hostile political climate, inept public relations, persistent environmental risks, and mounting regulatory pressures.

Visions of Revival

By early 2011, industry leaders and supporters were speaking confidently about a "nuclear renaissance."[1] One potent source of this optimism might be called the "other greenhouse effect." Capitalizing on growing national and international attention to global climate warming, in the 1990s, the industry initiated an aggressive campaign to promote commercial nuclear power as the most desirable economic and environmental alternative to the greenhouse gas (GHG) emissions associated with fossil fuel combustion to generate electric power. Another powerful stimulus was the federal government's vigorous political and economic initiatives since the George W. Bush administration.

The industry was enormously encouraged when the Bush administration declared in its 2001 National Energy Plan that a "dramatic improvement in US nuclear power plant performance over the last 25 years" had occurred and that the industry "has established a strong foundation for the expansion of nuclear energy in the next two decades."[2] In 2004, the DOE proposed building fifty new power plants and prolonging the operating life of numerous existing facilities to the year 2020. The Energy Policy Act's very substantial commitment to nuclear power development in 2005 seemed to the industry's advocates a confirmation that the industry was, at last, truly reviving.

In keeping with a half century tradition of massive federal governmental subsidies, research grants, and other economic patronage, the act provided financial incentives for the construction of advanced nuclear plants amounting to $18.5 billion, which the industry requested be increased to $100 billion. Barack Obama added additional momentum to the nuclear resurgence when, much to the disappointment of environmentalists, his campaign platform endorsed the continued development of commercial nuclear power, a commitment reinforced when his 2010 State of the Union speech advocated "a new generation of safe, clean nuclear power plants" and proposed to triple public financing for nuclear power.[3]

Underlying these decisions, and doubtless encouraging them, had been rising public approval for commercial nuclear power to the point where in mid-2009 the Gallup Poll reported "new high levels of support," with 59 percent of Americans favoring domestic nuclear energy.[4] Added good news was an anticipated 30 percent escalation of the US demand for electric power, a very substantial increase in nuclear output capacity, and the absence of a high-visibility facility accident or security lapse. The industry also anticipated that a planned new generation of reactor technologies (Generation III) would be considerably more efficient, safer, and economical than present operating models. As if to challenge history, moreover, the US Nuclear Regulatory Commission—less than a year *after* the Fukushima disaster—approved construction in Georgia of the first new commercial nuclear reactor since 1978.[5]

A Blighted Vision

Fukushima Daiichi has savaged visions of a bright nuclear future. The Japanese tragedy—rated 7 on the International Nuclear and Radiological Event Scale, comparable to the world's worst reactor accident, at Chernobyl—seemed to dramatize globally the ominous predictions about commercial nuclear electric power so long voiced by its domestic critics. The future of commercial nuclear power seemed blighted anew. Public support for commercial nuclear energy fell on a typical national poll from 71 to 50 percent.[6] The disaster "shook confidence in nuclear power around the world," reported one contemporary survey.[7]

Concerned about the vulnerability of US commercial reactors to severe earthquakes similar to the cause of the Japanese accident, the US Nuclear Regulatory Commission (NRC) rapidly initiated a safety survey of US commercial nuclear reactors and concluded that, while domestic reactors were generally safe, they could be better prepared for the kind of damage inflicted by the Japanese tsunami.[8] "All of the nation's 104 nuclear reactors will need to undergo analysis using cutting-edge technology and the most recent data to assess how well they can withstand earthquakes," the Nuclear Regulatory Commission also warned.[9] Plant operators will be required to study the safety of their facilities using a new seismic risk model created by the NRC, Electric Power Research Institute (EPRI), and US Geological Survey, which should be available later this year.[10]

Despite continued expressions of support for new commercial reactor development, the Obama administration reluctantly confronts an issue facing every presidency since Jimmy Carter and certain to arrive afresh at the door of the next presidency: what is to be done about commercial nuclear power? To illustrate the critical policy issues, the chapter begins with a description of the contemporary domestic nuclear industry, leading to a discussion of the political setting of commercial nuclear power and, finally, to an exploration of the strategic policy options now confronting the president and Congress.

THE COMMERCIAL NUCLEAR POWER INDUSTRY TODAY

In 2012, there were 104 operating nuclear reactors licensed to US electrical utilities, down from a peak of 112 in 1990.[11] Most reactors are located along the East Coast, in the Southeast, and in the Midwest (see Figure 5-1). These reactors currently represent about 22 percent of US net electricity-generating capacity. Under their original schedule, the licenses for these reactors were issued for forty years, and half of the reactors would have ended their legal operating lives between 2005 and 2015; the remainder would have shut down before 2075. By June 2009, the NRC had extended the licenses of 54 reactors, over half of the US total. The NRC is considering license renewals for a further 16 units, with more applications expected by 2013.

Commercial nuclear power began in the mid-1950s amid bright expectations—without the economic and technical problems that blighted the industry after 1970. These misfortunes included a twenty year plague of economically and politically damaging news: low generating capacity, sharply rising construction costs, revelations of serious plant and equipment safety deficiencies, the 1979 near reactor meltdown at Three Mile Island (Pa.), and the Soviet Union's 1986 Chernobyl Disaster, an international catastrophe. As early as 1973, utilities had canceled all existing orders for power reactors, and none were subsequently ordered after 1978. It seemed possible that commercial nuclear power might disappear within a few generations. The industry, however, slowly improved its safety record and operating performance during the 1990s thereby regaining a significant measure of economic and political credibility. After 1980, for example, the nuclear power industry's average "capacity factor" (the proportion of rated electric power capacity that is actually produced) had risen from an economically precarious 56 percent to

FIGURE 5-1

Commercial US Nuclear Power Reactors, Location and Age, 2012

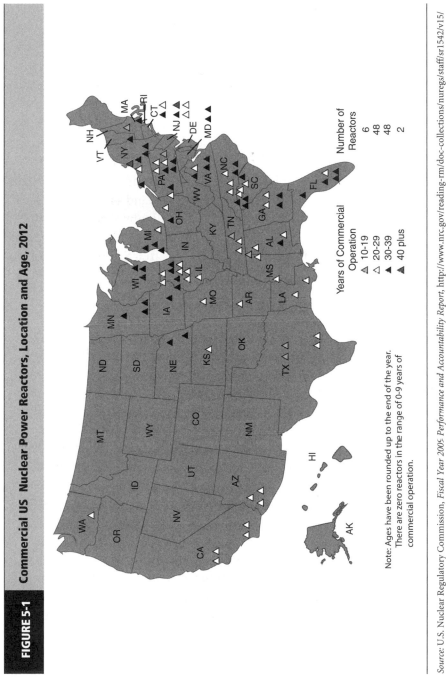

Years of Commercial Operation

△ 10-19
△ 20-29
▲ 30-39
▲ 40 plus

Number of Reactors
6
48
48
2

Note: Ages have been rounded up to the end of the year.
There are zero reactors in the range of 0-9 years of
commercial operation.

Source: U.S. Nuclear Regulatory Commission, *Fiscal Year 2005 Performance and Accountability Report*, http://www.nrc.gov/reading-rm/doc-collections/nuregs/staff/sr1542/v15/
sr1542v15.pdf.

more than 92 percent, relieving the industry of a major handicap in competition with other fuels.[12]

A Turn of Fortune

As the industry's performance continued to improve, the NRC began in 2000 to renew the existing utility licenses through a prolonged process involving extensive NRC safety reviews, public meetings, and state consultation. By mid-2011, the NRC had extended the licenses of sixty-six reactors and anticipated an additional twenty-two applications by 2013.[13] With the gradual return of public acceptance for nuclear power after 1990, the prospect of substantial federal financial support, and a new generation of better reactors, the industry could be guardedly optimistic about the future for the first time in several decades. With the prospect of a new generation of smaller, safer, more economically attractive reactors likely to become available, by 2010 applications to build twenty-six new plants at seventeen sites had been filed with the NRC by fourteen companies.[14]

The Federal Patron

Washington is largely responsible for the development of the nation's commercial nuclear power; federal policy has sustained the industry since its inception in the early 1950s with aggressive promotion, benign regulation, and massive financial infusions of subsidies, development grants, and research promotion.

The industry prospered in its first several decades due to this benevolent regulation, generous federal funding, public and political favor, and unique governmental concessions never given its competitors, such as the Price-Anderson Act (renewed in 2005), which limited the nuclear industry's total insurance liability to $12.6 billion, thus ensuring that the industry would obtain the necessary insurance coverage. Until the 1970s, all but a handful of scientists, economists, and public officials associated with the new technology seemed, according to economists Irvin C. Bupp and Jean-Claude Derian, so "intoxicated" by the enterprise that they largely ignored grave technical and economic problems already apparent to a few critical observers.[15] When problems could not be ignored, they usually were hidden from public view; when critics arose, they were discredited by Washington's aggressive defense of the industry.

Despite the industry's troubled history after the 1970s, by the beginning of the Obama presidency, the industry had received by conservative estimate more than $100 billion in federal subsidies—approximately 60 percent of the total federal energy research expenditures and far exceeding Washington's support for any other energy.[16] Critics have argued that without these direct and indirect subsidies, the industry was likely to have been uncompetitive in most markets. "Indeed . . . subsidies to the nuclear fuel cycle have often exceeded the value of the power produced," noted the Union of Concerned Scientists. "This means that buying power on the open market and giving it away for free would have been less costly than subsidizing the construction and operation of nuclear power plants."[17]

Federal financial backing is still the most potent driver of the nuclear industry's hope for a "renaissance" because this aid addresses the industry's chronically unsettled economic prospects. The largest current federal incentives for construction of new commercial nuclear facilities are provided by federal loan guarantees for new plant construction debt covering as much as 80 percent of construction cost, and, additional production tax credits.[18] Given the considerable economic risk involved in new plant construction, federal support is a crucial incentive for the construction of several "first starter" facilities that might prove the commercial success of the new reactor generation; otherwise, the industry has scant motivation to plan future facilities.[19]

The Problematic Economics of Nuclear Power

The gloss applied to the industry's public image by partisans of a nuclear renaissance cannot quite conceal some problematic economics. The cost of constructing and maintaining commercial nuclear power plants has climbed so steeply since 1980 that private capital has became increasingly scarce and costly. Even when an industry recovery seemed plausible after 2000, the managing director of a major national investment firm was warning that the "challenge of new construction is very difficult . . . Project sponsors must spend large amounts of capital for long lead-time procurement before the project has been licensed by the NRC and before the construction schedule is set. As a result, the project cost estimates have risen dramatically in the past year and are expected to continue rising.

In the eyes of lenders and investors, these projects will face the potential risk of serious delay and cost overruns."[20] Private investment is likely to be even more elusive in the aftermath of the 2007 economic recession and the bloating estimates for new plant construction. Early in 2008, the *Wall Street Journal* and several other publications carried headline news stories about the skyrocketing cost projections for new nuclear facilities, indicating that it might cost $9–$12 billion to build a single new nuclear power plant. Progress Energy's 2008 proposed plan for a Florida facility was predicted to cost $17 billion, triple the previous year's estimate.[21]

The industry's history already abounds with instances of huge construction cost overruns, low operating capacity, and failed market competitiveness. The Congressional Budget Office estimated, for example, that the average cost overrun for new nuclear plants in the 1970s and 1980s was about 200 percent.[22] Estimates of new plant construction costs are extremely tentative because the United States has had no experience in nuclear facility construction for thirty years. These construction costs are driven primarily by the expense of reactors. Among other, often unpredictable determinants of new facility economics are the comparative costs of alternative natural gas and coal for electric power generation, and, the impact of existing or future competition from other utilities in a specific market.[23] Nuclear power has been competitive with other fuels for electric generation, particularly in the northeastern and southern United States, where the domestic cost of competing fuels is highest.

Facility Safety Issues

The NRC's public admission, in the aftermath of the Fukushima Daiichi disaster, that the NRC lacked adequate information about the vulnerability of US commercial reactors to severe seismic shocks was a reminder that the national debate about reactor safety remains vigorous.

A major reason—often *the* reason—for the cost escalation of new plant construction is concern about public safety and environmental protection. Despite efforts to streamline the review process, surmounting the regulatory hurdles still requires four to eight years and may involve almost a hundred different federal, state, and local governmental permits. Industry officials also complain about the costs imposed during plant construction through regulatory ratcheting by the NRC (its habit of requiring facilities to make new safety modifications or other expensive design changes many years after plant construction). Additional costs have also been imposed on many utilities by protracted litigation involving environmental groups and others challenging various aspects of plant design and safety.[24]

Expensive technical problems continue to beset aging reactors, as illustrated by the prolonged shutdowns at First Energy Corporation's Davis-Besse Nuclear Power Station on Lake Erie and Exelon's Oyster Creek Nuclear Generating Station in New Jersey. Several technical problems have been especially damaging to the industry. Materials and design standards for many plants currently have failed essential safety requirements. Reactor parts, for instance, have aged much faster than anticipated. Steam generators meant to last a plant's lifetime—approximately fifty years—are wearing out much sooner than expected; this has been a particularly serious problem in New York, Florida, Virginia, Wisconsin, and South Carolina.[25] Mistakes have been made in plant specifications or construction. Pipes have cracked and "wasted" (the walls becoming thinner) from extended exposure to radiation.

Finally, continuing revelations of plant mismanagement, administrative bungling, and secrecy raise questions about the competence of plant managers and technicians. The industry must still contend with disclosures such as the NRC's announcement in early 2007 that it had downgraded the safety rating of the nation's largest nuclear plant. As the Associated Press reported:

> The NRC's announcement ended three years of problems in various safety systems at the Palo Verde nuclear plant west of Phoenix. Inspectors in September found that one of its emergency diesel generators had been broken for 18 days. Emergency generators are critically important at nuclear reactors, providing electricity to pumps, valves, and control rooms if the main electrical supply fails. Only FirstEnergy Corp.'s Perry nuclear plant in Ohio has a safety rating as bad as Palo Verde's, NRC spokesman Victor Dricks said.[26]

Proponents of nuclear power argue correctly that its safety record, notwithstanding the accident at Three Mile Island, is excellent and that critics have exaggerated its technical problems by seizing on these disclosures as if they characterized the entire industry. Still, revelations of technical difficulties continue.[27] Whatever their real significance, these problems have worked against the industry politically. The Union of Concerned Scientists' verdict seems fair:

> Is nuclear power in the United States safe enough today just because a reactor has not experienced a meltdown since 1979? The answer is a resounding no. In the 27 years since the TMI [Three Mile Island] meltdown, 38 US nuclear power reactors had to be shut down for at least one year while safety margins were restored to minimally acceptable levels. Seven of these reactors experienced two-year-plus outages. Though these reactors were shut down before they experienced a major accident, we cannot assume we will continue to be so lucky.[28]

The Waste Nobody Wants

Controversy about the safe disposal of radioactive reactor waste has become, like unsettled economics and safety, an intractable blight on the nuclear industry's visions of an imminent revival.

The waste problem was never anticipated when the federal government first promoted commercial nuclear power in the 1950s. To encourage private utilities to build nuclear power plants, Washington assured the industry that the federal government would provide a "reprocessing" technology for the radioactive wastes contained in the spent nuclear fuel rods used to generate reactor power. Thus, existing and planned commercial facilities were designed to store temporarily no more than three years of accumulated spent fuel rods in cooling ponds. However, the anticipated reprocessing proved an economic and technical failure.[29] Since the early 1970s virtually all commercial spent fuel has remained in the onsite cooling ponds (See Figure 5-2).[30] Until 1982, no comprehensive federal plan existed for the "permanent" storage of these nuclear wastes. Instead, federal and state governments had wrangled acrimoniously for more than a decade over the design and location of a permanent waste depository that no state wanted.

The Battle of Yucca Mountain. In 1982, Congress finally passed the Nuclear Waste Policy Act (NWPA), intended to create a process for designating and constructing the first permanent nuclear waste repository.

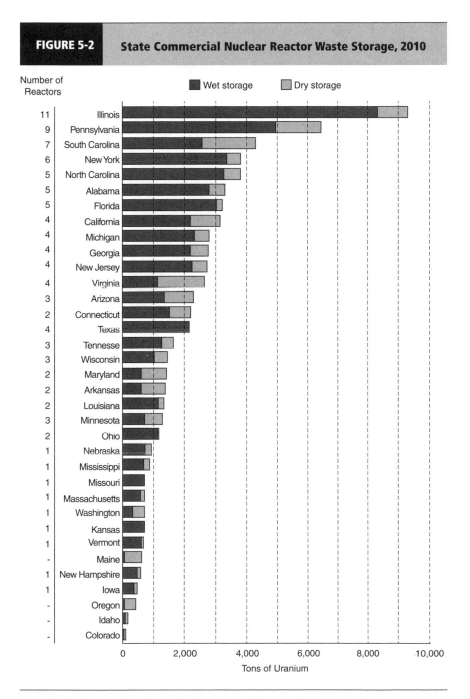

FIGURE 5-2   **State Commercial Nuclear Reactor Waste Storage, 2010**

Source: Nuclear Energy Institute, Nuclear Regulatory Commission. www.falloutreport.com/long-term-storage-of-nuclear-waste

The legislation assigned the site-selection task to the DOE and created what appeared to be a meticulously detailed, impartial, and open process by which all possible sites would be studied and reduced to a few from which the president would eventually select two for permanent repositories.

However, the political leadership in every eligible state fought vehemently in Congress and the courts to prevent its designation as an eligible waste site. Rather than abide the continuing controversy, Congress found a simpler solution. In December 1987, Congress suddenly renounced NWPA procedures, summarily designated Yucca Mountain, Nevada, to be the first permanent depository site, and assured the nuclear power industry that Nevada would be ready by 1998 to accept delivery of the spent fuel rods cooling at reactor sites.

Nevada residents and political leaders were outraged, and they're still angry. Nevada continues to resist the uncompleted Yucca Mountain facility with every available political and legal resource. This trench warfare, accompanied by fierce scientific controversy concerning Yucca Mountain's geologic safety, has slowed the facility's construction to a crawl.[31] The DOE abandoned its initial repository plan in 1989 because it lacked confidence in the technical quality of the proposal and predicted that the repository would be delayed until at least 2010 even though commercial utilities had already paid $3 billion in taxes to use the repository.[32] By 2007, the DOE was unprepared to receive wastes at even a temporary repository and a permanent site was still speculation.

Frustrated by these delays, the Bush administration in 2002 promised to open the site by 2010, requested a large budget increase to underwrite accelerated site construction, and was promptly sued by the state of Nevada and numerous other plaintiffs, thereby, relegating the Yucca Mountain facility to a judicial limbo and an uncertain future while controversy continued over the facility's safety. In an effort to settle the matter, in 2010, Secretary of Energy Steven Chu recommended to President Obama that the facility be terminated. But the repository's destiny was further muddled with Obama's pledge to eliminate its federal funding while simultaneously continuing its operation until the complex legal path to its termination is completed.

An alternative plan. The prospective close of the Yucca Mountain facility would require that some alternative storage space be available to accommodate the continuing increment of new waste at reactor sites. Any near-term solution must necessarily be temporary, pending the outcome of federal-state negotiations over the final deposition of commercial nuclear waste or a judicial order. The most plausible solution for the temporary containment of the high-level wastes that utilities may no longer be able to accommodate at their existing cooling ponds is "dry cask" storage.

"Dry cask storage," explains the Nuclear Regulatory Commission, "allows spent fuel that has already been cooled in the spent fuel pool for at least one year to be surrounded by inert gas inside a container called a cask. The casks are typically steel cylinders that are either welded or bolted closed. The steel cylinder provides a leak-tight containment of the spent fuel. Each cylinder is surrounded by additional steel, concrete, or other material to provide radiation shielding to workers and members of the public. Some of the cask designs can be used for both storage and transportation." (NRC.gov/waste) Dry-cask storage is already utilized in several states for high-level and low-level commercial waste. Debate lingers about the reliability of dry-cask waste sequestration and cask vulnerability to terrorism. However, dry casks have been approved for waste storage by the Nuclear Regulatory Commission, the Department of Energy, and an expert panel of the National Academy of Science.[33]

A number of states with commercial nuclear reactors, already uneasy about the safety of existing fuel rods that may remain in cooling ponds for at least several more decades, were further disconcerted when, in December 2010, the NRC modified its rules for onsite radioactive waste storage to double the storage time to 60 years after a facility goes out of service. The attorney generals of New York, Vermont, and Connecticut, expected to be the forerunners of future similar lawsuits by other states, have demanded that the NRC require commercial power companies to file environmental impact statements for the cooling ponds.[34] The contentious federalism that has characterized commercial nuclear power regulation for many decades seems destined to continue until, and *if,* the federal government can create a permanent nuclear waste depository.

Decommissioning. Once a civilian nuclear facility has finished its useful life, the NRC and the DOE require that the owners decommission the facility by removing from the site the radioactive materials, including land, groundwater, buildings, contents, and equipment, and by reducing residual radioactivity to a level permitting the property to be used for any other purpose. Before a nuclear power plant begins operations, the licensee must establish or obtain a financial mechanism—such as a trust fund or a guarantee from its parent company—to ensure that there will be sufficient money to pay for the ultimate decommissioning of the facility.[35] In 2012, twelve commercial nuclear power reactors were being decommissioned. At the end of 2012, ten commercial reactors were completely decommissioned and thirteen others were in earlier stages of dismantling.[36] The ten fully decommissioned sites are considered safe enough to be reclaimed for any purpose including agriculture, housing, or green space. Among the remaining reactors, six will be wholly decontaminated and six will be placed in "SAFSTOR" status where they will be sequestered until future full decontamination.

According to Paul Genoa, director of policy development of the Nuclear Energy Institute, a trade group for the nuclear power industry, "decommissioning costs typically run at $500 million per unit. But actual costs vary based on the plant's size and design, and some have reached over $1 billion—between 10 percent and 25 percent of the cost of constructing a nuclear reactor today."[37] Although the NRC requires utilities to set aside funds during the operating life of reactors in anticipation of future decommissioning costs, many utilities may be inadequately preparing for these costs. In 2009, the NRC notified about a quarter of the operating utilities that they may be not be setting aside sufficient funds for decommissioning.[38]

The Nuclear Regulatory Commission

Commercial nuclear power plants have been regulated by the Nuclear Regulatory Commission (NRC), an independent agency created by Congress and led by five commissioners appointed by the president and confirmed by the Senate for five-year terms. The NRC develops and implements regulations governing nuclear reactor and nuclear material safety: This mission involves oversight of these operations:

- *Reactors*—Commercial reactors for generating electric power and research and test reactors used for research, testing, and training
- *Materials*—Uses of nuclear materials in medical, industrial, and academic settings and facilities that produce nuclear fuel
- *Waste*—Transportation, storage, and disposal of nuclear materials and waste, and decommissioning of nuclear facilities from service[39]

In 2012, the NRC included a staff of approximately 4,000 and a budget of $1 billion. Among its most highly visible and often contentious responsibilities is the promulgation and enforcement of reactor safety standards for all domestic commercial nuclear reactors.

The NRC customarily works in a vortex of controversy and debate about its mission and performance, inspired not only by its own performance but also by the transcendent national debate over the future of commercial nuclear power. The agency was created in 1974 when Congress abolished the Atomic Energy Commission (AEC), the first federal regulatory agency for commercial nuclear power, which had the dual (and discordant) mission to promote commercial nuclear power and to regulate it simultaneously. Concerned that these missions were incompatible, Congress divided them and invested the NRC with the AEC's former regulatory authority. The new agency, however, could not readily dissolve the strong, congenial professional and institutional relationships linking former AEC staffers to the nuclear power industry, nor could it eliminate the impulse to promote and protect the industry so deeply rooted in the AEC's history.

Despite the 1979 near meltdown of the Three Mile Island reactor and the catastrophic 1986 Chernobyl disaster in the Soviet Union, the NRC's attention to reactor safety invited continued controversy. Throughout the 1980s, the agency seemed unable to overcome a promotional mindset toward the nuclear power industry. During the decade, as political scientist Robert Duffy observed, the NRC continued to "emphasize the licensing of new reactors while neglecting the performance of reactors already on line" and remained "reluctant to play the role of enforcer,

consistently stating that the primary objective of its enforcement program was corrective and not punitive."[40]

The agency remains enmeshed in the classic tangle of conflicting
loyalties and political pressures created for regulatory agencies seeking
to sustain a precarious balance between impartiality and "capture" by
the industries they regulate. Throughout the 1990s, successive NRC
commissioners and their staffs struggled with considerable success to
improve the agency's regulatory record and reputation despite budget-
ary limitations. By the George W. Bush administration, the agency had
improved its performance and image to the extent that a Government
Accountability Office (GAO) evaluation of the NRC in 2006 reported the
NRC "has generally taken a proactive approach to improving its Reactor Oversight Program" although it still needed to improve its ability to
identify and address declining reactor safety performance.[41]

Defenders of the NRC assert that many of its continuing regulatory lapses result from understaffing and underfunding, and that the
regulatory changes required by the NRC often take years for utilities to
accomplish. Some observers argue that the NRC must be doing its job
reasonably well because it is such a frequent target of criticism from the
nuclear power industry itself. The NRC remains divided over issues such
as the termination of the Yucca Mountain nuclear waste depository and
the safety of on-site storage of used nuclear fuel rods.[42] By the beginning
of Obama's second term, the NRC was further confronted by the political backlash from the Japanese nuclear disaster, uncertainty about the
feasibility of a new generation of reactors, and oversight of aging utility
reactors pressed into service for almost twice the period of their original
design.[43] And all the NRC's regulatory agenda is bundled into the most
compelling, transcendent issue: should the United States preserve the
"nuclear option?"

GOVERNANCE: CONFRONTING THE "NUCLEAR OPTION"

The Obama administration sent a message to electric utilities and potential
private investors that Washington was committed to continuing development of commercial power when it allocated $8.3 billion from the 2005
EPAct for construction of two new Georgia reactors and when Obama's
fiscal year (FY) 2012 budget requested $36 billion in loan guarantees

for more new reactor development. But the Fukushima reactor crisis revived a national debate about continuing commercial nuclear power development, the nuclear option. The federal government is the most essential participant in this decision, for without continued federal subsidies and other development incentives for commercial power, private investors are unlikely to gamble with the enormous economic risks entailed in new reactor construction.

Closing Out the Nuclear Option

Opponents of commercial nuclear power argue that the US experience with existing commercial reactors illustrate the problems, or likely problems, to be experienced with further industry development and make a compelling case to close out the nuclear option. In summary, these contentions include the following:

- *Nuclear technology will continue to involve unreasonable economic risks, including high construction and operating costs, continuing federal subsidies, and uncertain market competitiveness.* Commercial facilities are not profitable without large federal subsidies.[44] Moreover, the financial risk under current federal nuclear financing is largely displaced from private investors to the public and nuclear utility customers.
- *Renewable and low-carbon technologies should be funded instead.* Federal R&D money now invested in nuclear reactor development could be better spent to accelerate the commercial viability of low carbon, solar, wind, and other renewable energy technologies. The cost of alternative technologies has been steadily falling to the point where they can be economically competitive with coal, natural gas, and reactors with sufficient additional federal development support.
- *Commercial reactors are vulnerable to terrorism, technical failure, and natural disasters, which create unacceptable risk to human health, the environment, and national security.* The NRC domestic reactor study in the aftermath of the 2011 Japanese tsunami, for example, indicated that the vulnerability of US reactors to seismic shock has not been sufficiently evaluated.[45] Other concerns involve problematic emergency evacuation procedures at many facilitates (more than one hundred

million people living within a radius of fifty miles of a domestic nuclear power facility) and possible terrorist attacks.

- *A secure, permanent repository for high-level reactor waste is unpredictable.* The DOE cannot predict when it can dependably redeem its 1989 commitment to create a safe, secure, permanent repository for these existing wastes. New waste from potential future reactors would compound the existing disposal problems.
- *Nuclear power will not create a timely, significant reduction in domestic climate warming gas emissions.* Many other technologies will be needed to address global warming even if a major expansion of nuclear power were to occur. Moreover, "a major expansion of nuclear power in the United States is not feasible in the near term" and even "under an ambitious deployment scenario, new plants could not make a substantial contribution to reducing US global emissions for at least two decades."[46] Additionally, assert other critics, significant climate warming emissions are created by the whole production cycle for commercial nuclear fuel which diminishes the net impact of emission reductions from commercial facilities themselves.[47]

Sustaining the Nuclear Option

The federal government can follow different policy pathways to sustain the nuclear option. Washington can continue to implement existing commitments to reactor development by funding current legislation, such as the Energy Policy Act (2005), or by new legislation creating additional incentives. It can commit to a more limited development by reducing currently authorized expenditures without eliminating them. The federal government can decide to promote only favored technologies, to create different kinds of private-public development partnerships, or to implement many other policies likely to create incentives for new reactor development. Proponents of continued commercial reactor development assert there are still compelling reasons to keep the nuclear option alive.

Combating climate warming. No event has done more to sustain the nuclear power industry's visions for an early twenty-first century revival than the global climate issue. Climate warming is the industry's current political capital, the best hope for a political makeover.

Unlike carbon fuels, commercial nuclear reactors create no CO_2 emissions when generating electric power at a time when the United States produces more than 19 percent of all global CO_2. Moreover, the domestic nuclear power could produce showpiece facilities, such as the six US nuclear utilities rated among global leaders as combining very high power output with near zero CO_2 emissions.[48] Globally, the nuclear power industry has claimed to have reduced world CO_2 emissions from electric power generation by 20 percent.[49] The federal government's respected National Research Council recommended that nuclear reactors should be among the mix of "strategies for limiting domestic greenhouse-gas (GHG) emissions to a level with a global effort to hold future temperature increases to acceptable levels."[50] As noted earlier, the commitment by both the G. W. Bush and Obama administrations of very substantial federal research and development funding to finance new reactor development and commercialization reflects confidence in a future for the industry.

Numerous studies, however, suggest that the *full* cycle of nuclear power production may create significant CO_2 emissions. "When all is said and done," notes a careful summary of such research, "between mining the uranium, refining and enriching fuel, and building and operating the plant, a big 1,250 250-megawatt nuclear facility produces an estimated 250,000 tons of carbon dioxide during its lifetime, according to one analysis. If that's true, the entire US nuclear industry has produced something around 26 million tons of carbon dioxide."[51] Also, widely varying estimates exist concerning the length of time and cost required before sufficient new facilities can be constructed to significantly reduce future CO_2 emissions—*if* the new reactor designs can be commercialized—and how much emission reduction can be achieved.

New and improved reactors. Proponents of commercial nuclear power have maintained that these liabilities associated with the industry must be considered in the broader context of the foregone opportunities and risks created by a moratorium on all future commercial reactor development. Advocates assert that a new generation of safer reactors is now available, more efficient technically and economically than currently operating reactors, and even better technologies will soon appear.

By 2010, several industry consortia had submitted to the NRC applications to construct 26 new units, many based upon smaller, modular "Generation III" reactors. The greatest departure from previous designs is that many Generation III reactors and later designs incorporate "passive" or inherent safety features that require no active controls or operational intervention to avoid accidents in the event of malfunction but rely instead on gravity, natural convection, or resistance to high temperatures to abort meltdowns. Generation III and newer designs now being utilized in China, Korea, and Japan have other advantages that have prompted the United States to make these advanced designs the core elements of two international reactor initiatives created during the George W. Bush administration and implemented through the US Department of Energy. These new reactor innovations are said to include these features:

- Standard designs to expedite licensing and reduce capital cost and construction time
- Higher availability and longer operating life, typically sixty years
- Resistance to serious damage created by radioactive release from aircraft impact
- Greater fuel rod life and reduced waste[52]

These advanced reactors have elicited qualified support from some significant scientific and environmental spokesmen who believe some sort of nuclear option must remain for the United States.[53] In any case, nuclear power partisans believe it would be premature to prevent the technological resilience and economic implications of alternative reactor designs to be adequately tested. In addition to demonstrating the newer nuclear technology's technical and economic feasibility (if they exist), reactor development allows opportunity to develop governance structures appropriate for them.

Preserving a technology infrastructure. If the United States rejects further commercial reactor development, industry advocates believe this would virtually ensure the further demise of an already depleted scientific and industrial infrastructure whose recovery would be essential to sustain any domestic nuclear renaissance. Abandoning the nuclear option, it is asserted, would thereby concede global leadership in nuclear technology development to China, Korea, Japan, the European Union, the Russian Federation, and other nations, including politically volatile states in the Mideast including Iran, Egypt, and the United Arab Emirates.[54]

The United States still possesses the technological capability to create and test new reactors, but ambitious global development programs for several decades have been steadily drawing abroad the newer generation of nuclear engineers, facility specialists, and related skilled workers to a point where many domestic industry spokesmen consider this "brain drain" the industry's most acute contemporary problem.[55] Several reasons for this brain drain are apparent. First, the International Atomic Energy Agency (IAEA) noted as early as 2006 that the "USA faces the issue of a 'greying' workforce where literally half the current workers will be eligible to retire within the next five years."[56] Additionally, the majority of students now training in advanced US graduate programs to become nuclear engineers are not US citizens.[57] A high proportion of new US graduates in nuclear specialties is employed abroad or expects to be so employed upon graduation. The United States, assert industry supporters, cannot realistically contemplate options for a secure future involved in some way with commercial nuclear power if it must within a generation or so depend largely upon non-US resources for much of the development.

A changing energy marketplace. Proponents of commercial nuclear reactors also believe that the future marketplace for fuels to generate electric power is likely to be more advantageous for nuclear power than presently. They suggest that a new federal regulatory program to control industrial CO_2 emissions will certainly appear and significantly increase the cost of coal- and gas-fired electric power generation to the point that nuclear fuels will be much more competitive for electric power production, especially in the Northeast and southeastern United States.[58] Some comparisons also suggest that nuclear power is much less expensive per megawatt of generated electric power than most renewable energy alternatives including wind, solar, and biomass.[59]

A limited "renaissance"? The United States might create a limited moratorium—a sort of "little renaissance"—for several decades, during which federal funding and other development incentives could be limited to several "first starter" commercial facilities utilizing the newer reactor technologies. This would require sufficient federal support to convince several corporations or consortia to make the first commitments to facility design and operation, together with enough time and information to determine the technical and economic feasibility of the new utilities. Such a limited moratorium would probably require less federal investment in reactor development than is now planned. If these first starter reactors prove successful, they might become the assurance that draws other investors into the nuclear power marketplace.

Compared with the ambitious Obama proposal for a threefold increase in current federal support for nuclear power, a limited moratorium places American taxpayers at significantly reduced financial risk of loss from a failed nuclear renaissance.[60]

Solving the Waste Problem

The DOE's elusive permanent waste repository continues an expensive journey into a precarious future. The nuclear waste issue will not go away, whether the federal government keeps or abandons the nuclear option. Commercial nuclear utilities, collectively paying a required annual fee now exceeding $750 million to finance a facility long ago predicted to be operational, have collected more than $1.3 billion from Washington for breach of contract. At least seventy additional lawsuits are in the queue, and legal costs are estimated to reach $12 billion more if the facility isn't available by 2020. "The overall waste storage situation," noted a former Chairman of the NRC with considerable understatement, "does not bolster the credibility of our government to handle the matter competently."[61]

At the president's request, DOE Secretary Chu appointed a Blue Ribbon Commission on America's Nuclear Future in 2010 to recommend how to improve the current federal waste management plan.[62] By 2013, no White House decision had been made on any of the commission's recommendations. Thus, the White House and Congress continue to face several options, none of which provides a final solution to the waste problem:

- Move future commercial waste, and perhaps some of the existing waste in cooling ponds, to dry cask storage. Nationally, about fifty-five dry storage sites currently exist away from commercial reactor sites, and their volume or number can be increased. Dry casks are considered very safe for storage not exceeding twenty to twenty-five years.
- Chemically and physically separate the most dangerous radioactive fuel elements by "reprocessing" and subsequent disposal of the greatly reduced waste volume. However, the federal government in the past has rejected reprocessing as economically inefficient and potentially dangerous to national security because it creates a significant volume of weapons grade plutonium that may be difficult to sequester.
- Create monitored retrievable storage (MRS) sites. A MRS is a facility voluntarily accepted by communities to accept high-level nuclear waste until a final waste repository is created. However, attempts during the 1990s to create more than thirty MRS sites were rejected by communities throughout the United States.
- Modify the Yucca Mountain facility so that it will ultimately be technically acceptable for permanent waste deposition, meanwhile keeping wastes in existing ponds, dry casks, and other temporary storage.

CONCLUSION

The future of the nuclear power industry remains the most problematic and controversial of all the nation's major energy sources. Proponents of the industry believe it should be an important component of future US energy production. Compared to carbon fuels, nuclear energy is potentially a major source of CO_2-free electric power facilities and thus a plausibly important fuel in the long-term US strategy to mitigate global climate change. Moreover, the industry has developed, and continues to plan, innovative newer generations of smaller, safer, and more efficient reactor models that nuclear power advocates believe will overcome the operating and economic problems, which plagued the industry through its development from the 1950s through early 2000. Additionally, the technical and economic performance of many existing commercial nuclear facilities has become highly credible technically and economically. With the prospect of continuing federal subsidies and research support over at least another decade and the renewal of the operating licenses for a growing number of current operating plants, the short-term future of the industry appears, if not robust, at least secure. Finally, a governmental decision gradually to eliminate a domestic capacity to produce nuclear electric power could accelerate the migration of the nation's nuclear electric power infrastructure abroad and concede future nuclear innovation to other nations.

A national commitment to continued future development of commercial nuclear power also constitutes a risky gamble with the future. Controversy continues over the safety of nuclear reactor technologies, particularly their security from terrorism, their structural safety in the aftermath of the Fukushima disaster, and the reliability of new reactor designs despite assurances by their proponents. Disagreement prevails about the magnitude of current and future CO_2 emission reductions achievable with existing and planned power plants. Perhaps the most daunting of all issues clouding the future of a domestic nuclear industry, however, remain the enormous construction cost of new facilities and the bitter, decades long stalemate over where to store securely the relentlessly rising volume of radioactive waste presently cooling at reactor sites.

Altogether, these issues constitute the substance of the nation's current policy debate over the nuclear option: shall commercial nuclear power remain on the nation's future energy agenda? An answer to this question depends not only upon the contemporary status of the nuclear power industry considered in this chapter. Equally important is the technology, state of development, and policy options presented to policymakers by renewable energy, currently promoted as supplemental, and possibly an eventual alternative to nuclear energy for electric power and other energy production—the agenda for the next chapter.

RENEWABLE ENERGY AND ELECTRIC POWER

"We're still thinking about the future of renewable energy like it's 1990 or like it's the year 2000. Our thinking is just behind the reality of where renewables are today and where they are going based on existing market technology, cost, and finance trends."[1]

Eric Martinot
Senior Research Director
Institute for Sustainable Energy Policies

"It seems like for a few months we'll hear about solar and wind, and for a few months about [vehicle] electrification, and for a few months about another sector. I think what we have is an a la carte energy policy. . . . It doesn't have the focus, or shall I say, the gravitas it needs consistently."[2]

James Jones, former National Security
Advisor, 2009–2011

Before a national audience, newly elected President Barack Obama celebrated Earth Day 2009 from a wind tower assembly plant in Newton, Iowa, where he declared his intention to put the United States on "the clean energy superhighway" leading to a safer environment and greater energy efficiency. He envisioned "a new era of energy exploration for America" and predicted that by 2030 wind power could create 20 percent of all energy produced in the United States.

"After decades of dragging our feet," promised Obama, his new national energy agenda "will finally spark the creation of a clean energy industry that will create hundreds of thousands of jobs over the next few years, manufacturing wind turbines and solar cells."[3] To redeem that promise, the American Recovery and Reinvestment Act of 2009—the Obama administration's $781 billion economic stimulus package—dedicated $61 billion to promote wind energy and other clean energy alternatives. "Green energy" had now become a priority in the continually evolving politics and presidential energy policy.

A PATH NOT YET A HIGHWAY

Americans living during the second decade of the twenty-first century are on the threshold of what is predicted to be an expanding renewable energy economy. The route toward this renewable energy future is not likely to become Obama's "superhighway" or some other fast track envisioned by renewable energy's most ardent proponents but, instead, a slowly enlarging path which nonetheless moves the United States resolutely toward a new era of renewable energy development. And no presidency has more emphatically embraced the vision of a "clean energy" future, nor committed the federal budget more lavishly to such an abundance of renewable energy projects and proposals, nor invested quite so much political capital in the achievement of a green energy record, than the Obama administration.

Cautious predictions about future national energy production suggest that renewable energy generation will grow slowly but steadily. The highly respected U.S. Energy Information Administration (EIA), for instance, anticipates a growth of 1.7 percent a year and that renewables' total share of America's production will rise from 13 percent in 2011 to 16 percent in 2035 (Figure 6-1).

Like all projections of future energy development, predictions about future renewable energy are vulnerable to sudden or unexpected domestic economic and political shocks, unanticipated changes in US public policy, and changing global energy conditions. Still, most important private US investment institutions and advisors remain guardedly

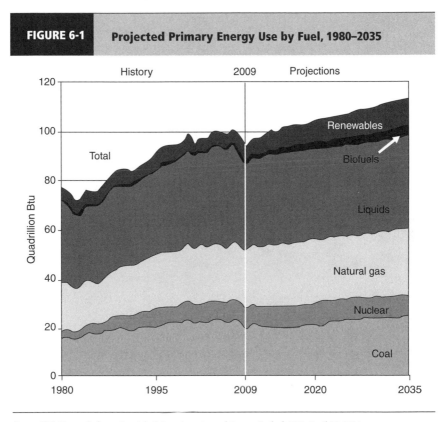

FIGURE 6-1   **Projected Primary Energy Use by Fuel, 1980–2035**

Source: U.S. Energy Information Administration, *Annual Energy Outlook 2011*, April 26, 2011.

optimistic about the long-term future for renewable energy nationally and internationally.

RENEWABLE ENERGY: THE RESOURCE

When it comes to US fuel production and consumption, Americans have been fossil fuel spendthrifts and renewable energy misers. Renewable energy resources include solar, wind, biomass, geothermal, and hydro-electric power. Currently, renewables account for less than a tenth of US energy production (Figure 6-2).

The most important current consumer of renewable energy, and likely to continue for at least another decade, is electric power production. As Figure 6-3 indicates, in 2012, renewables accounted for about 12 percent

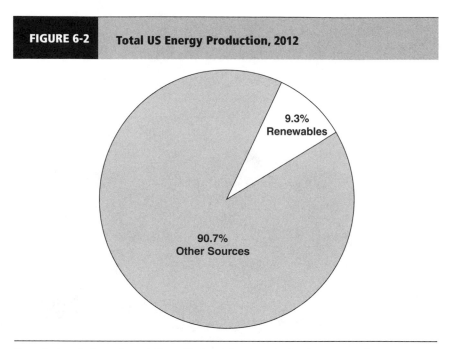

FIGURE 6-2 | **Total US Energy Production, 2012**

9.3%
Renewables

90.7%
Other Sources

Source: Institute for Energy Research, Renewable Energy, http://www.instituteforenergyresearch.org/energy-overview/renewable-energy/.

of total US electric power consumption, most of this energy produced by hydropower, wind, and solar sources.

A Varied and Abundant Resource

The United States is an international leader in renewable energy resources, if not in renewable energy use. While predictions of potential national renewable energy production vary widely, many plausible estimates suggest that the United States is capable of meeting a significant proportion of its future energy needs, or replacing much of its current fossil fuel consumption, with renewable energy. For example,

• a quarter of the US land area has winds strong enough to generate electricity at the same price as natural gas and coal;

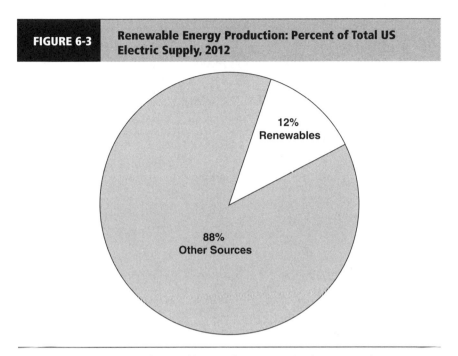

FIGURE 6-3 **Renewable Energy Production: Percent of Total US Electric Supply, 2012**

Source: Institute for Energy Research, Renewable Energy, http://www.instituteforenergyresearch.org/energy-overview/renewable-energy/

- seven states in the Southwest have the potential to provide ten times the current electric generating capacity through solar power;
- renewable energy sources could provide an additional 500 trillion kilowatt-hours of electricity per year by 2020 and perhaps an additional 1100 per year by 2035—total US electricity consumption at present is about 4000 per year;[4]
- based on the average US electricity fuel mix, one million watts of power per hour of wind energy displaces about 1,200 tons of CO_2. US wind capacity installed through 2008 will reduce CO_2 by about 44 million tons annually.[5]

Except for the numerous hydroelectric dams constructed by federal public works programs during the Great Depression of the 1930s, neither the American public nor its governments gave much attention to renewable resources until the energy shocks of the 1970s. Washington's enthusiasm for renewable energy promotion receded rapidly in the 1980s with the end of the domestic petroleum shortage. Waning federal funding inhibited renewable technology innovation through the 1990s, for renewable technologies usually depend upon federal research and development funding for their early development.

It required the catastrophic events of September 11, 2001, to revive national concern about America's energy insecurities and the strategic importance of renewable energy. Beginning with George W. Bush's administration, renewable energy in many different manifestations has become a continuing priority in federal and state government policies. Among renewables, solar radiation, wind, and biomass are expected to produce the most substantial energy to replace fossil fuels and nuclear reactor power.

Solar Power

Renewable solar energy technologies depend upon the sun to produce heat and electricity. These technologies include the following:[6]

- *Solar Thermal Systems for Heating Buildings and Water*—Solar thermal systems use solar collectors to absorb solar radiation to heat water or air for space and water heating.
- *Solar Thermal-Electric Power Plants*—Solar thermal-electric power plants use concentrating solar collectors to focus the sun's rays to heat fluid to a high temperature. This working fluid can then be used to generate steam to operate a turbine, which is then used to produce electricity in a generator.
- *Photovoltaic Systems*—Photovoltaic (PV) systems are based on solar electric cells, which convert solar radiation directly into electricity. Individual PV cells are configured into modules of varying electricity producing capacities. PV applications range from single solar cells for powering watches to large installations with hundreds of modules for electric power production.

Solar technologies currently account for little more than one percent of domestic renewable energy consumption but are expected to substantially grow in importance because they constitute a high priority renewable resource promoted by federal and state governments. With its large area and hemispheric spread, the United States experiences vast solar exposure with potential for conversion to heat and electric power through solar technologies. The southeastern and southwestern states are considered especially significant locations for large scale solar power developments. "Calculations show," notes the World Watch Institute, "that just seven states in the US Southwest could provide more than 7 million [megawatts] of solar generating capacity—roughly 10 times the total US generating from all sources today."[7]

Federal lands in the West, Southwest, and New England administered by the Department of the Interior and the Department of Agriculture are considered especially favorable for large scale solar development. Currently, federal lands provide about 6 percent of domestic renewable energy generation but have potential to create much more power. Large tracts in the Great Plains and Southwest receive large amounts of dependable solar radiation. Also, these tracts, notably in the southwestern deserts, are suitable for sprawling commercial "solar energy farms" containing thousands of solar electric panels covering hundreds of acres. The Bureau of Land Management (BLM) already has more than twenty-five solar facilities on public lands with a total estimated capacity (437 megawatts) to power more than four hundred thousand homes (a megawatt is estimated conservatively to provide power for from four hundred to nine hundred homes). More than fifty additional projects are scheduled for development in the next decade. The prospect of these large solar arrays, however, has been greeted with dismay by some environmentalists and residents near the prospective facilities who object to the intrusive technology in pristine natural settings and the threat to endangered native species—a matter to be further discussed shortly.

A number of states have initiated public policies to encourage the proliferation of solar technologies to generate heat and electric power for homes, businesses, and communities. California has created a public law requiring that 20 percent of the state's electric power must come from renewable resources after 2010, and several states have created "Renewable Portfolio Standards" (RPS) mandating a schedule requiring electric utilities to generate a significant proportion of their power from renewable resources.

Wind

Wind energy was once used extensively, especially in rural America, to drive windmill pumps and wind electric generators, until the 1930s when federal rural electrification programs replaced farm-based wind technologies. Not until the 1980s did federal and state governments begin to create incentives for the return of wind power on a significant scale throughout the United States. Starting in the early 1980s, federal and state governments began modest programs to revive wind power generation, including research and development funding for wind technologies, federal and state tax incentives, subsidies, and Renewable Portfolio Standards.

Today, most wind energy "comes from turbines that can be as tall as a 20-story building and have three 200-foot-long (60-meter-long) blades. These contraptions look like giant airplane propellers on a stick," explains *National Geographic*. "The wind spins the blades, which turn a shaft connected to a generator that produces electricity. Other turbines work the same way, but the turbine is on a vertical axis and the blades look like a giant egg beater."[8] The wind turbine, usually combined in large arrays called "wind farms," is the primary technology upon which planning is based to generate wind-powered electricity in sufficient strength to displace significant fossil fuel combustion. Large wind turbine farms, most of them located on private property, may contain dozens, or hundreds, of tall (as high as 200 feet) turbines with blades customarily at least one hundred feet in diameter; the largest commercial turbines can provide electric power to as many as six hundred homes.[9] Smaller turbines located on private property can supply power to single homes or small businesses.

Estimates of US wind energy potential vary widely, depending upon differing assumptions concerning the technology's durability, future economic conditions, and land availability.[a] The American Wind Energy Association believes, very optimistically, that American wind resources with

---

[a] "Wind turbines will only operate satisfactorily if there is enough sustainable wind speed, the ideal conditions being a minimum of about 8 mph for at least 18–20 hours per day. When the wind is not blowing, the turbine cannot produce electricity." Environment 911, "14 Wind Turbine Facts," available at http://www.environment911.0rg/127.14_Wind_Turbine_Facts.

appropriate technologies could generate sufficient power annually equal to ten times current national electric power consumption. "Today's wind farms," notes the Association, "produce enough electricity to power all of Virginia, Oklahoma, or Tennessee" and "Iowa existing wind projects could produce 20 percent of the state's electricity."[10] More conservatively, the Department of Energy has estimated that wind resources could replace at least 20 percent of current national electricity consumption by 2030.[11] Wind energy is already a significant source of electric power in many states, such as Texas, California, and Iowa, the current leaders in state wind energy production. Many states, as Table 6.1 indicates, have significant potential for wind power generation.

Biomass

Beer drinkers with an environmental conscience will find a new reason to celebrate upon discovering that the Anheuser-Busch Brewery and Ameresco, a renewable energy corporation, were operating in 2012

TABLE 6-1 Top Ten States in Wind Potential		
State	Megawatts (MW) of wind turbines	Gigawatt hours (GWh) a year of wind power
Texas	1,901,530	6,527,850
Kansas	952,371	3,646,590
Montana	944,004	3,228,620
Nebraska	917,999	3,540,370
South Dakota	882,412	3,411,690
North Dakota	770,196	2,983,750
Iowa	570,714	2,026,340
Wyoming	552,073	1,944,340
Oklahoma	516,822	1,788,910
New Mexico	492,083	1,644,970

Source: Renewable Energy Focus.com, Potential for US Wind Energy Is 10.5 GW, February 19, 2010, http://www.renewableenergyfocus.com/view/7446/potential-for-us-wind-energy-is-105-gw/.

an unusual six-mile pipeline in Houston to generate steam energy for the brewery's power plant. The pipeline carries biogas, processed from the large east Houston McCarty Road Landfill, to provide more than 55 percent of the brewery's fuel demand, which was formerly met with fossil fuels.[12] Biogas, a mixture of methane and carbon dioxide produced by bacterial degradation of organic matter, such as garbage and animal waste, can be converted to generate electricity, heat, or steam or even to an alternative vehicle fuel. The Houston pipeline is an early illustration of a growing trend in biogas utilization that has made Texas a leader in state biogas production and consumption.

Biomass energy, such as Houston's biogas, has gradually emerged as a priority in American governmental renewable energy projects. This biomass consists primarily of three energy sources:

Wood. This includes wood chips from forestry operations; residues from lumber, pulp or paper, and furniture mills; and fuel wood for space heating. The largest single source of wood energy is "black liquor," a residue of pulp, paper, and paperboard production.

Municipal solid waste and biogas. Garbage, or municipal solid waste (MSW) contains biomass (or biogenic) materials like paper, cardboard, food scraps, grass clippings, leaves, wood, and leather products; and other non-biomass combustible materials, mainly plastics and other synthetic materials made from petroleum. MSW can be recycled, composted, sent to landfills, or used in waste-to-energy plants. As of October 2010, there were about 490 landfills that recover biogas, or methane, which forms as waste decomposes in the low-oxygen (anaerobic) conditions. The gas can be converted and used in many ways: to generate electricity, heat, or steam; or as an alternative fuel for vehicles.

Biofuels. Biofuels include alcohol fuels, such as ethanol, and "biodiesel," a fuel made from grain oils and animal fats. Most biofuel used in the United States is fuel ethanol produced from corn.[13]

While ethanol and other alcohols produced from grain are the most familiar examples of domestic biomass energy, wood and wood waste are the largest sources of national biomass fuel. Virtually any organic material, however, is a potential source of biomass energy. Biomass still constitutes only 4 percent of US energy production, more than half of which is used industrially. "In the United States," a recent study notes,

> The production of biogas from animal manure alone represents an enormous potential energy resource, on the order of 0.9 quadrillion BTU (quad) annually, or nearly 1% of total US energy consumption. In addition, only 15% of the wastewater treatment flow in the US produces biogas that is used as a source of energy; the rest of the wastewater flows either do not produce biogas at all or produce biogas that is wastefully flared instead of captured for heat or power.[14]

Other sources of domestic renewable energy include hydropower and geothermal technology. Hydroelectric power is especially important in generating more than 71 percent of all electric power produced by renewable sources and about 6 percent of all electric power generated in the United States. The nation's hydroelectric power resources, however, are not expected to increase significantly, and some hydroelectric dams have been, or will soon be, removed from operation for environmental reasons. Geothermal energy continues to be a comparatively low federal energy policy priority.

GOVERNANCE: THE POLICY CHALLENGE OF RENEWABLES

The renewable sector of the US energy economy has been especially dependent upon federal funding, through policies such as tax subsidies, R&D money, and federal energy purchases, to sustain its growth. It is also vulnerable to all the formidable liabilities packaged with governmental funding: shifts in partisan control of Congress and the White House, changes in the public mood, economic and political crises, international events, the inherent incrementalism of American policymaking, constitutional divisions of power, federalism, and much else. Nonetheless, federal support for renewable energy, particularly R&D funding for renewable technologies and, within the last several decades for commercialization of renewables, has been significant in the federal budget (between 1978 and the inception of the Obama administration in 2008, for example, the renewable energy share of DOE's technology research and development budget averaged about 11 percent).[15]

The Importance and Growth of Federal Incentives

Renewable energy development has been highly sensitive to federal budget support and other policies for several reasons. Private entrepreneurs are reluctant to invest in renewable technologies until a technology's technical feasibility and commercial viability have been demonstrated. Moreover, investors usually plan on the basis of long-term capital commitments and prefer assurance of various federal tax subsidies and other concessions diminishing the long-term capital risks. Additionally, the commercial potential for many renewable energy technologies may depend upon the international markets and national trade policies heavily influenced by Washington.

Finally, federal renewable energy policy has often been inconsistent and episodic, threatening to create "orphan" technologies unable to survive on their own. Investors are likely to favor technologies that do not require decades for creation, development, and commercial demonstration. "In the United States," observe economists David Victor and Kassia Yanosek,

> *every few years, key federal subsidies for most sources of clean energy expire. Investment freezes until, usually in the final hours of budget negotiations, Congress finds the money to renew the incentives—and investors rush in again. As a result, most investors favor low-risk conventional clean-energy technologies that can be built quickly before the next bust.*[16]

A Variety of Policy Options

Over the decades since the energy shocks of the 1970s, federal policymakers have debated, created, and modified a variety of basic policy options to encourage the domestic growth of renewable energy. These include the following:

Research and development grants (R&D). Federal R&D is usually associated with work conducted by the private sector or academic institutions, although federal agencies and laboratories may also receive support.[17] President Obama committed about $1.9 billion in the fiscal year (FY) 2012 budget for renewable energy R&D, or roughly 64 percent of the DOE's total R&D request.

Renewable energy production tax credit (PTC). The PTC is an inflation-adjusted tax credit for electricity produced from qualifying renewable energy sources or technologies.

Income tax credits for renewable energy systems. Tax credits up to 30 percent of the cost of qualifying renewable energy systems are available through 2016.

Renewable portfolio standards (RPS) and state mandates or goals. An RPS is a requirement that a percentage of electric power generation or sales come from renewable energy. Some states have specific mandates for power generation from renewable energy while others have voluntary goals. By the end of 2009, there were 42 states plus the District of Columbia with an RPS, state mandate, or goal.

Loan guarantees. Federal insurance, of variable amount, provided against failure or default in debt incurred by private sector companies engaged in technology development or commercialization.

Green Power programs. US consumers in many states can purchase electricity generated by renewable energy resources, termed green power. There are about 600 electric utilities in 47 states now offering green power to their customers. Most of these programs sell power produced by new wind and landfill gas-to-energy projects.

State financial incentives. Many states subsidize the installation of renewable energy equipment through a variety of measures. For example, in California, a state "buy-down" program (a grant for the purchase of small renewable energy systems) for photovoltaic (PV) equipment greatly increased the number and size of PV systems installed on houses and buildings.

Net metering programs. Net metering allows electric utility customers to install grid-connected renewable energy systems on their property and get credit for the amount of excess electricity the systems produce.

Forty-two states and the District of Columbia now have state-wide net metering programs.

Ethanol and other renewable motor fuels. A variety of federal and state requirements and incentives exist for the production, sale, and use of ethanol, biodiesel, and other fuels made from renewable biomass. The Federal Energy Independence and Security Act of 2007 requires that 36 billion gallons of biofuels be used in the United States per year by 2022. Several states have their own renewable fuel standards or requirements.[18]

The decade of 2000–2010 marked the greatest increase in federal support of renewable technology in the nation's history. Beginning with the George W. Bush administration, the scale of federal support for renewable energy enlarged rapidly. The Bush administration's Energy Policy Act (2005) was a major leap ahead in federal renewable energy promotion. The act, for example,

- authorized loan guarantees for innovative technologies that avoid greenhouse gases, such as renewable energy technologies;
- increased the amount of biofuel (primarily ethanol) that must be mixed with gasoline sold in the United States to 7.5 billion US gallons by 2012;
- authorized subsidies for wind and other alternative energy producers;
- authorized $50 million annually over the life of the law for biomass grants.

The Energy Independence and Security Act of 2007, which quickly followed the 2005 legislation, further enlarged federal participation in renewable energy development. Its provisions included extending the requirement for biofuel mixture in gasoline to 36 billion gallons by 2022, granting programs to encourage the development of cellulosic biofuels, and increasing federal support for research, production, and infrastructure development of ethanol fuels.

The Resilient States

State governments, once considered laggards in energy policymaking, have become in the last several decades important policy innovators, in many instances seizing the initiative in renewable energy policymaking when the federal government mired itself in institutional rivalries, partisan conflict, and the glacial pace of bureaucratic regulation. In most states, mandated renewable energy usage is accomplished by gubernatorial orders, legislation, or state public utility commissions. Each state public utility commission collaborates with the Federal Energy Regulatory Commission (FERC) in policymaking. The public utility commissions have become national leaders in renewable energy innovation, in part because of the broad scope of their authority. These commissions are responsible for regulating

- retail sales of electricity and natural gas,
- construction of energy facilities and local pipelines,
- local and regional power systems and cooperatives,
- nuclear power plants,
- pipeline safety,
- electric transmission and reliability,
- abandoned oil facilities.

The states have been especially important in promoting renewable energy use by requiring "Renewable Portfolio Standards" (RPS) for electric utilities, and by initiating regional agreements to limit greenhouse gas emissions.[19] An RPS, as noted earlier, requires electricity providers to obtain a minimum percentage of their power from renewable energy resources by a certain date. Currently, twenty-four states plus the District of Columbia have RPS policies in place. Together these states account for more than half of the electricity sales in the United States. Five other states, North Dakota, South Dakota, Utah, Virginia, and Vermont, have nonbinding goals for adoption of renewable energy instead of an RPS.

The states, as noted in chapter 4, have also become the leaders in early national efforts to control greenhouse gas emissions. GHG emission control policies could have a potentially vast impact upon renewable energy development by promoting the replacement of coal with renewable sources to generate electric power and provide industrial energy.

The future of state GHG regulatory initiatives remains problematic. Much depends upon what the federal government does during Obama's second term. If the Obama administration is successful in using the Clean Air Act to regulate domestic CO_2 emissions, this could supplement, or perhaps replace, much state regulation. Failure of the federal plan, in contrast, would leave the states as the nation's default GHG regulators.

The Obama Administration's "Green Agenda"

The Obama administration, determined to implement rapidly an unprecedented green energy agenda, ambitiously enlarged both the diversity of projects and the magnitude of federal spending for renewable energy through Obama's first term and proposed an equally aggressive agenda after Obama's reelection.

The first term. The realities of the national recession compelled a retreat from many of the administration's expansive and expensive renewable energy projects. Nonetheless, the administration had by mid-2013 invested more federal dollars in renewable energy development than any previous presidency. Using money already authorized for renewable energy development by the Bush administration, the White House added $16.8 billion from the American Recovery and Reinvestment Act of 2009 for the DOE's Office of Energy Efficiency and Renewable Energy, a tenfold increase in the DOE Office's previous year's authorization.

Among the Obama administration's most vigorously promoted renewable energy programs was a massive increase in federal support for renewable development on federal public lands. Between 2008 and 2010, the administration quadrupled the electric generating capacity of projects approved on public lands including sixteen new solar projects, four new wind farms, and seven new geothermal plants.[20] Among these innovations are the following:

- The Sonoran Solar Energy Project, about 3,700 acres of Bureau of Land Management managed land near Buckeye, Arizona, planned to generate enough electricity to power about 90,000 homes

- The Tule Wind Project in southeastern San Diego County, about seventy miles east of San Diego, expected to produce 186 megawatts of electricity (enough to power 65,000 homes) using sixty-two wind turbines[b]
- A proposal, announced in 2010, to make 677,400 acres of public lands in six Western states available as solar energy zones and appropriate for solar energy development[21]

The administration also gave high priority to economic incentives encouraging the accelerated development of solar, wind, and biomass technologies. Thus, the president's proposed FY 2012 renewable energy budget included an almost 46 percent increase in the DOE's authorization for renewable programs.[22] More than 2,600 projects received tax dollars under the initiative to promote wind and solar power created in the 2009 stimulus bill. The program, run by the Treasury, enabled developers to receive as much as 30 percent of the cost of a project.

However, some of the administration's most highly promoted clean energy projects were casualties to the economic recession, partisan congressional infighting, inflated expectations, and questionable judgment. The most publicized and politically damaging detour along the "energy superhighway" was Solyndra, the California based developer of solar panels, which received $535 million in federally guaranteed loans from the Obama administration but proved unable to create the economies of scale necessary to compete in a suddenly shrinking global marketplace. Critics charged that the administration's political intervention in the loan decision produced the failure, while project partisans blamed unanticipated market conditions. The slow development of other wind and solar energy projects left very improbable the president's goal in his 2011 State of the Union message to generate 80 percent of the nation's electricity with renewable energy.

---

[b] The project still needs to gain approval from the California Public Utilities Commission, Bureau of Indian Affairs, California State Lands Commission, and the County of San Diego.

Back to the "Superhighway." The Obama energy agenda for his second term, declared in The President's Climate Action Plan in mid-2013, proposed to advance renewable energy even further along his envisioned energy superhighway than he proposed to travel in his first term. His most significant renewable energy priorities included

- doubling US renewable electric power generation by 2020,
- accelerating renewable energy permitting on the public lands by 2020,
- increasing installed renewable energy capacity in federal government agencies and the military, and
- upgrading the nation's electric grid.[23]

For every light that beckons to policymakers at the end of the renewable energy tunnel, there is often another tunnel beyond the light. The Obama administration's challenges in transforming its renewable energy agenda into reality are predictable, as the history of many preceding presidencies demonstrates. Each renewable energy technology is bundled with its unique mix of technical complexities, which may defy easy management yet demand a policy-based solution.

Policy Constraints

Often, the technical characteristics inherent to a technology—for example, the amount and predictability of the wind required to power efficiently a large wind tower—will determine where wind energy development is politically plausible. In addition to technical problems, however, renewable energy policymakers face other formidable challenges shaping and constraining policy decisions and common to most renewable technologies.

Economic and commercial feasibility. It is one thing to create a renewable energy technology—a highly efficient solar cell, for example—and another matter to scale the technology up to a technical level sufficient to operate dependably and commercially in a highly competitive national and international energy market. "Big changes in the energy industry do not happen overnight," caution economists Victor and Yanosek.

The bold goals of energy independence and of radically shifting to renewable energy may be attractive to politicians who prize what is popular over what actually works in the long run. Short-term motivations have created boom-bust patterns that have hurt the clean-energy industry; they have produced business models that depend too much on subsidies and on technologies that cannot compete at scale with conventional energy.[24]

National economic growth or its absence can significantly alter the availability of private capital upon which many technologies depend for startup or early marketability. Wind farms need space to accommodate giant wind turbines and customarily rely on bank financing for as much as 50 percent of project costs. The severe recession beginning in 2006 severely diminished bank financing to the point that capital available for new renewable energy projects shrank by more than 50 percent in early 2009.[25] "I thought if there was any industry that was bulletproof, it was that industry," lamented Rich Mattern, the mayor of West Fargo, North Dakota, where DMI Industries makes towers for wind turbines. "Though the flat Dakotas are among the best places in the world for wind farms, DMI had to cut its work force by 20 percent because of falling sales."[26] Renewable technologies are often vulnerable, as well, to the vicissitudes of the global economy. The Obama administration's problems with the ill-fated Solyndra project were compounded by a recession in the European market for solar panels.

Renewable technologies may require long start-up periods, perhaps years or more than a decade, before they are even ready for commercial introduction.

For solar power to become a significant contributor to energy supply, and hence greenhouse gas emissions reductions, the industry has to achieve high annual growth rates for decades. The challenge cannot be overstated, especially once subsidies can no longer be relied upon to drive industry growth. Several barriers, including high costs, lack of reliable demand, supply chain dynamics, and utility integration issues, threaten to prevent adoption rates from rising as fast as is required. In particular, high costs are a major barrier, since solar power must soon be cost competitive unsubsidized.[27]

Economics can trump technology and ecology when it comes to producing feasible renewable energy. It was significant that president Obama's 2011 State of the Union message included a reminder to Congress and the nation: "Now, clean energy breakthroughs will only translate into clean energy jobs if businesses know there will be a market for what they're selling."

While federal financial incentives may facilitate technology startups, a full development and production cycle may require additional, longer-term private commitments of investment without which federal funding may not materialize. Private investors, however, may be wary about the federal government's history of technology development. The technological graveyard is unfortunately abundant in projects that succumbed to erratic federal funding—and federal support may become especially volatile when the White House and Congress are fiercely divided by partisan conflict, as they have been since 2010.

Environmental impacts. Shortly after Barack Obama's first election, the Department of the Interior announced new rules that might have seemed predestined to confirm among environmentalists their high expectations for the new administration. The DOE rules removed the last federal administrative obstacles to erecting the first offshore wind turbines in the United States—a symbolic down payment on the president's anticipated green energy superhighway. However, many environmentalists and their allies were displeased, very displeased, because the DOE decision was expected to hasten construction of the Cape Winds turbine farm on Nantucket Sound off Cape Cod.[28]

Cape wind or ill wind? Cape Wind, located about five miles off the south Cape Cod coast would be big: twenty-four square miles including 130 horizontal-axis wind turbines. Peak generation capacity could create electricity estimated to serve 420,000 homes. Moreover, the project developers estimated that Cape Wind power would annually offset about a million tons of climate-warming CO_2 emissions and 113 million gallons of petroleum consumption.[29] Despite support from Massachusetts

Governor Deval Patrick and other state political leaders, the project had been bitterly opposed from the beginning in 2001 by numerous Cape Cod residents, local environmentalists, and other prominent state residents including Senator Ted Kennedy and his family.[30] Opponents considered the project an environmental menace, destroying irreplaceable natural beauty, obstructing the horizon, adversely displacing native animal and plant habitat, and requiring expensive public and private maintenance. Late in the struggle, the opponent's legal ranks were fortified by the Wampanoag Tribe, indigenous native Americans who asserted that

> the wind farm will destroy historical, cultural and spiritual tribal resources located on Horseshoe Shoal which was once exposed land [and] . . . will obstruct views across Nantucket Sound that are used by tribal members for spiritual rituals and contemplation."[31]

Opponents and supporters of Cape Wind battled in the media, in the Massachusetts legislature, in innumerable public debates between various organizational proxies for each side, in environmentalist and electric utility conferences, and (inevitably) the courts. The Cape Wind contention pitted environmentalists, communities, and federal bureaucracies against each other, delayed a Bush administration green energy showpiece, and delivered years of political and legal wrangling instead of renewable energy. The final legal hurdle was not crossed until 2011. A decade of costly, exhausting contention ended when both sides quit the battle. Cape Wind appeared, finally, headed for development.

The Cape Wind conflict is a sharp reminder that almost all renewable energy technologies, no matter how impeccably green their credentials, are likely to create controversial and sometimes undesirable environmental impacts as well. Wind farms on the Great Plains often provoke opposition from environmentalists, local communities, and residents in proximity to proposed projects because towers were predicted to be potent bird killers or to threaten endangered species, or, because they're unsightly or transmission lines are a health hazard. Massive ethanol production allegedly increases soil erosion, reduces desirable aphid predators, and produces significant CO_2 emissions, among other problems.[32] Some studies suggest that biogas "could end up increasing global greenhouse-gas emissions instead of reducing them."[33]

Whose public lands? By mid-2013, the DOE's Bureau of Land Management had issued permits, or was considering them, for solar, wind, and geothermal projects covering an area of 310,000 acres, about the size of Wyoming's expansive Grand Teton National Park.[34] The doubling of renewable electric power production proposed by Obama in mid-2013 would alone provide power for an estimated 4.4 million homes. However, the public lands where federal government renewable energy projects are planned are becoming contested territory between Washington, environmentalists, local residents, and cultural conservationists, especially in the Southwest, where a variety of groups believe large solar arrays threaten numerous endangered desert species, blight historic sites, and destroy natural beauty.[35]

The federal government will increasingly confront this politically difficult problem in reconciling environmental claims with Washington's determination to increase the speed of renewable electric power development, particularly when the environmentalist community itself is divided about where, and how, to locate large solar arrays and wind farms. Moreover, in many instances, regulatory federalism is involved. The states are often active stakeholders in issues about the disposition of public lands within their boundaries and expect to be included in decisions about the planning of large renewable power arrays and the distribution of the anticipated electric power.

Technological issues. Renewable energy use requires both a production technology and a technological infrastructure to distribute the energy. Technical issues have to be confronted and appropriate policy responses crafted—if they can be created—to convert the concept of renewable energy to reality.[36]

One fundamental technical issue common to renewable energy technologies, such as solar, wind, biogas, geothermal, and biomass, is whether the technology can be "scaled up" from small to commercial size.

The large amount of land required for utility-scale solar power plants, for instance, creates potential problems of adverse environmental impacts, available land, and the durability of the solar units. The "life cycle" cost and impact of a technology's manufacture, use, and disposal may pose problems. The amount of fossil fuel energy required to produce the components of solar and wind technologies, as well as the greenhouse gas emissions through a life cycle of use may become constraints that policymakers must confront.

The combustion of biomass produces carbon monoxide, nitrogen oxides, soot, and ash whose volume varies widely among different combustion systems. Different technologies pose different levels of control costs. "Emissions from conventional biomass-fueled plants are generally similar to emissions from coal-fired power plants . . . the most serious problem is their particulate emissions, which must be controlled with special devices." And installations that burn raw municipal waste "present a unique pollution-control problem. This waste often contains toxic metals, chlorinated compounds, and plastics, which generate harmful emissions that must be regulated with specialized emission control devices."[37]

Since renewable energy systems need to operate efficiently and economically over many decades, a technology's durability and replacement cost are likely to enter into the policy calculus when evaluating the comparative merit of competing technologies. Wind tower technology and large wind farms have not been utilized long enough in the United States to demonstrate the cost-effectiveness of some innovative new technologies, and this may be a substantial consideration in decisions about where to locate towers and upon the appropriate scale.

ELECTRIC POWER

"The U.S. electrical grid," writes author Jennifer Weeks,

> is the world's largest interconnected machine. With 300,000 miles of long-distance transmission lines and even more miles of local distribution networks, it carries power from more than

9,200 generating plants to homes and business nationwide. The system is so large and essential that the National Academy of Engineering ranks national electrification as the greatest engineering achievement of the 20th Century.[38]

The national electric grid has also become a great technological challenge now confronting designers of a renewable energy future, the more politically formidable because the imperative for the grid's comprehensive upgrading is vaguely understood by the public, very expensive, and without political glamour.

The Resource: Electric Power and Renewable Energy

The electric utilities linked by this grid are both consumers and producers of enormous energy resources; thus, few industries are more strategic to the development of America's energy economy. Additionally, the industry is a crucial economic intersection for almost every major domestic energy resource; with the exception of the nuclear power, all other domestic renewable and nonrenewable energy is consumed in some form by conventional electric utilities. Decisions about future sources of electric power and its distribution can profoundly shape the nation's energy economy because the industry

- consumes 94 percent of all US coal and largely creates the economic, environmental, and technological impact of coal combustion;
- purchases about 30 percent of natural gas production;
- generates 45 percent of national energy production with coal; and
- creates more than 90 percent of the domestic CO_2 emissions associated with global climate warming.

Size alone would thrust the electric power industry to the forefront of any discussion of the nation's renewable energy future. Moreover, because of the industry's size, changes in the configuration of national power generation has a multiplier effect as the impact spreads across the industry's many energy interdependencies.

The strategic role assumed by electric utilities in the future regulation of national climate warming emissions has been explored in chapter 4 and will be further examined in chapter 7. The industry's impact on the rapidly transforming economic status of coal and natural gas industries was discussed, as well, in chapter 7. The industry has an equally important place in any discussion of the present and future status of America's renewable energy.

Electric utilities are especially important to renewable energy advocates not only because of the industry's strategic location in the energy economy but also because utilities currently use comparatively little renewable sources to generate electricity. As Figure 6-4 illustrates, only about 11 percent of domestic electric power is produced by renewable energy sources. Since hydropower generates more than half this renewable production, the remaining renewables account for less than 5 percent of all the fuel consumed by electric utilities.

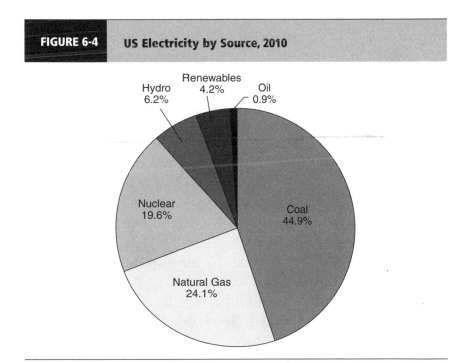

FIGURE 6-4   **US Electricity by Source, 2010**

Source: Climate Warming Central, "US Electricity (Only) by Source," *Energy Profiles,* http://www.climatewarmingcentral.com/energy_page.html.

Hydropower production is not expected to significantly increase in the future. While other forms of renewable energy consumed by utilities are expected to more than double in the next several decades, they will nonetheless remain a relatively small source of utility fuel without significant changes in federal, state, and local electric power policies (See Figure 6-4).

Predictions are not destiny, however, and many energy analysts and renewable energy advocates believe the potential capacity of renewable sources to create future electric power is underestimated and underexploited. Estimating the scale of electric power potential of renewable energy, however, depends upon a variety of contingencies including, especially, many future policy options in various combination. Since the nation lacks a nationally coordinated renewable energy strategy for electric power, a reasonable answer to the question "how much renewable electricity is possible?" is, "It depends, and it will very likely change over time."[39]

In any case, the *potential* electric generating capacity of renewable energy resources is considerable. The federal Government Accountability Office, for instance, estimated conservatively that in the Midwestern United States, there is enough wind power to meet "a significant portion of the nation's electricity needs."[40]

Significant constraints must be confronted in electric power development. One of the most formidable technical problems in linking renewable energy to electric power production is connecting sources to the national power grid. Because wind towers and solar cells create variable power depending upon the availability of sunshine and wind at the source, they can pose reliability issues for utilities with significant potential renewable sources. Moreover, the national electric power grid is an aging and highly stressed infrastructure already vulnerable to reliability problems when power demand cannot be shifted quickly among regional grids when peak demands exceed some regional grid capabilities. Some experts believe that any very large increase in the magnitude of electric power from renewables is unlikely unless the present aging grid is also made more resilient and efficient.

These infrastructure problems are compounded by a lack of compelling interest among the public and public officials. While the Obama administration is vigorously promoting a comprehensive renovation for the grid, constructing a new "smart grid" lacks the urgency and visibility to provide the political propulsion for a more comprehensive and incisive governmental response to the power grid challenge.[41]

Governance: Regulatory Federalism

No domestic energy resource better illustrates the impact of governance by federalism than the electric power industry. Electric utilities are economically regulated by federal, state, and local governments more comprehensively and consistently than any other domestic energy system. For more than a century, this intricate structure of interrelated laws and regulatory commissions has largely licensed, established service rules, determined economic market conditions, defined and implemented standards for public service for both publicly and privately owned utilities, and otherwise created the policy framework within which Americans produce, consume, and pay for electricity.

Federal Regulation

The Federal government constitutes the top tier of electric power governance, which constitutes a veritable alphabet soup of different regulatory institutions. The two foundations are the Federal Power Act (1935) and the Federal Energy Regulatory Commission (FERC). The Federal Power Act created a Federal Power Commission, which became in 1970 the FERC, a bipartisan and independent commission with oversight of the entire private utility industry. The FER Commission's responsibility is "to assure that electric power rates are reasonable, nondiscriminatory, and just to the consumer." Virtually every aspect of electric power production and distribution lies within the ambit of the FERC's authority, which includes

- the sale and transmission of power in interstate wholesale electricity markets;
- utility sales, mergers, acquisitions, and interconnections;
- oversight of the national electric grid's reliability; and
- the security of the national electric power grid.

The electric power industry, however, serves many other federal masters as well. The National Electric Reliability Council (NERC) is responsible for creating and enforcing reliability standards, educating and certifying industry personal, and assuring the accuracy of long-term electric power demand forecasts. Some of the most familiar domestic aspects of electric power consumption for the average American lie within federal authority of the Federal Communications Commission (FCC) including the structural integrity, safety, security, and reliability of utility poles linking together the nation's energy infrastructure.

And there are a multitude of relevant environmental regulations.

The electric power industry must comply with literally hundreds of environmental regulations, including dozens of rules created under the federal Clean Air Act and Clean Water Act. The U.S. Environmental Protection Agency (EPA) has primary responsibility for developing and enforcing most federal environmental regulations. Other federal agencies have broad authority over electric company facilities crossing federal lands or affecting unique interests, such as historical sites or endangered species.[42]

State Regulation

Below the federal level, state utility commissions perform regulatory roles similar to FERC in regulating sales of electricity at the retail level to end-use customers, as well as ensuring financial stability and reliability. The retail markets are where traditional utilities and other service providers sell energy and other services to end-user consumers, such as homeowners, businesses, units of government, schools, hospitals, manufacturers, and others. Generally, services and other aspects of these markets are regulated by state public utility commissions in states that do not allow retail.

Promoting Competition and Markets

In addition to their responsibilities for regulating standards of service, market pricing, consumer protection, and the security of electric power infrastructures, since the 1990s, federal and state policymakers in many sections of the nation have been concerned with promoting competition and enlarging markets for the electric power industry. Throughout the 1990s, the nation generally enjoyed ample energy supply, stable energy prices, and other market conditions. Most of the decade between these two was characterized by relatively little public or private interest in national energy policy. "Overall, the U.S.'s energy consumption portfolio changed very little during the decade. Energy demand continued to grow moderately, energy intensity continued to decline modestly, and the mix of fuels satisfying demand changed remarkably little."[43]

Beginning shortly after 2000, the aging national energy grid, together with increasing demand for electric power, and mounting concern over the environmental impact of carbon-based electric power prompted the federal and state governments to give more attention to developing a larger supply of renewable fuels to be able to use more renewable energy for electric power production.

The "Smart Grid"

The present national electric grid, essentially an interconnected network of regional power transmission and distribution infrastructures capable of switching electric generating capacity among regional networks to avoid regional overloads and blackouts, must be gradually replaced with a new, smart grid if renewable energy and energy efficiency are to have major impact on national production and consumption of electric power. In 2009, President Obama announced that the federal government would offer $3.4 billion in stimulus money for projects demonstrating how to improve power transmission and distribution to achieve greater efficiency, speed, and resiliency and, in 2013, pledged substantial additional funding for grid improvement.

If demonstration projects prove that a smart grid is technically and commercially feasible, the process of national conversion will be necessarily gradual and highly expensive. Smart grid designs involve installing advanced digital technologies throughout the electric power transmission and distribution system and reaching from large electric utilities to commercial and residential locations. A smart grid usually assumes the installation of smart meters in homes and businesses.

These meters display the price of electricity as it fluctuates during the day and "communicates" with electric utilities through wireless technology eliminating the familiar meter reader. With these and other technological innovations, energy consumers will presumably have the information and incentive to reduce the cost of their electric power usage. Smart grids are also assumed essential to increasing the use and nationwide integration of electric power from numerous renewable energy sources into a national grid system. Smart grids, however, may be vulnerable to cyberattacks and other forms of electronic sabotage. The transmission lines necessary to integrate large solar- and wind-energy production into the grid can also be controversial because they are allegedly unsightly, intrusive, possibly threatening to endangered species, or otherwise ecologically undesirable. In Wyoming and Nebraska, for example, the prospect of extensive, large electric transmission lines intended to connect wind towers with existing electric grids has incited considerable opposition in some communities.

Among the states, some of the most aggressive and innovative policy initiatives have also appeared to improve both the quality of the nation's electric power infrastructure and the growth of renewable energy demand by electric utilities.

State and Local Government Initiatives: RPS and FITs

In the last several decades, state and local governments have become important innovators and initiators in developing renewable sources for electric power. This active engagement in renewable energy development has been intensified by state and local efforts to regulate GHG emissions, since the two goals are complementary. The most common policy instrument currently adopted, or actively considered, by the states for renewable energy development is the Renewable Portfolio Standards (RPS), already noted in chapter 4, concerning coal combustion. In essence, a RPS requires that an electric power company have a certain proportion of its power generation or sales created by renewable energy. By the end of 2012, forty-two states plus the District of Columbia had mandated or recommended an RPS. Figure 6-5 identifies states with a RPS standard, the mandated amount of renewable energy required, and the deadlines for achieving these standards.

Some state governments, such as Indiana, Minnesota, and Michigan, and many local governments are now considering a "feed-in-tariff" (FIT) to increase electric power production with renewable energy. In essence, a FIT involves a long-term contract between an electric utility and private

FIGURE 6-5

State Renewable Portfolio Standards, Mandates, or Goals, 2010

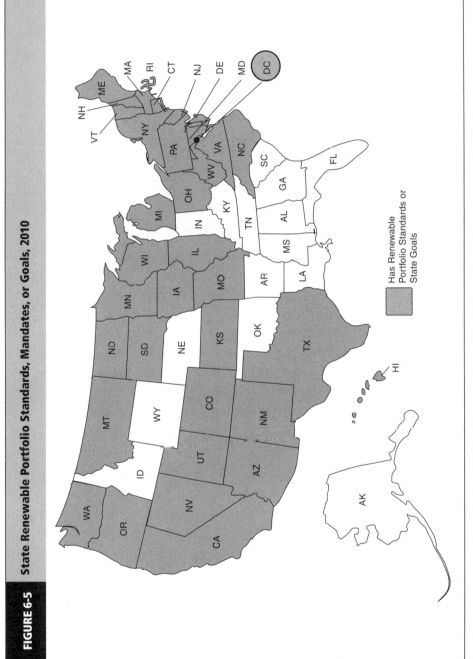

Has Renewable
Portfolio Standards or
State Goals

Source: "Are Energy Companies Getting Too Gassy?," *Millennial Living,* http://www.millennialliving.com/content/are-energy-companies-getting-too-gassy.

producers of electricity created with renewable technologies in which the utility agrees to purchase the renewable produced electricity at a unit price (usually per kilowatt) based on the producer's cost of production, which varies with the type of technology involved. "Technologies such as wind power, for instance, are awarded a lower per-kilowatt price, while technologies such as solar photovoltaic and tidal power are offered a higher price, reflecting higher [production] costs."[44]

FITs can be offered to large- or small-scale energy producers, including sources as modest as a single home or small business. The contracts must be carefully negotiated to avoid violating federal law, but the European and Canadian experience suggest that FITs are technically practical and relatively simple to administer. The city of Gainesville, Florida, is among the first to implement an FIT. "Gainesville residents with photovoltaic panels on their roofs will get 32 cents a kilowatt-hour when they produce energy. (By contrast, homeowners in Florida paid on average 12 cents a kilowatt hour for their electricity, according to Department of Energy statistics)."[45]

CONCLUSION

The upward road toward the renewable energy future is likely to broaden quite gradually. Renewable energy, once politically and economically marginalized, has become a slowly but progressively increasing national energy resource. It will be well past the middle of the century, however, before renewable energy is predicted to constitute more than a small proportion of the nation's total energy consumption, which will continue heavily dependent on coal, petroleum, or natural gas. Renewables, however, may assume greater importance because of their impact in the electric power sector. By midcentury, renewable energy generated from solar arrays and wind farms is conservatively predicted to incrementally increase until it produces at least 16 percent of national electric power production although proponents of renewable electricity assert that with favorable governmental support and improving technological innovation solar and wind sources can produce more than 30 percent of national electric power by midcentury.[46]

A bright future for renewable energy depends, however, upon important state and federal government policies. Continued and generous federal support, in the form of R&D funding, tax subsidies, and loan guarantees, will be essential for the development and commercialization of renewable energy technologies. Sustained incentives for private sector investment in future renewable energy will also be needed. State and local governments can also contribute substantially to the expansion of the renewable energy sector. They can creatively use their utility regulatory authority and taxing power to encourage electric utilities to generate more power from renewable energy sources and also to provide incentives for homeowners and commercial enterprises to consume more renewable energy on site.

The electric power industry's role in the future of renewable energy is likely to depend significantly upon how quickly and comprehensively the national electric power grid is modernized. The Obama administration's energy agenda places a high priority upon investment in creating an efficient, expanded "smart grid" which will facilitate the integration of renewable energy into national, state, and local energy transmission and provide more capacity to upload consumer produced renewable energy into local electric power arrays. Despite its potential to increase considerably the scale and efficiency of national renewable energy production and consumption, the impact of federal and state support for a smart grid is problematic. The grid has not assumed a compelling priority on governmental energy agendas. Moreover, investment by private utilities in the grid will be substantially influenced by the uncertain course of future government policy.

7

AMERICAN AND GLOBAL ENERGY

"Oil is a global market in which America is a big consumer but a
small supplier. We consume about 20 percent of the world's
oil but hold only 2 percent of the oil reserves. That means we
are, in economics jargon, 'price takers.' Domestic production
has increased during the Obama administration, but it has
had minimal effects on global prices because, as producers,
we are just too small to matter much. And even if domestic oil
companies further increased production, they would sell
to the highest global bidder."

Richard Thaler,
"Why Gas Prices Are Out of Any President's Control"[1]

It is early in 2012. With the national media obsessively tracking the
combative Republican presidential primaries and speculating on
Barack Obama's reelection prospects, the website PollingReport.com,
a supermarket of polling information, presented sixteen national polls
concerning the campaign issues most important to the public during the
prior four months. A typical poll reported the public preoccupied over-
whelmingly with the economy, and, to far lesser extent, with the federal
budget, health care, immigration, and other issues.[2] Energy was never
mentioned. Moreover, energy issues failed to merit more than marginal
discussion throughout the 2012 presidential election debates.

The collapse of public concern about national energy security that
concluded the 1970s seems to resonate again in the second decade of

the twenty-first century. Energy issues commonly linger, as they have since the Jimmy Carter presidency, at the margins of public attention. However, energy has always claimed a place, often a precarious one, on presidential policy agendas since the 1970s. Energy issues have always been vulnerable to displacement on White House agendas by apparently more urgent issues like foreign wars, public welfare, or unemployment. Even Obama's enormous political investment in promoting renewable energy development and energy conservation had to yield during his 2012 presidential campaign to the more compelling problems of the national economic recession.

Nonetheless, energy is embedded in some manner in almost every major issue of contemporary national importance. Energy issues relentlessly resurface, often by proxy as military crises erupting in the Middle East, international trade deficits, inflationary surges, or environmental disasters confront national policymakers. In short, energy, acknowledged or not, has become inseparable from any informed discourse about the future of American public policy. Put differently, most major issues facing American policymakers in the decade ahead are destined to involve energy governance in one way or another.

Many of the most compelling energy issues to challenge US energy governance are the result of profound, swiftly evolving transformations in the global energy economy. The United States is now inextricably embedded within this complex and expanding international economy to such an extent that domestic and global energy issues are increasingly interdependent. This chapter explores several of the major challenges posed by this confluence of the domestic and global energy economies.

RISING GLOBAL ENERGY DEMAND

Until well after World War II, the United States was almost self-sufficient in virtually all important energy resources, especially petroleum, and a major exporter of oil to the international market. The global energy market was dominated by a few major petroleum exporting countries, such as the United States, Saudi Arabia, Iran, Russia, and several South American nations. The United States and Western Europe were the world's major petroleum consumers. The energy crises of the 1970s shocked Americans into the realization that they had become heavily dependent upon imported petroleum as domestic oil production had gradually declined while petroleum demand was steadily rising. National energy policy was focused from the 1970s through the end of the century primarily on promoting more domestic oil, producing more, and decreasing dependence upon petroleum imported from insecure Middle Eastern sources.

Surging Energy Consumption

The United States now faces a rapidly changing international energy economy characterized by steadily increasing energy demand from rapidly developing nations, especially in Asia and Africa. The result has been increasing global competition for energy resources. This has incited mounting US concern about the adequacy of global energy resources, considerable debate about the impact of this global competition on the domestic energy market, and increasing interest in the development of more energy conserving and efficient technologies. The rise of energy demand from non-Western, expanding national economies is illustrated in Figure 7-1, which compares global demand for petroleum among primary Western nations (labeled Organisation for Economic

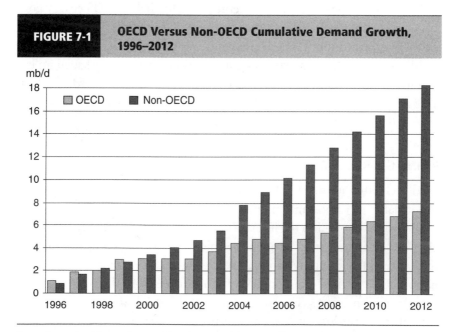

| FIGURE 7-1 | OECD Versus Non-OECD Cumulative Demand Growth, 1996–2012 |

Source: International Energy Agency, *Oil Market Report,* http://omrpublic.iea.org/.

Co-operation and Development, or "OECD"), and non-Western countries ("non-OECD").

The two national economies expected to have the greatest impact upon global demand and supply in the next decade are China and India. "China already consumes more total energy than the United States," notes global energy expert Daniel Yergin. "The same will be true of oil perhaps by the end of the decade, as China becomes more motorized. This year, 20 million new cars will be sold in China, compared to about 15 million in the United States. Some think that number could grow to 30 million."[3] Projections of future oil consumption by these two populous nations, illustrated in Figure 7-2 below, indicate an enormous growth within a few decades.

FIGURE 7-2 Projected Oil Consumption for the United States, China, and India

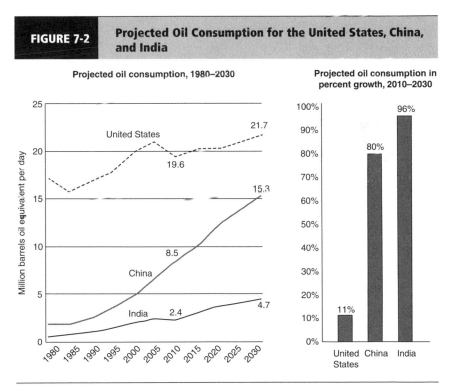

Source: Energy Information Administration, Office of Energy and End Use, "World Petroleum Consumption, Annual Estimates, 1980–2008," October 6, 2009, http://www.eia.gov/emeu/international/recentpetroleumconsumptionbarrelsperday.xls; EIA, International Energy Outlook, 2009, Table A5, "World Liquids Consumption by Region, Reference Case, 1990–1930," May 2009, http://www.eia.doe.gov/oiaf/ieo/excel/ieoreftab_5.xls.

In addition to this burgeoning energy consumption among developing economies, Europe's current dependence upon imported oil, now about 52 percent of total consumption, is also predicted by the IEA to increase to 79 percent by 2020. Estimates of future global energy supply and demand are always tentative. Nonetheless, a continually increasing magnitude of global energy consumption seems almost inevitable for at least another decade.

The Policy Challenges

Growing international energy demand creates both opportunities and risks for the United States. Assuming prudent policy choices and favorable circumstances, rising global energy demand can even create long-term growth in the domestic energy economy. Conversely, a failure to make timely and appropriate responses can produce economic and political instability in long-term US energy governance. The most important policy issues facing US policymakers as global energy consumption expands include the following:

- *Expand domestic petroleum production and, especially, accelerate development of new "fracking" technologies (discussed in chapters 1 and 3), with sufficient scope and speed to profit by increasing new petroleum exports in response to rising global oil demand.* The new fracking technology is widely predicted to be a "game changer" producing rising US petroleum exports and creating long-term growth of the US economy thus able to take advantage of the international increase in energy consumption.
- *Develop fracking technologies quickly enough to significantly diminish US imports of petroleum.* Fracking is expected to create a remarkably quick decrease in US dependence on imported petroleum. Fracking also poses significant environmental risks that must be managed, and its potential productivity depends upon political and economic stability in the international energy market.
- *Approve the complete Keystone XL pipeline and continue to develop other sources of Canadian petroleum, which presently accounts for more than 25 percent of total US oil imports.* Pressure will continue on Washington to increase Canadian fossil fuel imports as a hedge against future global energy market instabilities.

- *Continue to increase domestic energy efficiency and conservation over sufficient time to diminish domestic dependence upon fossil fuels.* The anticipated growth of energy conservation and renewable energy consumption is expected to be gradual during the next several decades; it is expected to increase to about 11 percent of US energy consumption by 2030. It might produce enough domestic energy savings to significantly decrease US dependence upon imported petroleum of the politically unstable Middle East, South America, and Africa.

GLOBAL CLIMATE CHANGE

The atmosphere is a global commons where the United States is always vulnerable to the environmental consequences of climate change. Daniel Yergin, an internationally respected energy economist and a thoughtful, prudent analyst concerning global energy trends, reminded American energy experts and policymakers about this vulnerability when he asserted early in Barack Obama's second administration that climate change has become *the* most important influence in global energy economics. "The interaction of environmental concerns with energy will continue to shape the energy marketplace," he predicted. "The biggest question is climate change and carbon. Over 80 percent of world energy is supplied by carbon-based fuels—oil, natural gas, and coal. About 75 to 80 percent of world energy is generally expected to be carbon based two decades from now."[4] The import of the message seemed unmistakable. Whether or not climate change proves to be the most transcendent force in global energy economics, it is now so compelling a reality that US policymakers must increasingly and continually address the implications for America's global energy policymaking.

The US and Global Climate Change

US energy policymakers have reason to be deeply concerned about the US's capacity to appropriately confront the domestic impact of the climate issue. The climate issue has incited a divisive discord resulting from conflict between the increasing scientific evidence of profound global climate transformations, the persistent political dissension over the credibility of this climate science, and the imperative to initiate timely, potent, long-term governmental measures to mitigate the adverse consequences of climate change.[5] The result has impeded, and sometimes paralyzed, essential governmental responses to the climate issue.

One cogent reason why global climate change is so important to the United States itself was spelled out by the Intergovernmental Panel on Climate Change (IPCC), the most influential international scientific entity currently involved in climate change research, as shown in its *Fourth Assessment Report* (FAR) and summarized in Box 7-1.[6] For the policymakers and the scientific community that are promoting an aggressive national response to the issue, a major part of the work continues to be creating political credibility for the science undergirding these conclusions and finding a strategy to overcome the politically polarizing impact of the climate issue in Congress and among the public.

BOX 7-1	Global Climate Change Impacts in the United States: Key Findings

1. Global warming is unequivocal and primarily human induced.

Global temperature has increased over the past fifty years. This observed increase is due primarily to human-induced emissions of heat-trapping gases.

2. Climate changes are underway in the United States and are projected to grow.

Climate-related changes are already observed in the United States and its coastal waters. These include increases in heavy downpours, rising temperature and sea level, rapidly retreating glaciers, thawing permafrost, lengthening growing seasons, lengthening ice-free seasons in the ocean and on lakes and rivers, earlier snowmelt, and alterations in river flows. These changes are projected to grow.

3. Widespread climate-related impacts are occurring now and are expected to increase.

Climate changes are already affecting water, energy, transportation, agriculture, ecosystems, and health. These impacts are different from region to region and will grow under projected climate change.

4. Climate change will stress water resources.

Water is an issue in every region, but the nature of the potential impacts varies. Drought, related to reduced precipitation, increased evaporation, and increased water loss from plants, is an important issue in many regions, especially in the West. Floods and water quality problems are likely to be amplified by climate changes in most regions. Declines in mountain snowpack are important in the West and Alaska where snowpack provides vital natural water storage.

5. Crop and livestock production will be increasingly challenged.

Agriculture is considered one of the sectors most adaptable to changes in climate. However, increased heat, pests, water stress, diseases, and weather extremes will pose adaptation challenges for crop and livestock production.

6. Coastal areas are at increasing risk from sea-level rise and storm surge.

Sea-level rise and storm surge place many US coastal areas at increasing risk of erosion and flooding, especially along the Atlantic and Gulf Coasts, Pacific Islands, and parts of Alaska. Energy and transportation infrastructure and other property in coastal areas are very likely to be adversely affected.

7. Threats to human health will increase.

Health impacts of climate change are related to heat stress, waterborne diseases, poor air quality, extreme weather events, and diseases transmitted by insects and rodents. Robust public health infrastructure can reduce the potential for negative impacts.

8. Climate change will interact with many social and environmental stresses.

Climate change will combine with pollution; population growth; overuse of resources; urbanization; and other social, economic, and environmental stresses to create larger impacts than from any of these factors alone.

9. Thresholds will be crossed, leading to changes in climate and ecosystems.

There are a variety of thresholds in the climate system and ecosystems. These thresholds determine, for example, the presence of sea ice and permafrost, and the survival of species, from fish to insect pests, with implications for society. With further climate change, the cross of additional thresholds is expected.

10. Future climate change and its impacts depend on choices made today.

The amount and rate of future climate change depend primarily on current and future human-caused emissions of heat-trapping gases and airborne particles. Responses involve reducing emissions to limit future warming, and adapting to the changes that are unavoidable.

Source: U.S. Global Climate Change Research Project, "Executive Summary," Global Climate Change Impacts of the United States (New York: Cambridge University Press, 2009), 12.

Another significant reason for greater US engagement in mitigating global climate change is that the US is second only to China as the most important source of the global CO_2 emissions, as Figure 7-3 indicates, and thus a major contributor to its own climate warming problems.

US efforts to promote a comprehensive international treaty creating a rigorous, practical regime to regulate global climate warming emissions have also been thwarted by America's own refusal to sign such an agreement and to initiate tough, thorough regulation of its domestic emissions.

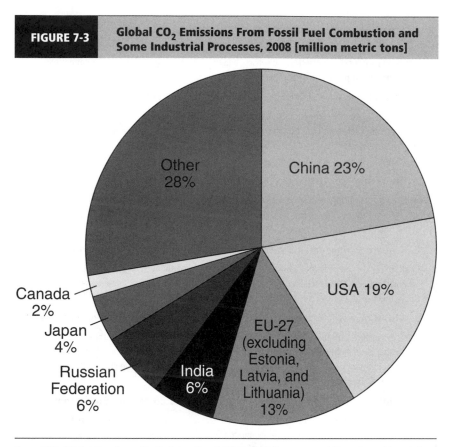

FIGURE 7-3 Global CO$_2$ Emissions From Fossil Fuel Combustion and Some Industrial Processes, 2008 [million metric tons]

Source: EPA, "Global Greenhouse Gas Emissions Data," *Climate,* http://www.epa.gov/climatechange/ghgemissions/global.html.

China and India, whose participation is critically important to the success of any such international agreement, have been reluctant to sign such a treaty until the United States initiates more stringent domestic emissions controls and signs such a treaty itself. The United States can expect continuing international pressure to commit to such a rigorous global regulatory regime.

The Policy Challenges

Since 2000, the United States has belatedly initiated significant governmental and private sector measures to mitigate the expected impact of climate change. The United States reduced its domestic CO_2 emissions by 7 percent since 2005 due to growing substitution of natural gas for coal in industry and electric power generation, increased auto fuel efficiency standards and other energy efficiencies, and the impact of the 2007–2009 economic recession. As the economy recovers, however, related emissions are likely to climb again.

The Obama administration has been the first presidency committed to a very aggressive, ambitious policy agenda to reduce domestic CO_2. Faced with legislative deadlock over a rigorous "cap-and-trade" regulatory strategy to control CO_2 emissions, in 2010 the White House bypassed Congress, asserted that the Clean Air Act (CAA) created authority for the Environmental Protection Agency (EPA) to regulate national greenhouse gas (GHG) emissions, and directed the EPA to proceed with the task. In 2012, the EPA proposed regulations that would, for the first time, set national limits on carbon emissions from new power plants.

Shortly after his second inauguration in 2013, Obama proposed to expand the scope of the new EPA regulations to include existing power plants and to set new goals of reducing all US climate warming emissions 17 percent by 2030.[7] Concurrently, many states, impatient with Washington's sluggish response to climate warming, have initiated their own regulatory programs to control CO_2 emissions. State partnerships have created three cap-and-trade regional regulatory programs.[8]

Thus, by 2014, the United States was clearly moving cautiously toward more active and comprehensive governance of its climate warming emissions. At the same time, policymakers still face several daunting challenges to ensure that the US response to climate warming will be sustained and effective across the full breadth of the US economy. The major challenges include the following:

- *Creating a comprehensive national regulatory program for all major sources of climate warming emissions.* Effective national emission controls across the entire US economy will require congressional legislation involving a more complex, broader, regulatory effort than the Obama administration can achieve using EPA authority alone. A commonly proposed solution is some version of a cap-and-trade regulatory regime discussed in chapter 4 or another equally controversial, politically daunting approach.[9]

- *Negotiating and signing an international treaty requiring the United States to accept rigorous and enforceable domestic emission controls, based on standards relevant to the global scope of climate warming and its mitigation.* A strong international regulatory regime is essential to the United States because the global scale of climate warming requires internationally coordinated emission reductions beyond the capacity of the United States to achieve alone.

IMPROVING ENERGY SECURITY

Between 2010 and 2013, a swift, surprising change in the mind-set of policymakers and experts surfaced. After more than four decades of outspoken apprehension about Americans' energy security, a rapidly growing number began to speak about an impending era of national energy "independence" or "energy security." Based upon recent evidence of rising US oil exports, increasing domestic oil production, and a significant decline in petroleum imports, the anticipation of a new energy era just over the horizon may soon become the accepted wisdom about future US energy development.

The big game changer in this bright vision of America's energy future is presumed to be the oil and natural gas boom created by fracking technologies discussed in chapters 1 and 3. This, coupled with improving domestic energy efficiency, seems to imply that the United States will become less vulnerable to the economic shocks, military insecurities, and political risks associated with heavy dependence on imported petroleum from the volatile Middle East and South America. Still, the United States will experience significant energy security risks to challenge policymakers even if optimistic predictions about fracking's productivity and its impact on future US oil exports prove reliable.

These security risks remain for several reasons. A significant portion of the petroleum the United States will continue to import in the near future will still come from politically unstable regions (see Figure 7-4) where sudden or severe changes in petroleum supply or price can create considerable economic shocks in the world energy market to which the United States is vulnerable.[a]

---

[a] The Strategic Petroleum Reserve does provide emergency crude oil storage for use when domestic production or imports are disrupted. At current crude oil consumption rates, the SPR can supply up to 30% of total refining crude oil feed for about 5 months.

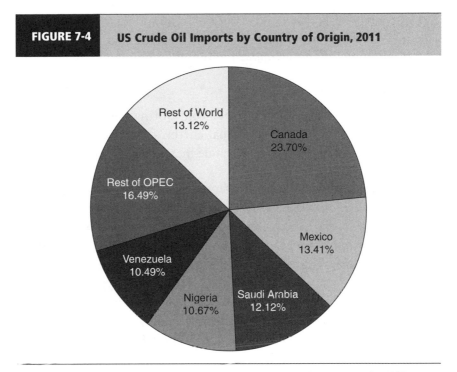

FIGURE 7-4   US Crude Oil Imports by Country of Origin, 2011

Source: Energy Information Administration, *Petroleum Supply Monthly,* March 30, 2011. Graph available at http://www.danielstrading.com/resources/newsletter/2011/04/12/. Adapted from EIA, *US Imports by Country of Origin,* June 6, 2013, www.eia.gov/dnav/pet/pet_move_impcus_a2_nus_ep00_im0_mbbl_m.htm

The International Energy Administration (EIA), a highly respected global energy analyst, has emphasized that "U.S. dependence on the long-haul Middle East has fallen sharply . . . [but] since oil is a global market, the relevant measure for that vulnerability is not U.S. dependence, but world dependence on Middle East oil—and that has not shrunk."[10] Also, more than 30 years will be required before energy efficiency in the transportation sector—where more than 70 percent of all US petroleum is consumed—will have the cumulative impact required to achieve the magnitude of national energy conservation desired for long-term energy security.[11]

Additionally, fracking's future productivity may depend upon its intensely debated but still undetermined environmental impact.[12] Finally, predictions about the energy future, global or domestic, always rest insecurely on political and economic assumptions at risk to unanticipated future events, to unexpected technological and environmental problems, to miscalculated energy reserves or much else.

The Policy Challenges

The significant challenges that still confront national policymakers despite the improvement in US global energy security that may arrive with a continuing fracking boom include these:

- *Continuing to rapidly reduce US dependence upon imported petroleum from unstable Middle Eastern, South American, and African sources.* This implies, especially, an active governmental engagement in accelerated development and dispersion of renewable energy technologies and gradually increased efficiency requirements in the transportation sector.
- *Creating a national regulatory regime for the environmental impacts of fracking technology, rather than relying primarily upon state and local governments to initiate regulation.* The boom in fracking technology is rapidly spreading on a geographic scale that will require national regulatory standards whatever the character of environmental impacts. National regulatory governance, however, must include regulatory federalism that ensures a role for state and local governments similar to the collaborations in other federal environmental programs.
- *Improving the efficiency of electric power production and consumption, as well as the national electricity infrastructure, specially the national power grid.* State and local governments have important opportunities to achieve significant energy conservation through efficiency innovations promoted by state and local utility regulators. The federal government can create large-scale energy savings by improvements in the national electric power infrastructure, beginning with the national energy grid.

"RIDING THE WAVE" OF TECHNOLOGY INNOVATION

The growth of energy consumption among the large, rapidly expanding non-Western economies including, especially, China, Russia, and India, has been accompanied by a growing investment in research and development of new energy technologies, many pressing the frontiers of energy innovation. "Historically, the U.S. has been a technology leader in energy," noted the President's Council of Advisors on Science and Technology in its report to the Obama White House, but this leadership will "not be the case for energy over the coming decades, as the developing world adds energy infrastructure at a dizzying pace. We must 'ride the wave' and be in the forefront of energy technology innovation over the next decade to renew our own energy infrastructure with cleaner, more efficient and more economic technologies, and to set markets abroad. The alternative will be uncharacteristically to become a 'technology taker' with the implied economic and leadership consequences."[13]

Since "riding" a wave of a technology innovation may require as much as a half century or more between its initial design and its successful implementation, innovative energy technologies intended for the latter twenty-first century must be initiated and their commercialization planned within the next several decades. The challenge for US energy policymakers living with a recovering but still fragile economy is to join foresight with initiative to sustain governmental support for promising technologies at the edge of energy development.

One innovative energy technology whose development is often considered important for both energy conservation and sustained US leadership in global energy development is the "smart grid." The US national electric power network is aging, increasingly inefficient, and poorly adapted for the integration of growing renewable energy sources, such as wind and solar power, with traditional electric power transmission.

Another innovation considered vital to efficient and economical future energy production is low-carbon technologies that reduce GHG emissions, particularly from electric power plants, that improve the production and utilization of biofuels and that promote advanced battery designs and hydrogen based fuels. An important component in creating such evolving low-carbon systems is expected to be nanotechnology, the rapidly developing international science involving "research and technology development at the atomic, molecular or macromolecular levels at the nanoscale . . . to create and use structures, devices and systems that have novel properties and functions because of their small and/or intermediate size."[14] (A "nano" is one billionth of a meter. A sheet of paper is about 100,000 nanometers thick).[15] Nanotechnology is considered to have numerous important energy efficiency and conservation applications.[16]

Finally, hydrogen as an alternative to fossil fuels for generating energy continues to be an important, if still experimental and controversial, resource in current international research. Interest has focused especially on the potential of hydrogen fuel cell vehicles to reduce GHG emissions and to diminish domestic dependence on imported oil. Fuel cells "combine hydrogen and oxygen to produce electricity, heat, and water. Fuel cells are often compared to batteries. Both convert the energy produced by a chemical reaction into usable electric power. However, the fuel cell will produce electricity as long as fuel (hydrogen) is supplied, never losing its charge."[17] Liquid hydrogen has been used by NASA since the early 1970s to power the space shuttle and other rockets into space.

The Policy Challenges

Support in developing these innovative energy technologies is challenging because they require enormous, sustained public investment before their economic benefits and technical practicability can be demonstrated. Government may have to make virtually all the initial investment and assume all the considerable risk. Federal spending on the most innovative technologies, especially, are always vulnerable to criticism that the innovations are too speculative, too financially risky, and too marginal compared to more important priorities such as social welfare or economic recovery. The future of such investment strategy may ultimately depend upon how well US policy advocates can make a persuasive case that the United States confronts increasingly competent challenges to crucial future energy innovation in the global energy market. The challenges include the following:

- *Investing as much as needed over the several decades to ensure the full development of a national smart-grid infrastructure.* The grid is an "electricity network that uses digital and other advanced technologies to monitor and manage the transport of electricity from all generation sources to meet the varying electricity demands of end-users. Smart grids coordinate the needs and capabilities of all generators, grid operators, end-users, and electricity market stakeholders to operate all parts of the system as efficiently as possible, minimizing costs and environmental impacts while maximizing system reliability, resilience, and stability."[18] While the federal government is already investing substantially in the grid, the early initiatives represent only a small portion of the very large, continuing national investment essential over several decades.[19]

- *Continuing federal R&D support for the development of energy related nanotechnology development and testing.* Nanotechnology innovations and applications related to energy conservation and efficiency will need continuing federal R&D support, particularly during their early experimental and prototype development, if they are to be relevant to national energy policy within the next several decades. "Transmission and storage of energy, particularly electrical power and hydrogen, is a major societal need, and holds the most promise in solutions with new nanotechnologies," notes a major report on nanotechnologies from Rice University's Baker Institute. "It is in this area that we believe nanoscience can bring the most immediate benefits, with nanotubing and other nano-based materials creating new opportunities to transport electricity efficiently and at lower cost over very long distances."[20]
- *Continuing federal R&D funding for hydrogen fuel cell and related technologies.* Despite evidence of hydrogen's potential as a vehicle propellant and substitute for other forms of fossil energy, formidable challenges remain in translating fuel cell technology into an economically viable and energy efficient component of the energy economy. Fuel cells have yet to prove economically and technically feasible for mass marketing in transportation vehicles. If hydrogen is likely to have a plausible role in America's long-term energy future, the federal government must assume an important role in its development.[21]

CONCLUSION: THE GLOBAL IMPERATIVE

The American energy economy has never been isolated in fact, nor in the thinking of US energy policymakers, from the global energy markets. For more than a half century, the history of the domestic energy economy has been a tale of increasing interdependence with global energy affairs progressively enlarging the US's vulnerability to even slight economic and political shocks among any of the major energy importing and exporting nations. The new challenges, freighted with significant long-term economic and security implications, have become increasingly apparent since the turn of the century.

Among the most important of these emerging challenges is atmospheric climate warming, evidence that environmental problems are becoming increasingly globalized and, with that, an inherent message that national energy policymakers can expect to confront environmental issues embedded in energy policy with increasing frequency. This gradual infusion of global environmentalism into discussions of national energy issues, while inevitable, represents a profound change in the historic scale and substance of what was once considered purely domestic policymaking. This change requires a profound shift in the culture of national energy policymaking—in fact, in the culture of all domestic policymaking. If domestic policymakers are to respond appropriately to this new reality, the challenge will be, in large part, to become increasingly alert and responsive to the implications and to define response in terms of appropriate policy.

A second challenge posed by the globalization of energy affairs is the increasing economic and political importance in the global energy market of rapidly developing national economies, particularly those in China and India. Domestic policymakers confront opportunities to stimulate domestic economic growth by exporting the growing domestic petroleum and natural gas supply in response to rising global energy demand. At the same time, the United States is still sufficiently dependent upon imported petroleum that, despite a predicted decrease in future petroleum exports, the United States needs to continue developing domestic energy resources to decrease dependence on petroleum imports. An important contribution to improved domestic energy resources, in addition to more natural gas and petroleum production, is promotion of increasing renewable energy technologies and energy efficiency.

Finally, the United States is now competing with Russia, China, India, and several other nations in the development of innovative new energy technologies. This amounts to an undeclared and often subtle technology race loaded with potentially high economic and political stakes for the participants and the potential to influence powerfully the future importance of competing nations in the world energy market. The challenge of this technology competition to the future status of the United States in the global energy market is the more important because the future implications may not carry the political weight to claim the attention, nor to demonstrate the importance, necessary to secure a significant place of evolving national policy agendas.

ENDNOTES

CHAPTER 1

1. Quoted in Mara Liasson, "On Obama's Team, Ex-Clinton Staffers Get Do-Over," NPR News, December 23, 2008, accessed October 10, 2010, http://www.npr.org/templates/story/story.php?storyId=98593976.
2. David Barstow, David Rohde, and Stephanie Saul, "Deep Water Horizon's Final Hours," *New York Times,* December 26, 2010, A1.
3. U. R. Sumaila et al., "Impact of the Deepwater Horizon Well Blowout on the Economics of US Gulf Fisheries," *Canadian Journal of Fisheries and Aquatic Sciences,* 2012; "Deepwater Disaster Could Have Billion Dollar Impact," *Science Daily,* February 17, 2012, http://www.sciencedaily.com/releases/2012/02/120217115553.htm.
4. National Commission on the BP Deepwater Horizon Oil Spill and Offshore Drilling, *Deepwater: The Gulf Oil Disaster and the Future of Offshore Drilling* (Washington, DC: National Commission on the BP Deepwater Horizon Oil Spill and Offshore Drilling, 2011), 136, accessed January 3, 2013, www.oilspillcommission.gov.
5. Ibid.
6. Ibid.
7. Pew Research Center, Project for Excellence in Journalism, "100 Days of Gushing Oil: A Different Kind of Disaster Story," August 25, 2010, accessed May 10, 2013, http://www.journalism.org/analysis_report/oil_spill_was_very_different_kind_disaster_story.
8. For this and numerous other public polls concerning the Gulf event, see Karlyn Bowman and Jennifer Marsico, *Polls on the Environment, Energy, Global Warming and Nuclear Power* (Washington, DC: AEI Public Opinion Studies, 2013), 93–97.
9. For polling examples, see ibid., 100.
10. Jennifer Weeks, "Gulf Coast Restoration: The Issues," *CQ Researcher,* August 26, 2011, 21, no. 29, 685.
11. The implications of "punctuated equilibrium" for energy management is explored in Jeff D. Colgan, Robert O. Keohane, and Thijs Van de Graaf, "Punctuated Equilibrium in the Energy Regime Complex," *Review of International Organization* 7, no. 2 (July 2011): 117–143.
12. National Commission on the BP Deepwater Horizon Oil Spill and Offshore Drilling, *Deepwater: The Gulf Oil Disaster and the Future of Offshore Drilling: Final Report* (Washington, DC: National Commission on the BP/Deepwater Horizon Oil Spill and Offshore Drilling Commission, 2011), vii.
13. Polls found in James Lucier, "A Growing Season Gone," *Global Interdependence Center,* August 16, 2010, accessed May 10, 2013, www.interdependence.org/resources/a-growing-season-gone-the-political-impact-of-the-deepwater-horizon-oil-spill/.
14. National Commission on the BP Deepwater Horizon Oil Spill and Offshore Drilling, *Deepwater: The Gulf Oil Disaster and the Future of Offshore Drilling: Final Report* (Washington, DC: National Commission on the BP/Deepwater Horizon Oil Spill and Offshore Drilling Commission, 2011); and National Academy of Engineering and National Research Council, Committee on the Analysis of Causes of the Deepwater Horizon Explosion, Fire, and Oil Spill to Identify Measures to Prevent Similar Accidents in the Future, "Summary," in *Macondo Well Deepwater Horizon Blowout* (Washington, DC: National Academies Press, 2011), 3–9; see also Jonathan Simon and Jennifer Owen, "The Policy and Regulatory Response to Deepwater Horizon: Transforming Offshore Oil and Gas

Leasing?," *Environmental Law Reporter*, 40 (November 2010): 11084; and Brittan J. Bush, "Addressing Regulatory Collapse Behind the Deepwater Horizon Oil Spill: Implementing a 'Best Available Technology' Regulatory Regime for Deepwater Oil Exploration Safety and Cleanup Technology," *Journal of Environmental Law and Litigation*, 26 (2011): 535–568.

15. Richard E. Neustadt, *Presidential Power* (New York: John Wiley and Sons, 1960).

16. Charles Lindblom, "The Science of 'Muddling Through,'" *Public Administration Review*, 19, no. 2 (Spring 1959): 86.

17. James L. True, Bryan Jones, and Frank R. Baumgartner, "Punctuated-Equilibrium: Explaining Stability and Change in Public Policymaking," in Paul A. Sabatier, ed., *Theories of the Policy Process*, 2nd ed. (Cambridge, MA: Westview Press, 2007), 136.

18. Frank R. Baumgartner and Bryan D. Jones, *Agendas and Instability in American Politics*, 2nd ed. (Chicago, IL: University of Chicago Press), 11.

19. Institute for Energy Research, *Fiscal Revenues from Mineral Production on Federal Lands*, accessed July 20, 2013, http://www.instituteforenergyresearch.org/2012/12/20/the-government-can-raise-revenues-by-leasing-federal-lands-just-check-its-data/.

20. General Accounting Office (GAO), *National Energy Policy*, 11.

21. Carl Hulse, "A Senator Whom Colleagues Are Hesitant to Cross," *New York Times*, October 25, 2003, accessed November 20, 2011, www.nytimes.com/2003/10/25/us/a-senator-whom-colleagues-are-hesitant-to-cross.html?pagewanted=all&src=pm.

22. Steven Mufson, "Democrats Struggling for Consensus on Climate Bills," *The Washington Post*, June 15, 2009, A5.

23. Information about DOE's mission and organization can be found at the Department's website, www.allgov.com/agency/Department_of_Energy. See also GAO, *Major Challenges and Risks: Department of Energy* (Washington, DC: General Accounting Office, 2011).

24. On the DOE's responsibilities for nuclear waste management, see Walter A. Rosenbaum, *Environmental Politics and Policy*, 8th ed. (Washington, DC: CQ Press, 2011), Chapter 8.

25. About the Department of the Interior, see Jeanne N. Clarke and Daniel McCool, *Staking Out the Terrain: Power Differentials among Natural Resource Management Agencies*, 2nd ed. (Albany: SUNY Press, 2000); Paul J. Culhane, *Public Lands Politics* (Baltimore, MD: Johns Hopkins University Press, 1981); Ross W. Gorte, Carol Hardy Vincent, and Marc Humphries, *Federal Lands Managed by the Bureau of Land Management (BLM) and the Forest Service (FS): Issues for the 110th Congress* (Washington, DC: Congressional Research Service, 2008), Report RL33792; Martin A. Nie, *The Governance of Western Public Lands: Mapping Its Present and Future* (Lawrence: University of Kansas Press, 2009).

26. "About the Department of the Interior," http://www.doi.gov/facts.html.

27. Institute for Energy Research, "Fiscal Revenues from Mineral Production on Federal Lands," accessed July 20, 2013, http://www.instituteforenergyresearch.org/2012/12/20/the-government-can-raise-revenues-by-leasing-federal-lands-just-check-its-data/.

28. Ross W. Gorte, Carol Hardy Vincent, and Marc Humphries, *Federal Lands*, 3.

29. U.S. Department of the Interior, U.S. Department of Agriculture, *New Energy Frontier: Balancing Energy Development on Federal Lands* (Washington, DC: U.S. Department of Agriculture, 2011), 13.

30. http://www.doi.gov/facts.html.

31. William Reilly, former EPA administrator. Quoted in John M. Broader, "E.P.A. Chief Stands Firm as Tough Rules Loom," *New York Times*, July 5, 2011, A13.

32. Mark Holt and Carol Glover, *Energy Policy Act of 2005: Summary and Analysis of Enacted Provisions* (Washington, DC: Congressional Research Service, 2006), Document RL33302.

33. Michael W. Grainey, "Energy Conservation: The Federal-State Nexus," *American University Law Review*, 27 (1977): 611–634.

34. Alaska Department of Natural Resources, *Division of Oil and Gas Royalty Revenue, 2010*, http://www.dog.dnr.alaska.gov/oil/.

35. "U.S. News: States Vie for Share of Clean-Coal Cash," Rebecca Smith, *Wall Street Journal* (Eastern Edition), March 23, 2009, A3.

36. Chelsea Conaboy, "Regional Cap and Trade Is Working—and Maligned," *The Philadelphia Inquirer*, October 4, 2010. See also Barry Rabe, "Racing to the Top, the Bottom, or the Middle of the Pack?: The Evolving State Government Role in Environmental Protection," in Michael E. Kraft and Norman J. Vig, *Environmental Policy: New Directions for the Twenty-First Century* (Washington, DC: CQ Press, 2010), 27–50.

37. See, for example, Karlyn Bowman and Jennifer Marsico, *Polls on the Environment*, 105–106.
38. Scott Bittle, Jonathan Rochkind, and Amber Ott, *The Energy Learning Curve* (Washington, DC: Public Agenda, 2009), 5, www.publicagenda.org/reports/energy or www.planetforward.org.
39. Jon Krosnick, "Energy, Environment, and Elections: Mapping Voter Behavior in 2008: A Conversation with Jon Krosnick," *Resources* (Summer 2008), www.rff.org/Publications/Resources/Pages/EnergyEnvironmentandElections.aspx.
40. Pew Research Center for the People and the Press, *Economy Dominates Public's Agenda, Dims Hopes for the Future*, January 20, 2011(Washington, DC: Pew Research Center), accessed May 7, 2013, http://www.people-press.org/2011/01/20/economy-dominates-publics-agenda-dims-hopes-forthe-future/; see also Karlyn Bowman, Andrew Rugg, and Jennifer Marsico, *Polls on the Environment, Energy, Global Warming, and Nuclear Power* (April 2013), accessed May 25, 2013, www.aei.org/article/politics-and-public-opinion/polls/polls-on-the-environment-energy-global-warming-and-nuclear-power-april-2013/.
41. Karlyn Bowman and Jennifer Marsico, *Polls on the Environment*, 106–108.
42. Environmental Law Institute, "Estimating U.S. Government Subsidies to Energy Sources: 2002–2008," 27–28.
43. Paul Gilman, "Science, Policy, and Politics: Comparing and Contrasting Issues in Energy and the Environment," *Social Research*, 73 no. 3 (Fall, 2006): 103.
44. Stephen Power, "Dispute on Oil Spill Panel Flares Before First Meeting," *Wall Street Journal* (Eastern Edition), July 10, 2010, A5.
45. Yale Project on Climate Change Communication, *Global Warming: Democrats, Republicans, Independents, and the Tea Party* (Washington, DC: George Mason University, Center for Climate Change Communication, 2011), 3–4.
46. U.S. Environmental Protection Agency (EPA), Technology Transfer Network, National Emissions Inventory Air Pollutant Emissions Trend Data, "1970–2011 Average Annual Emissions, All Criteria Pollutants in MS Excel," http://www.epa.gov/ttn/chief/trends/index.html; American Lung Association, "Electric Utilities," http://www.lungusa.org/healthy-air/outdoor/protecting-your-health/what-makes-air-unhealthy/electric-utilities.html.
47. GAO, *Information on the Number of Hardrock Mines, Cost of Cleanup, and Value of Financial Assurances* (Washington, DC: GAO, 2011), Document No. GAO-11-834T.
48. Stephen Power, "Currents: In a Small Fish, a Large Lesson in Renewable Energy's Obstacles," *Wall Street Journal* (Eastern Edition), June 16, 2009, A11.
49. Quoted at www.quotegarden.com/government.html.
50. Center for Responsive Politics, "Energy and Nuclear Power," www.opensecrets.org/lobby/issuesum.php?lname=Energy+%26+Nuclear+Power&year=.
51. Center for Responsive Politics, *Energy/Natural Resources: Long-Term Contribution Trends*, accessed May 12, 2013, www.opensecrets.org/industries/totals.php?cycle=2012&ind=E.
52. Ibid.
53. "About NPC: National Petroleum Council, Origins and Operations," www.npc.org/background.html. The Federal Advisory Committee Act (FACA) contains a data base of an average of 1,000 advisory committees at www.fido.gov/facadatabase/default.asp.
54. Thomas E. Cronin, *The State of the Presidency*, 2nd ed. (Boston: Little, Brown and Co., 1980), 169.
55. *New York Times*, May 4, 1985.
56. See, for example, Daniel Yergin, "Ensuring Energy Security," *Foreign Affairs*, 85, no. 2 (2006): 71: "The United States must face the uncomfortable fact that its goal of 'energy independence'—a phrase that has become a mantra since it was first articulated by Richard Nixon four weeks after the 1973 oil embargo was put in place—is increasingly at odds with reality."

CHAPTER 2

1. Neil King Jr., "Energy: A Past President's Advice to Obama: Act with Haste—Jimmy Carter Says New Administration Needs to Harness the Benefits of a Crisis Mentality to Tame Energy Policy," *Wall Street Journal* (Eastern Edition), December 11, 2008, A16.
2. On the history of US energy policy, see Robert Engler, *The Brotherhood of Oil* (Chicago, IL: University of Chicago Press, 1977); David E. Nye, *Consuming Power* (Cambridge, MA: MIT Press, 1999); Richard H. K. Vietor, *Energy Policy in American Since 1945* (New York: Cambridge University Press,

1984), and Daniel Yergin, *The Quest: Energy, Security, and the Remaking of the Modern World* (New York: Penguin Press, 2011).

3. Don E. Kash and Robert W. Rycroft, *U.S. Energy Policy: Crisis and Complacency* (Norman, OK: University of Oklahoma Press, 1984); Karen R. Merrill, *The Oil Crisis of 1973–74: A Brief History with Documents* (New York: Bedford/St. Martin's, 2007).

4. Neil King Jr., "A Past President's Advice to Obama: Act with Haste," *Wall Street Journal*, December 11, 2008, A16.

5. On the Reagan energy policies generally, see John L. Palmer and Isabel V. Sawhill, eds., *The Reagan Record* (Cambridge, MA: Ballinger Publishing, 1984), chaps. 1 and 5.

6. Paul L. Joskow, "U.S. Energy Policy During the 1990s." NBER Working Paper Series, vol. w8454 (2001), http://ssrn.com/abstract=281859.

7. On the history of energy policy, see Colin Campbell, Bert A. Rockman, and Andrew Rudalevige, eds., *The George W. Bush Legacy* (Congressional Quarterly Press, 2007); John D. Graham, *Bush on the Home Front: Domestic Policy Triumphs and Setbacks* (Indiana University Press, 2010); Armin Rozencranz, "U.S. Climate Policy Under G. W. Bush," *Golden Gate University Law Review* 32, no. 4 (December 2002): 479–491.

8. Mark Holt and Carol Glover, *Energy Policy Act of 2005: Summary and Analysis of Enacted Provisions* (Washington, DC: Congressional Research Service, 2006), Document RL33302.

9. Fred Sissine, *Energy Independence and Security Act of 2997: A Summary of Major Provisions* (Washington, DC: Congressional Reference Service, 2007), Document RL34294.

10. Neil King Jr., "A Past President's Advice to Obama: Act with Haste," *Wall Street Journal*, December 11, 2008, A16.

11. Richard Simon and Jill Zuckman, "The Nation: Inauguration's Theme: Green; Many Organizations Will Celebrate Their Pet Causes on Jan. 20. But It'll Be the Environment That Cleans Up," *Los Angeles Times*, January 11, 2009, A14.

12. Concise, informative explanations of the difference between markets and governmental regulation can be found in Charles Wolf Jr., *Markets or Governments: Choosing Between Imperfect Alternatives* (Cambridge, MA: MIT Press, 1990), especially chapters 1 and 8; and Deborah Stone, *Policy Paradox: The Art of Political Decision Making*, 2nd ed. (New York: W. W. Norton & Co, 2010), chapter 1.

13. A list of federal agencies involved with energy policy would include at least the Department of Energy (DOE), Federal Energy Regulatory Commission (FERC), North American Electric Reliability Corporation (NERC), Nuclear Regulatory Commission (NRC), Bureau of Ocean Energy Management, Regulation, and Enforcement (BOEMRE), Chemical Safety and Hazard Investigation Board, Environmental Protection Agency (EPA), Mine Safety and Health Administration (MSHA), National Institute of Standards and Technology (NIST), Office of Surface Mining, Reclamation, and Enforcement (OSM), and the Occupational Safety and Health Administration (OSHA).

14. Useful summaries of major federal energy regulations can be found in Federal Energy Regulatory Commission, "Introduction," *Energy Primer: A Handbook of Energy Market Basics* (Washington, DC: Federal Energy Commission, 2012).

15. Maeve P. Carey, "Counting Regulations: An Overview of Rulemaking, Types of Federal Regulations, and Pages in the Federal Register," *Congressional Reference Service Report* R43056 (Washington, DC: Congressional Research Service, May 1, 2013).

16. Environmental Law Institute, *Estimating U.S. Government Subsidies to Energy Sources: 2002–2008* (Washington, DC: Environmental Law Institute, 2010), 6.

17. Estimates of total federal energy subsidies vary enormously, depending upon how a "subsidy" is defined. See, for example, US EIA, *Direct Federal Financial Interventions and Subsidies in Fiscal Year 2010* (Washington, DC: Department of Energy, 2010).

18. Maura Allaire and Stephen P. A. Brown, *U.S. Energy Subsidies: Effects on Energy Markets and Carbon Dioxide Emissions* (Pew Charitable Trusts, August 2012).

19. US Energy Information Administration, "Executive Summary," in *Direct Federal Financial Interventions and Subsidies in Energy in Fiscal Year 2010* (Washington, DC: 2011), xiii. Also available online, accessed July 5, 2013, http://www.eia.gov/analysis/requests/subsidy/.

20. See, for example Doug Koplow, *Nuclear Power: Still Not Viable Without Subsidies* (Washington, DC: Union of Concerned Scientists, 2011).

21. Yuki Noguchi, "Solyndra Highlights Long History of Energy Subsidies," *NPR Morning Edition*, November 16, 2011, accessed January 27, 2012, http://www.npr.org/2011/11/16/142364037/solyndra-highlights-long-history-of-energy-subsidies.
22. This legislation was the Connally Hot Oil Act of 1935. For a brief, informative review of federal interventions in the domestic petroleum market, see Peter Van Doren, "A Brief History of Energy Regulation," in *Downsizing the Federal Government*, Cato Institute (2009), accessed February 10, 2013, www.downsizinggovernment.org/energy/regulations#sthash.VKOICzuC.dpuf.
23. Department of Energy, Office of Fossil Energy, "Strategic Petroleum Reserve," Petroleum Reserves, accessed February 20, 2013, http://energy.gov/fe/services/petroleum-reserves.
24. See, for example, Executive Office of the President, President's Council of Advisors on Science and Technology, *Report to the President on Accelerating the Pace of Change in Energy Technologies Through an Integrated Federal Energy Policy* (Washington, DC: Exec Office Pres., November 2010), ix.

CHAPTER 3

1. Michael Winter, "U.S. Exported More Gasoline Than Imported Last Year," *USA Today*, February 29, 2012, accessed April 5, 2013, http://content.usatoday.com/communities/ondeadline/post/2012/02/us-exported-more-gasoline-than-imported-last-year/1#.UfLAuW0SYs0.
2. Energy Information Administration (EIA), *Energy in Brief*, May 10, 2013, accessed May 14, 2013, http://www.eia.gov/energy_in_brief/article/foreign_oil_dependence.
3. Dennis Blair, former deputy secretary of state, quoted in Annie Snider, "War Game Preps for Unimaginable But Hits Close To Home," *Greenwire E&E Reporter*, July 14, 2011, accessed December 11, 2011, www.eenews.net/gw/2011/07/14.
4. Asjylyn Loder, "Fracking Pushes U.S. Oil Output to Highest Since 1992," *Bloomberg*, July 10, 2013, at: www.bloomberg.com/news/2013-07-10/fracking-pushes-u-s-oil-output-to-highest-since-january-1992.html (accessed July 21, 2013).
5. EIA, "How Dependent Are We on Foreign Oil?," *Energy in Brief*, July 23, 2012, accessed September 17, 2012, http://www.eia.gov/cfapps/energy_in_brief/foreign_oil_dependence.cfm.
6. David Frum, "'Peak Oil' Doomsayers Proved Wrong," CNN, March 4, 2013.
7. EIA, *Annual Energy Outlook 2013: Executive Summary*, at http://www.eia.gov/forecasts/aeo/chapter_executive_summary.cfm; see also, *EIA AEO2013 Early Release Overview: Executive Summary* (Washington, DC: Energy Information Administration, 2013), 2–6.
8. David Kocieniewski, "As Oil Industry Fights a Tax, It Reaps Subsidies," *New York Times*, July 4, 2010, A1.
9. "Report: Offshore Energy Development Could Create 6,700 Jobs and Bring North Carolina up to $577 Million Annually," *PR Newswire*, July 27, accessed July 5, 2011, http://www.prnewswire.com/news-releases/report-offshore-energy-development-could-create-6700-jobs-and-bring-north-carolina-up-to-577-million-annually-62239592.html.
10. Mike Soraghan, "Drilling Regulators Pull Double Duty as Industry Promoters," *Greenwire E&E Reporter*, November 20, 2011, accessed June 12, 2011, www.eenews.net/special_reports/ground_rules. See also: Jason DeParle, "Minerals Service Had a Mandate to Produce Results," *New York Times*, August 8, 2010, A1.
11. Peter van Doren, "A Brief History of Energy Regulations," *Cato Institute*. February 2009, accessed November 7, 2011, www.downsizinggovernment.org/energy/regulations.
12. Environmental Law Institute, *Estimating U.S. Government Subsidies to Energy Sectors, 2002–2008* (Washington, DC: Environmental Law Institute, 2009), 3.
13. David Victor, "The Energy Trap: Why the United States Is Doomed to Be an Energy Outlaw," *Newsweek*, March 3, 2008, accessed January 19, 2011, www.newsweek.com/2008/03/02/the-energy-trap.html#.
14. Marc Humphries, *Outer Continental Shelf: Debate Over Oil and Gas Leasing and Revenue Sharing* (Washington, DC: Congressional Reference Service, 2008), Document RL33493, "Summary." Another 86 billion barrels of oil and 420 trillion cubic feet (tcf) of natural gas are classified as undiscovered resources.
15. Ibid.

16. Ted Barrett and Alan Silverleib, "Senate Rejects GOP Oil Drilling Plan," CNN, May 18, 2011, accessed July 16, 2010, http://articles.cnn.com/2011–05–18/politics/senate.oil.drilling_1_drilling-moratorium-oil-gas-prices/2?_s=PM:POLITICS.

17. Defenders of Wildlife, "Arctic National Wildlife Refuge," accessed May 1, 2007, http://www.savearcticrefuge.org.

18. Rachael D'Oro, "Alaska Environment, Development Co-Exist," November 17, 2003, accessed May 1, 2007, www.lists.envirolink.org/pipermail/ar-news/Week-of-Mon-20031117/010930.html.

19. Charli Coon, "Tapping Oil Reserves in a Small Part of the ANWR: Environmentally Sound, Energy Wise," August 1, 2001, accessed April 14, 2004, www.heritage.org/research/energyandenvironment/em763.cfm.

20. For a legislative history of ANWR, see M. Lynne Corn and Bernard A. Gelb, "Arctic National Wildlife Refuge (ANWR): Controversies for the 108th Congress," Report no. 1B10111, Congressional Research Service, Washington, DC, 2003; see also Lisa Demer and Richard Mauer, "U.S. House OKs Opening ANWR to Oil Drilling," The Anchorage Daily News, February 17, 2012, accessed March 1, 2012, http://www.mcclatchydc.com/2012/02/17/139185/us-house-oks-opening-anwr-to-oil.html.

21. The National Academies, Energy: Emerging Technologies: Alternatives to Conventional Oil," accessed November 19, 2010, http://needtoknow.nas.edu/energy/energy-sources/emerging-technologies/conventional-oil-alternatives.php.

22. Michael McDermott, "Oil Pipeline Work Near Finish, Augusta Gazette, September 24, 2010, accessed May 27, 2011, http://www.augustagazette.com/newsnow/x552732354/Oil-pipeline-work-near-finisGovernment of Alberta. See also: Alberta's Oil Sands: Opportunity, Balance (2008), accessed December 16, 2011, http://www.environment.alberta.ca/documents/oil_sands_opportunity_balance.pdf; and US Department of State, Bureau of Oceans and International Environmental and Scientific Affairs, Executive Summary: Final Environmental Impact Statement for the Proposed Keystone XL Project, August 26, 2011, accessed December 7, 2011, http://www.keystonepipeline-xl.state.gov/clientsite/keystonexl.nsf?Open.

23. The National Academies, Our Energy Sources: Emerging Technologies Alternatives to Conventional Oil, accessed October 5, 2011, http://needtoknow.nas.edu/energy/energy-sources/emerging-technologies/conventional-oil-alternatives.

24. Erin N. Kelly, David W. Schindler, Peter V. Hodson, Jeffrey W. Short, Roseanna Radmanovich, and Charlene C. Nielsen, "Oil Sands Development Contributes Elements Toxic at Low Concentrations to the Athabasca River and Its Tributaries," Proceedings of the National Academy of Sciences, 2010, accessed October 6, 2011, http://www.pnas.org/content/107/37/16178.ful.

25. Tennille Tracy and Edward Welsch, "Keystone Poses 'No Significant Impacts' to Most Resources Along Path—US," Wall Street Journal, August 26, 2011, retrieved August 27, 2011, http://online.wsj.com/article/SB10001424053111904787404576532473486763738.html.

26. "Obama Administration Delays Keystone XL Pipeline Approval," PBS News Hour, accessed November 10, 2011, www.pbs.org/newshour/bb/science/july-dec11/pipeline_11–10.html.

27. "Obama Administration Delays Keystone XL Pipeline Approval," PBS News Hour, accessed November 10, 2011, www.pbs.org/newshour/bb/science/july-dec11/pipeline_11–10.html.

28. "Obama Administration Delays Keystone XL Pipeline Approval," PBS Newsour, November 10, 2011, accessed November 14, 2011, http://www.pbs.org/newshour/bb/science/july-dec11/pipeline_11–10.html.

29. Steve Hargreaves, "Keystone Oil Sands Pipeline Rejected, for Now," available at http://money.cnn.com/2012/01/18/news/economy/keystone_pipeline/index.htm?hpt=hp_t3.

30. Mark Holt and Carol Glover, Energy Policy Act of 2005: Summary and Analysis of Enacted Provisions (Washington, DC: Congressional Research Service, 2006), Document No. RL33302.

31. Frank Morris, "Ethanol Industry Torn Over Losing Subsidy Billions," NPR Morning Edition, July 21, 2011, accessed September 10, 2011, http://www.npr.org/2011/07/21/138543233/ethanol-industry-torn-over-losing-subsidy-billions.

32. However, near-term barriers to the marketing of E15 may slow the transition to higher blends due to concerns over potential mis-fueling, associated liabilities, and other issues.

33. Max Borders and H. Sterling Burnett, "The Environmental Costs of Ethanol," Brief Analysis, National Center for Policy Analysis, August 2, 2007, accessed August 9, 2011, www.ncpa.org/pub/ba591.

34. Frank Morris, "Ethanol Industry Torn."

35. "U.S. Ethanol Industry to Launch First-Ever National TV Ad Campaign, *Growth Energy,* April 12, 2010, accessed August 4, 2011, http://www.growthenergy.org/news-media-center/releases/us-ethanol-industry-to-launch-first-ever-national-tv-ad-campaign.
36. Proved reserves of natural gas are estimated quantities that analyses of geological and engineering data have demonstrated to be economically recoverable in future years from known reservoirs.
37. EIA, *Annual Energy Outlook, 2011 With Projections to 2035,* accessed July 23, 2011, http://www.eia .gov/for ecasts/aeo/source_natural_gas.cfm.
38. Rebecca Smith, "Progress to Shutter 11 Plants Using Coal," *Wall Street Journal,* December 2, 2009, B4.
39. Clifford Krauss, "Drilling Boom Revives Hopes for Natural Gas," *New York Times.* (Late Edition, East Coast), August 25, 2008, A1.
40. A comprehensive discussion of the environmental issues associated with fracking can be found in US Government, Environmental Protection Agency, US Geological Survey, *Risks and Rewards: The Controversy About Shale Gas Production and Hydraulic Fracturing, Ground Water Pollution, Toxic and Carcinogenic Chemical Dangers, Marcellus Shale, Hydrofrac and Fracking* (E-publisher: Progressive Management Publications, 2011), Amazon Digital Service [Kindle e-reader].
41. The Energy Policy Act (2005), passed during the Bush Administration, specifically exempts fracking operations from EPA regulation under the Clean Water Act or the Safe Drinking Water Act.
42. Caterine Tsai, "Halliburton Exec Sips Fracking Fluid at Conference," *Huffpost Green,* August 22, 2011, accessed September 18, 2003, http://www.huffingtonpost.com/2011/08/22/halliburton-executive-drinks-fracking-fluid_n_933621.html.

CHAPTER 4

1. Lorelei Scarbro, "Coal River Activist: 'We Are All Being Used,'" *CNN,* accessed April 7, 2010, http://articles.cnn.com/2010–04–07/opinion/scarbro.coal.mine.tragedy_1_coal-river-mountain-coal-mining-coal-industry?_s=PM:OPINION.
2. Christa Marshall, "Coal Country: W. Va. Ponders Its Mining Future Amid Hills and Valleys of Climate Debate," *E&E Climate Wire,* accessed April 6, 2010, http://www.eenews.net/public/climatewire/2010/04/06/1.
3. Rebecca Smith and Stephen Power, "After Washington Pulls Plug on FutureGen, Clean Coal Hopes Flicker," *Wall Street Journal* (Eastern edition), February 2, 2008, A7.
4. David Mercer, "Illinois Town Backs Out of FutureGen: Mattoon Says Changes in 'Clean' Coal Plant a Deal Breaker," *Huff Post Chicago,* August 11, 2010, accessed September 16, 2010, http://www.huffingtonpost .com/2010/08/11/illinois-town-backs-out-o_n_679344.html.
5. Clifford Krauss, "Coal Industry Pins Hopes on Exports as U.S. Market Shrinks," *New York Times,* June 14, 2013, A1; Lisa Palmer, "Facing Tough Market at Home, U.S. Coal Giant Pushes Overseas," *Environment360,* accessed July 29, 2013, http://e360.yale.edu/feature/facing_tough_market_coal_ giant_peabody_energy_pushes_overseas/2676/.
6. U.S. Environmental Protection Agency, *Clean Energy,* accessed February 19, 2011, www.epa.gov/cleanenergy/energy-and-you/affect/air-emissions.html.
7. Paul Billings, *Emissions of Hazardous Air Pollutants From Coal-Fired Power Plants* (Needham, MA: Environmental Health and Engineering, 2011), 11; American Lung Association, *Toxic Air: The Case for Cleaning Up Coal-fired Power Plants* (Washington, DC: American Lung Association, 2011); EPA, *Air Emission Sources,* accessed August 27, 2010, www.epa.gov/cgi-bin/broker?_service=data&_ debug=0&_program=dataprog.national_1.sas&polchoice=SO.
8. United States Geological Survey, *News Room: Mining-Related Contaminants Persist in Some Appalachian Coal Region Water Wells,* Released December 28, 2006, accessed August 13, 2010, www.usgs .gov/newsroom/article.asp?ID=1597; see also World Coal Association, *Coal Mining & the Environment,* available at www.worldcoal.org/coal-the-environment/coal-mining-the-environment/.
9. Union of Concerned Scientists, *Clean Energy,* accessed April 12, 2011, www.ucsusa.org/clean_energy/coalvswind/c02d.html.
10. Wendy Koch, "Study: Drinking Water Polluted by Coal-Ash Dump Sites," *USA Today Greenhouse,* accessed November 11, 2010, http://content.usatoday.com/communities/greenhouse/post/2010/08/coal-ash-dump-sites/1.
11. World Coal Association, *Climate Change,* accessed January 20, 2011, www.worldcoal.org/coal-the-environment/climate-change/; see also U.S. EPA, *Inventory of U.S. Greenhouse Gas Emissions and*

Sinks,1990–2009 (Washington, DC: Environmental Protection Agency, April 2011), Document 430-R-11–005.

12. Energy Information Administration, *Major U.S. Coal Producers,* Report No. DOE/EIA-0584, February 3, 2011, accessed March 18, 2011, http://38.96.246.204/cneaf/coal/page/acr/table10.html.

13. The National Mining Association's official website, www.nma.org/about/info.asp, offers an informative overview of the NMA's economic and political agenda.

14. Dan Eggen, "Mining Interests Are Heavily Invested in Capitol Hill," *Washington Post,* April 8, 2010, accessed December 28, 2011, http://www.washingtonpost.com/wp-dyn/content/article/2010/04/07/AR2010040704707.html.

15. However, other regions are starting to mine coal more efficiently and at lower prices, and that's shifting production to other parts of the country. Central Appalachia accounted for roughly 18 percent of all US coal production in 2009, but that share is expected to decline to 11 percent by 2015, and 8 percent by 2035, see Annalyn Censky, "Coal 'Ghost Towns' Loom in West Virginia," *CNN Money,* accessed May 26, 2011, money.cnn.com/2011/05/26/news/economy/west_virginia/index.htm.

16. Christa Marshall, "W. Va. Ponders Its Mining Future Amid Hills and Valleys of Climate Debate," *The New York Times,* April 6, 2010, http://www.nytimes.com/cwire/2010/04/06/06climatewire-wva-calculates-survival-in-a-new-climate-19658.html?pagewanted=all.

17. Rick Reis, "Appalachian Dems Seek Distance From Obama on Coal, Climate," *E&E Reporter,* August 26, 2010, accessed September 1, 2010, http://www.eenews.net/public/Greenwire/2010/08/26/1.

18. National Academy of Sciences, Committee on Health, Environmental, and Other External Costs and Benefits of Energy Production and Consumption, National Research Council, *Hidden Costs of Energy: Unpriced Consequences of Energy Production and Use* (Washington, DC: National Academy Press, 2009), 4.

19. "Coal Forum: West Virginia Coal Forum Seeks Middle Ground Between Environmentalists, Producers," accessed August 20, 2008, www.wvcoalforum.org/content/view/17/1/.

20. White House, "Energy and Environment Latest News: Blueprint for a Secure Energy Future," accessed September 18, 2013, at http://www.whitehouse.gov/energy/news.

21. Office of Surface Mining Reclamation and Enforcement, *Surface Mining Law,* accessed December 13, 2011, http://www.osmre.gov/topic/smcra/smcra.shtm.

22. U.S. Department of the Interior, Office of Surface Mining Reclamation and Enforcement, "Abandoned Mine Land Reclamation: Update on the Reclamation of Abandoned Mine Land Affected by Mining That Took Place Before the Surface Mining Law Was Passed in 1977," (Washington, DC, 2003), 20, http://www.osmre.gov/aml/remain/zintroun.htm.

23. U.S. Department of the Interior, Office of Surface Mining, *References and Guidance: Children's Workbook,* accessed November 23, 2011, www.osmre.gov/browse.shtm.

24. Manuel Quinones, "Regulators, Advocates Weigh Merits of Merging Mining Agency, BLM," *E&E Daily,* October 26, 2011.

25. David Biello, "Mountaintop Removal Mining: EPA Says Yes, Scientists Say No," *Scientific American Observations,* January 8, 2010, http://www.scientificamerican.com/blog/post.cfm?id=mountaintop-removal-mining-epa-says-2010–01–08. See also Margaret A. Palmer et al., "Mountaintop Mining Consequences," *Science,* 327 (January 8, 2010): 148–149.

26. Jennifer Weeks, "Coal's Comeback," *CQ Researcher,* October 5, 2007, 825.

27. Ibid.

28. Uday Desai, "Assessing the Impacts of the Surface Mining Control and Reclamation Act," *Policy Studies Review* 9 (autumn 1989): 104–105.

29. David A. Fahrenthold, "Still Unresolved, Tennessee Coal-Ash Spill Only One EPA Hurdle," *Washington Post,* December 22, 2009, A1.

30. "Toxic Metals From Coal Ash Found in Groundwater at TVA Power Plants," *Fairwarning,* July 26, 2011, accessed October 17, 2011, http://www.fairwarning.org/2011/07/coal-ash-contamination-found-in-groundwater-near-9-tva-power-plants/.

31. Shaila Dewan, "Huge Coal Ash Spills Contaminating U.S. Water," *New York Times,* January 7, 2009, accessed September 5, 2009, www.nytimes.com/2009/01/07/world/americas/07iht-sludge.4.19164565.html.

32. Center for American Progress, *Coal Capture and Sequestration, 101,* accessed June 18, 2011, www.americanprogress.org/issues/2009/03/ccs_101.html.

33. Mountaineer was to employ so-called chilled ammonia technology, which relies on ammonium carbonate chemistry to pull CO_2 out of the exhaust gases . . . Mountaineer takes the captured CO_2 and

compresses it to at least 2,000 pounds per square inch, liquefying it and pumping it roughly 8,000 feet down into the ground. That deep, the liquid CO_2 flows through the porous rock formations, adhering to the tiny spaces, slowly spreading out over time and, ultimately, chemically reacting with rock or brine. David Biello, "Burying Climate Change: Efforts Begin to Sequester Carbon Dioxide From Power Plants," *Scientific American,* September 22, 2009, www.scientificamerican.com/article .cfm?id=burying-climate-change#comments.

34. David Biello, "Advanced CO_2 Capture Project Abandoned Due to 'Uncertain' U.S. Climate Policy," *Scientific American,* July 14, 2011, accessed January 11, 2012, http://blogs.scientificamerican.com/observations/2011/07/14/advanced-c02-capture-project-abandoned-due-to-uncertain-u-s-climate-policy/.

35. Rebecca Smith and Stephen Power, "After Washington Pulls the Plug on Future Gen, Clean Coal Hopes Flicker," *Wall Street Journal,* February 2, 2008, A7.

36. For example, Summit Power has estimated that to build a CCS facility for its use near Odessa, Texas, would cost about $1.6 billion, about ten times as much as a modern gas fired power plant. Rebecca Smith, "States Vie for Share of Clean-Coal Cash," *Wall Street Journal* (Eastern edition), March 23, 2009, A3. See also: GAO, *Climate Change: Federal Actions Will Greatly Affect the Viability of Carbon Capture and Storage as a Key Mitigation Option,* 1 (Washington, DC: Government Accountability Office, 2008), Document No. GAO-08–1080, September 2008, "Highlights."

37. Robynne Boyd, "Obama Looks to Clean Air Act as Inspiration for Tackling Climate," *Scientific American,* June 25, 2013, http://blogs.scientificamerican.com/plugged-in/2013/06/25/addressing-climate-is-similar-to-embracing-the-clean-air-act-of-the-70s/; Justin Gillis, "Taking a Risk Over Climate," *New York Times,* June 26, 2013, A1. See also: Executive Office of the President, *The President's Climate Action Plan,* June 2013, http://www.nytimes.com/interactive/2013/06/25/us/obama-climate-action-plan.html?ref=earth.

38. Pew Center on the States, *Climate Change 101: Cap and Trade* (Washington, DC: The Pew Center, 2008), 1–4.

39. Ibid.

40. See also, U.S. Environmental Protection Agency (EPA), Office of Air and Radiation, "Cap and Trade," January 18, 2010, http://epa.sownar.com/airmarkets/cap-trade/index.html; Eileen Claussen and Robert W. Fri, *A Climate Policy Framework: Balancing Policy and Politics* (Queenstown, Md.: The Aspen Institute, 2004); A. Denny Allerman, Paul L. Jaskow, and David Harrison Jr., *Emissions Trading in the United States* (Arlington, Va.: Pew Center on Climate Change, 2003), Pt. III.

41. Committee on Energy and Commerce, "Climate Change Legislation Design White Paper: Appropriate Roles for Different Levels of Government," Washington, DC, February 2008, http://energycommerce.house.gov/Climate_Change/white%20paper%20st-lcl%20roles%20final%202–22.pdf.

42. Adapted from "State Legislation from around the Country," Pew Center on Global Climate Change, accessed February 12, 2010, www.pewclimate.org/what_s_being_done/in_the_states/state_legislation.cfm.

CHAPTER 5

1. See, for example, Matthew W. Wald, "After 35-Year Lull, Nuclear Power May Be in Early Stages of a Revival," *New York Times* (Late Edition, East Coast), October 24, 2008, B3; Mark Williams, "The Renaissance of Nuclear Power Appears Inevitable: Nuclear Power Renaissance Faces Serious Obstacles," *Huffpost Green,* February 2, 2010, www.huffingtonpost.com/2010/02/26/nuclear-power-renaissance_n_477934.html; Sally Adee and Erico Guizzo, "Nuclear Reactor Renaissance," August 2010, http://spectrum.ieee.org/energy/nuclear/nuclear-reactor-renaissance.

2. U.S. Department of Energy/Nuclear Power Industry, "Strategic Plan for Light Water Reactor Research and Development," (Washington, DC: USDOE, February 2004), Executive Summary.

3. World Nuclear Power Association, "Nuclear Power in the USA."

4. Jeffrey M. Jones, "Support for Nuclear Energy Inches Up to New High, Majority Believes Nuclear Power Plants Are Safe," Gallup, March 20, 2009, accessed June 14, 2009, http://www.gallup.com/poll/117025/support-nuclear-energy-inches-new-high.aspx.

5. Hannah Northey, "NRC Approves Construction of First New Reactors Since 1978," *E&E Reporter,* February 9, 2012.

6. Marcia Clemmitt, "Nuclear Power: Can Nuclear Energy Answer Global Power Needs?," *CQ Researcher* 21, no. 2, accessed December 12, 2011, www.cqresearcher.com, 507.

7. Christopher Joyce, "Commission: U.S. Must Make Nuclear Plants Safer," *NPR*, August 19, 2011, www .npr.org/2011/07/19/138513212/commission-u-s-must-redefine-nuclear-plant-safety.

8. Near-Term Task Force Review of Insights From the Fukushima Dai-Ichi Accident, *Recommendations for Enhancing Reactor Safety in the 21st Century* (Washington, DC: Nuclear Regulatory Commission, 2011).

9. U.S. Nuclear Regulatory Commission, *Briefing on NRC Response to Recent Nuclear Events in Japan, March 21, 2011,* accessed October 8, 2011, www.nrc.gov/reading-rm/doc-collections/ . . . /tr/ . . . /20110321.pdf

10. Christopher Joyce, "Commission."

11. There are 69 pressurized water reactors (PWRs) with combined capacity of 66,697 megawatts electricity (MWe) and 35 boiling water reactors (BWRs) with combined capacity of 33,885 MWe—for a total capacity of 100,582 MWe. World Nuclear Power Association, *Nuclear Power in the USA Appendix 1: US Operating Nuclear Reactors* (Washington, DC: World Nuclear Power Association, 2010). Almost all the US nuclear generating capacity comes from reactors built between 1967 and 1990.

12. "The performance of the 104 U.S. nuclear plants since 2003 has been excellent. The total number of kilowatt hour (kWh) produced by the reactors has steadily increased over those five years. The fleet-averaged capacity factor since 2003 has been maintained at about 90%." John M. Deutch et al., *Update of the MIT 2003 Future of Nuclear Power* (Cambridge, MA: Massachusetts Institute of Technology), 5.

13. World Nuclear Association, "Nuclear Power in the USA," accessed March 24, 2011, http://www.world-nuclear.org/info/inf41.html.

14. Union of Concerned Scientists, *Nuclear Power: A Resurgence We Can't Afford* (Cambridge, MA: Union of Concerned Scientists, 2009), 1; Jeff Donn, "How Long Can Nuclear Reactors Last? US, Industry Extend Spans," *Environment on MSNBC.com,* http://www.msnbc.msn.com/id/43556350/ns/us_news-environment/t/how-long-can-nuclear-reactors-last-us-industry-extend-spans/#.TuQjuNXntBg.

15. Irvin C. Bupp and Jean-Claude Derian, *The Failed Promise of Nuclear Power* (New York: Basic Books, 1978), chapter 5.

16. Estimates of federal nuclear power subsidies vary greatly because of different methods of calculation. The conservative estimate is based upon Doug Koplow, "Nuclear Power in the US: Still Not Viable Without Subsidy," Earth Track, Inc. (Cambridge, MA: Earth Track, Inc., 2005); see also Marshall Goldberg, "Federal Energy Subsidies: Not All Technologies Are Created Equal," *Renewable Energy Policy Project* Research Report No. 11 (Washington, DC: Renewable Energy Policy Project, 2000). See also Doug Koplow, *Nuclear Power: Still Not Viable Without Subsidies* (Washington, DC: Union of Concerned Scientists, 2011).

17. Doug Koplow, *Nuclear Power*, 1.

18. Congressional Budget Office, *Nuclear Power's Role in Generating Electricity* (Washington, DC: Congressional Budget Office, May 2008), Publication No. 2986.

19. Notes the National Research Council of the National Academy of Sciences, "The handful of plants that could be built in the United States before 2020, given the long time needed for licensing and construction, would need to overcome several hurdles, including high construction costs, which have been rising rapidly across the energy sector in the last few years, and public concern about the long-term issues of storage and disposal of highly radioactive waste. If these hurdles are overcome, if the first new plants are constructed on budget and on schedule, and if the generated electricity is competitive in the marketplace, the committee judges that it is likely that many more plants could follow these first plants. Otherwise, few new plants are likely to follow." National Research Council, 447; see also Union of Concerned Scientists, *Nuclear Power: A Resurgence We Can't Afford.*

20. John Gilbertson, Managing Director, Goldman Sachs. *Statement of John Gilbertson.* Hearing of the Clean Air and Nuclear Safety Subcommittee of the Senate Environment and Public Works Committee. Subject: Nuclear Regulatory Commission's Licensing and Relicensing Processes for Nuclear Plants. Available from neinuclearnotes.blogspot.com/2008_07_01_archive.html.

21. Rebecca Smith, "New Wave of Nuclear Plants Faces High Costs," *Wall Street Journal,* May 12, 2008, 1; Michael Grunwald, "Nuclear's Comeback: Still No Energy Panacea," *Time,* December 31, 2008, http://www.time.com/time/magazine/article/0,9171,1869203-1,00.html.

22. Cited in Union of Concerned Scientists, *Nuclear Power*, 2.

23. Energy Information Administration (EIA), *Annual Energy Outlook for 2011* (Washington, DC: Energy Information Administration, 2010), 75.

24. EIA, *Annual Energy Review 2002* (Washington, DC: U.S. Government Printing Office, 2002), 254. See also Max Schulz, "Nuclear Power Is the Future," *Wilson Quarterly* (autumn 2006): 98–107.

25. Matthew L. Wald, "As Nuclear Reactors Show Age, Owners Seek to Add to Usable Life," *New York Times,* June 22, 1989, A1.

26. "Safety Rating for Nation's Biggest Nuclear Plant Lowered," *Associated Press,* February 22, 2007, www.cnn.com/Nuke%20Safety%20Problem07.html.

27. A concise, comprehensive discussion of reactor safety and related issues is found in Marcia Clemmitt, "Nuclear Power: Can Nuclear Energy Answer Global Power Needs?," *CQ Researcher,* 21, no. 2, accessed December 12, 2011, www.cqresearcher.com. See also David Lochbaum, *The NRC and Nuclear Power Plant Safety in 2010: A Brighter Spotlight Needed,* Union of Concerned Scientists, March, 2011, www.ucsusa.org/assets/documents;nuclear_power/nrc-2010-full-report.pdf.

28. David Lochbaum, *Nuclear Tightrope: Unlearned Lessons of Year-plus Reactor Outages* (Washington, DC: Union of Concerned Scientists, 2006), 1.

29. The federal government, in fact, gave surprisingly little attention to the whole problem of reactor waste disposal. See Robert J. Duffy, *Nuclear Politics in America* (Lawrence, KS: University of Kansas Press, 1997), 184–189.

30. http://www.reuters.com/article/2011/06/13/idUS178883596820110613.

31. Among the major Yucca Mountain problems, the uranium in the fuel waste "in SNF is not stable under the oxidizing conditions in Yucca Mountain and would convert rather rapidly to more soluble higher oxides. Substantial amounts of water exist in the pores and fractures of the volcanic tuff. The geologic complexity of the Yucca Mountain site, including seismicity and relatively recent volcanism, and the proposed reliance on engineered barriers, notably titanium drip shields to protect the casks from water, make the safety analysis complicated and less than convincing." Rodney C. Ewing and Frank N. Von Hippel, "Nuclear Waste Management in the United States—Starting Over," *Science,* July 10, 2009, 151, accessed May 18, 2011, *www.sciencemag.org/content/325/5937/151.*

32. US Nuclear Regulatory Commission, *Decommissioning Nuclear Power Plants,* www.nrc.gov/reading-rm/doc-collections/fact-sheets/decommissioning.html.

33. US Nuclear Regulatory Commission, *Fact Sheet on Dry Cask Storage of Spent Nuclear Fuel,* 2009. accessed June 20, 2010, http://www.nrc.gov/reading-rm/doc-collections/fact-sheets/dry-cask-storage.html; see also National Academy of Sciences, Committee on the Safety and Security of Commercial Spent Nuclear Fuel Storage, National Research Council, *Safety and Security of Commercial Spent Nuclear Fuel Storage: Public Report (2006),* accessed January 14, 2010, http://www.nap.edu/catalog/11263.html.

34. Abby Luby, "As U.S. Moves Ahead with Nuclear Power, No Solution for Radioactive Waste," *Inside Climate News,* March 3, 2011, accessed December 18, 2011, http://insideclimatenews.org/news/20110302/us-nuclear-power-energy-radioactive-waste-storage-yucca-mountain.

35. Nuclear Regulatory Commission, Office of Public Affairs, *Fact Sheet on Decommissioning Nuclear Power Plants* (Washington, DC: Nuclear Regulatory Commission, 2011).

36. Lisa Song, "Decommissioning a Nuclear Plant Can Cost $1 Billion and Take Decades," *Reuters,* June 13, 2011, accessed December 12, 2011, http://www.reuters.com/article/2011/06/13/idUS178883596820110613.

37. Ibid.

38. Doug Koplow, *Nuclear Power,* 93.

39. U.S. Nuclear Regulatory Commission, "The Commission," accessed March 5, 2011, http://www.nrc.gov/about-nrc/organization/commfuncdesc.html.

40. Robert J. Duffy, *Nuclear Politics in America,* 171.

41. GAO, *NRC Has Made Progress in Implementing Its Reactor Oversight and Licensing Processes but Continues to Face Challenges* (Washington, DC: Government Accountability Office, 2007), Report No. GAO-08-114T, "Summary."

42. Stephen Tetreault, "NRC Staff Blasts Bid to Shutter Yucca Project," *Las Vegas Review Journal,* June 24, 2011, accessed July 15, 2011, http://www.lvrj.com/news/nrc-staff-criticizes-jaczko-over-yucca-124522529.html.

43. On continuing concerns about oversight of existing commercial reactors, see Near-Term Task Force Review of Insights From the Fukushima Dai-Ichi Accident, *Recommendations for Enhancing Reactor Safety in the 21st Century* (Washington, DC: Nuclear Regulatory Commission, 2011) vi, vii.

44. Energy Information Administration, "Levelized Cost of New Generation Resources," *Annual Energy Outlook 2011*, 21, no. 2, 505–528, www.eia.gov/oiaf/aeo/pdf/20161evalized _costs_aeo.

45. Near-Term Task Force Review of Insights From the Fukushima Dai-Ichi Accident, *Recommendations for Enhancing Reactor Safety in the 21st Century.*

46. Union of Concerned Scientists, *Position Paper: Nuclear Power and Global Warming* (Cambridge, MA: Union of Concerned Scientists, 2007), 2.

47. Greenpeace, *Open Letter and Questions Concerning the Relevance of Nuclear Power in Addressing the Problem of Global Warming,* April 26, 2007, accessed November 8, 2011, www.greenpeace.or.jp/ . . . / climate/ . . . /Open_Letter_to_Lovelock.pdf.

48. The six utilities: South Texas (TX), Limerick (PA), Vogtle (GA), Byron (IL), Braidwood (IL). Science News, "Carbon Dioxide Emissions From Power Plants Rated Worldwide," *Science Daily,* November 14, 2007, http://www.sciencedaily.com/releases/2007/11/071114163448.htm.

49. World Nuclear Association, "Nuclear Energy: Meeting the Climate Change Challenge," accessed May 10, 2012, http://www.world-nuclear.org/climatechange/nuclear_meetingthe_climatechange_ challenge.html.

50. Robert W. Fri, "The Technological Challenge of Climate Change," *The Bridge,* Fall 2010, accessed May 10, 2012, http://www.nae.edu/Publications/Bridge/24514/24533.aspx. See also, National Academy of Engineering, *Limiting the Magnitude of Future Climate Change* (National Academies Press, 2009); G8+5 Academies' Joint Statement, *Climate Change and the Transformation of Energy Technologies for a Low Carbon Future, 2011,* accessed May 12, 2012, www.nasonline.org/about-nas/leadership/president/statement-climate-change.pdf; and Lisbeth Gronlund, David Lochbaum, and Edwin Lyman, *Nuclear Power in a Warming World* (Cambridge, MA: Union of Concerned Scientists, 2007).

51. Jeffrey M. Smith, "The Pro and Cons of Nuclear Power," *The Daily Green,* accessed May 20, 2012, www.thedailygreen.com/environmental-news/latest/nuclear-power-pro-con.html. See also Kurt Kleiner, "Nuclear Energy: Assessing the Emissions," *Nature Reports: Climate Change,* October 2008, no. 10, accessed May 14, 2012, www.nature.com/nclimate/archive/issue.html?year=2008&month=10.

52. World Nuclear Association, *Advanced Nuclear Power Reactors,* accessed November 19, 2011, www.world-nuclear.org/info/inf08.html.

53. See, for example, James and Anniek Hansen's letter to Barack Obama and his wife concerning global warming, quoted at Weather Underground, *Climate Change Research,* accessed August 28, 2011, www.wunderground.com/blog/streamtracker/show.html.

54. Many of the newer, near-term reactor projects, such as the Westinghouse AP1000 and the GE Hitachi Nuclear Energy Advanced Boiling Water Reactor, are based upon designs developed by collaboration between US and foreign manufacturers, such as the General Electric-Hitachi and Mitsubishi-Arveda; they have also received domestic Design Certification from the US Nuclear Regulatory Commission. At least nine additional, longer-term Generation IV designs are under development through the same corporate collaboration. Domestic nuclear manufacturers continue to envisage Generation IV reactors, but the United States has so far been far less assertive than many foreign countries in providing credible incentives for their development. Many of the present US companies with current COL filing, for instance, appear to be creating "place holders" to satisfy state requirements to keep the "nuclear option" open but not necessarily to construct Generation III and III-plus reactors.

55. *National Research Council, Committee on Nuclear Engineering Education, U.S. Nuclear Education: Status and Prospects.* (Washington, DC: National Academy Press, 1990), accessed May 20, 2010, http://www.nap.edu/catalog/1696.html.

56. Enterprise Informatics, *Solving the Brain Drain of the Nuclear Power Industry,* accessed June 23, 2010, nuclearstreet.com/ . . . /nuclear . . . /white-paper-solving-the-brain-drain-of-the-nuclear-industry-1812.aspx.

57. Engineering Trends, *Degrees Since 1945,* accessed December 30, 2011, http://www.engtrends.com/degrees1945.html 2010.

58. Energy Information Administration, "Levelized Cost of New Generation Resources," *Annual Energy Outlook, 2011,* accessed March 15, 2011, www.eia/gov/olaf/aeo/pdf/20161evelized_costs_ae02011 .pdf.

59. Ibid.

60. One alternative investment, for example, would accelerate the construction of new combined-cycle turbines that rely upon what appears to be an unexpected increase in natural gas reserves.

61. Rebecca Smith, "Atomic Waste Gets 'Temporary' Home," *Wall Street Journal*, June 1, 2010, accessed September 22, 2013, http://online.wsj.com/article/SB1000142405274870471700457526911133175457 0.html.

62. Blue Ribbon Commission on America's Nuclear Future, *Report to the Secretary of Energy* (Washington, DC: Department of Energy, 2012), accessed July 7, 2013, www.brc.gov.

CHAPTER 6

1. Alli Gold, "The Case for Optimism About a Renewable Energy Future," *MIT News*, May 1, 2013, accessed July 10, 2013, http://web.mit.edu/newsoffice/2013/the-renewable-energy-future.html.

2. Stephen Power, "Gen. Jones Bemoans 'A La Carte' Energy Policy," *Wall Street Journal Washington Wire*, April 21, 2011, accessed May 5, 2011, http://blogs.wsj.com/washwire/2011/04/11/gen-jones-bemoans-a-la-carte-energy-policy/.

3. Market Watch, "Text of President Barack Obama's Speech on Energy," April 22, 2009, accessed December 3, 2009, www.marketwatch.com/story/text-president-obamas-speech-energy.

4. Committee on America's Energy Future; National Academy of Sciences; National Academy of Engineering; National Research Council, *America's Energy Future: Technology and Transformation: Summary Edition 2009*, 2 (Washington, DC: National Academy Press, 2009).

5. Center for Sustainable Systems, *U.S. Renewable Energy* (Ann Arbor, MI: Center for Sustainable Systems, 2011).

6. See Energy Information Administration, "Renewable Energy Explained," 2012, http://www.eia.gov/energyexplained/index.cfm?page=renewable_hom.

7. Janet L. Swain et al., *American Energy: The Renewable Path to Energy Security* (Washington, DC: Worldwatch Institute, 2006), 30.

8. National Geographic, *Wind Power*, accessed October 24, 2011, http://environment.nationalgeographic.com/environment/global-warming/wind-power-profile/.

9. Ibid.

10. American Wind Energy Association, *Clean, Affordable, Homegrown: American Wind Power* (Washington, DC: American Windpower Association, 2011), accessed March 22, 2011, www.powerofwind.com.

11. US Department of Energy, *20% Wind Energy by 2030* (Washington, DC: National Renewable Energy Laboratory, 2008), also available at www. nrel.gov/docs/fy08sti/41869.pdf.

12. PR Newswire, "Republic Services' McCarty Road Landfill to Begin Sending Biogas to Anheuser-Busch Brewery in Houston," June 24 (no year), accessed January 3, 2012, http://www.prnewswire.com/news-releases/republic-services-mccarty-road-landfill-to-begin-sending-biogas-to-anheuser-busch-brewery-in-houston-61859757.html.

13. Energy Information Administration, *Renewable Energy Sources: A Consumer's Guide*, n.d., accessed December 20, 2011, ftp://ftp.eia.doe.gov/brochures/brochure/renew05/renewable.html.

14. Amanda D. Cuellar and Michael E. Webber, "Policy Incentives, Barriers and Recommendations for Biogas Production, Paper presented at the 2009 3rd International Conference on Energy Sustainability," *ASME Digital Library*, accessed January 2, 2012, http://scitation.aip.org/getabs/servlet/GetabsServlet?prog=normal&id=ASMECP002009048890000049000001&idtype=cvips&gifs=yes&ref=no. http://proceedings.asmedigitalcollection.asme.org/proceeding.aspx?articleid=1647716.

15. Fred Sissine, "Renewable Energy R&D Funding History: A Comparison With Funding for Nuclear Energy, Fossil Energy, and Energy Efficiency R&D," *CRS Report to Congress*, April 9, 2008, 1, Document RS22858.

16. David G. Victor and Kassia Yanosek, "The Crisis in Clean Energy," *Foreign Affairs*, 90, no. 4, July/August 2011, 114–115.

17. For a summary explanation of research and development funding, see Kirstin R. W. Matthews, Neal Lane, and Kenneth M. Evans, *U.S. Scientific Research and Development 202: A Critical Look at the Federal Research and Development Funding System*, Center for American Progress, July 21, 2011, accessed January 4, 2011, http://scienceprogress.org/2011/07/u-s-scientific-research-and-development-202/.

18. Adapted from Lynn J. Cunningham and Beth A. Roberts, "Renewable Energy and Energy Efficiency Incentive Resources," *CRS Report to Congress*, March 23, 2009 (Washington, DC: Congressional Reference Service, 2009), Document R40455; and Richard J. Campbell, Lynn J. Cunningham, and Beth

A. Roberts, "Renewable Energy and Energy Efficiency Incentives: A Summary of Federal Programs," *CRS Reports* (Washington, DC: Congressional Research Service, 2009), Document 7–5700.

19. Union of Concerned Scientists, *State Policies Fact Sheet: Renewable Energy Standards at Work in the States* (Cambridge, MA: Union of Concerned Scientists, 2009); see also DOE, *Energy Efficiency and Renewable Energy: States With Renewable Portfolio Standards,* accessed December 10, 2011, http://apps1.eere.energy.gov/states/maps/renewable_portfolio_states.cfm.

20. Quadrupled Renewable Energy on Public Lands, *CleanTechnica.com,* accessed January 5, 2012, http://cleantechnica.com/2011/12/31/obama-has-nearly-quadrupled-renewable-energy-on-public-lands/.

21. Susan Culver-Graybeal, "Obama Administration Approves New Renewable Energy Products," accessed January 5, 2012, http://news.yahoo.com/obama-administration-approves-renewable-energy-products-193000973.html.

22. Dept. of Energy, Office of Chief Financial Officer, *FY 2012 Congressional Budget Request: Budget Highlights,* February 2012, 26, accessed January 5, 2012, http://energy.gov/about-us/budget-performance.

23. Executive Office of the President, *The President's Climate Action Plan,* June 2013, at: http://www.whitehouse.gov/sites/default/files/image/president27sclimateactionplan.pdf.

24. David G. Victor and Kassia Yanosek, "The Crisis in Clean Energy," 120.

25. Russell Gold, "Clean-Energy Doldrums," January 5, 2012, accessed January 5, 2012, intrabecc.cocef.org/ . . . /cccleanenergyindustrytheddoldrums.pdf.

26. Kate Galbraith, "Dark Days for Green Energy," *New York Times,* February 4, 2009, B1.

27. Sam Newman et al., "Accelerating Solar Power Adoption: Compounding Cost Savings Across the Value Chain," *Rocky Mountain Institute,* 2009, accessed January 6, 2012, http://www.rmi.org/Knowledge-Center/Library/2009–03_AcceleratingSolarPowerAdoption.

28. Jim Tankersley, "Offshore Wind Turbines Get Further Boost From Obama Administration," *Los Angeles Times,* April 22, 2009, B1.

29. Cape Wind Associates, "Frequently Asked Questions," 2012, accessed January 9, 2012, http://www.capewind.org/FAQ-Category4-Cape+Wind+Basics-Parent0-myfaq-yes.htm.

30. See Robert Kennedy, Jr., "An Ill Wind off Cape Cod," *New York Times,* December 16, 2005, accessed March 5, 2010, http://www.nytimes.com/2005/12/16/opinion/16kennedy.html; "Save Our Sound," accessed January 10, 2012, http://www.saveoursound.org/myths_vs_facts/; and Beth Daly, "Cape Wind Backers Blew Right by Cost," *Boston Globe,* October 10, 2010, accessed December 14, 2011, http://www.boston.com/lifestyle/green/articles/2010/10/10/cape_wind_backers_blew_right__by_cost/.

31. Beth Daly, "Wampanoag Tribe Sues Over Cape Wind," *Boston Globe,* July 11, 2011, accessed August 10, 2011, http://articles.boston.com/2011–07–11/lifestyle/29761941_1_cape-wind-wind-farm-horseshoe-shoal.

32. Henry Fountain, "Growing More Corn for Ethanol Makes Pest Control Harder," *New York Times* (Late East Coast Edition), December 23, 2008, D3.

33. Bryan Walsh, "Tallying the Real Environmental Cost of Biofuels," *Time,* October 23, 2009, accessed February 27, 2010, http://www.time.com/time/health/article/0,8599,1931780,00.html.

34. Sam Pearson, "Desert Storm: Battle Brews Over Obama Renewable Energy Plan," *National Geographic Daily News,* July 24, 2013, accessed August 1, 2013, http://news.nationalgeographic.com/news/energy/2013/07/130725-obama-renewable-energy-plan-public-lands/.

35. See, for example, Desert Watch, accessed January 10, 2012, http://www.docstoc.com/docs/28893362/Desert-Watch-July-06_3pub; and Peter Maloney, "Solar Projects Draw New Opposition, *New York Times,* September 24, 2008, accessed January 9, 2012, http://www.nytimes.com/2008/09/24/business/businessspecia12/24shrike.html?pagewanted=print.

36. Union of Concerned Scientists, "Environmental Impacts of Renewable Energy Technologies," *Clean Energy,* accessed January 6, 2011, http://www.ucsusa.org/clean_energy/technology_and_impacts/impacts/environmental-impacts-of.html.

37. Jennifer Weeks, "Modernizing the Grid," *CQ Researcher* 20, no. 7 (2010), 147, accessed January 10, 2012, www.cqresearcher.com.

38. Jennifer Weeks, "Modernizing the Grid," *CQ Researcher* 20, no. 7 (2010), 147, accessed January 10, 2012, www.cqresearcher.com.

39. "No centralized authoritative body or organization currently exists to develop and enforce standards for renewable electricity resource assessment methodologies and assumptions used to calculate

estimates. Renewable electricity resource estimates come from multiple organizations. As a result, renewable electricity generation potential estimates are derived using different methodologies and different assumptions which, in turn, produce different estimates." Philip Brown and Gene Whitney, *U.S. Renewable Electricity Generation: Resources and Challenges* (Washington, DC: Congressional Research Service, 2011), Publication R41954.

40. GAO, *Renewable Energy: Wind Power's Contribution to Electric Power Generation and Impact on Farms and Rural Communities* (Washington, DC: GAO, 2004), Report No. GAO-04–756, 1.

41. "Connecting renewable electricity generation facilities to the electric power grid can raise potential technical challenges. In particular, a high percentage penetration of variable sources—such as solar and wind—can cause serious power quality and reliability problems. The power system requires constant, 24/7 minute-by-minute monitoring and control. The introduction of variable electricity generation may pose power system reliability challenges associated with moment-by-moment balancing of electricity supply and demand." Brown and Whitney, *U.S. Electric Power Generation*, 34.

42. *The Regulation of Shareholder-Owned Electric Companies*, accessed May 24, 2012, www.eei.org/whoweare/AboutIndustry/ . . . /KeyFacts-Regulation.pdf.

43. Paul L. Joskow, "American Economic Policy During the 1990s," paper prepared for the Conference on American Economic Policy During the 1990s, sponsored by the John F. Kennedy School of Government, Harvard University, June 27 to June 30, 2001, accessed May 24, 2012, econ-www.mit.edu/files/1144.

44. Karlynn Cory, Toby Couture, and Claire Kreycik, *Feed-in Policy: Design, Implementation, and RPS Policy Interactions* (Washington, DC: National Renewable Energy Laboratory, 2009), Report NREL/TP-6A2–45549.

45. Kate Galbraith, "Feed-In Tariffs Contemplated in the U.S.," *New York Times*, February 9, 2009, accessed January 20, 2012, http://green.blogs.nytimes.com/2009/02/09/feed-in-tariffs-contemplated-in-the-us/.

46. Energy Information Administration, *AEO2013 Early Release Overview*, Figure 12: "Electricity Generation By Fuel, 1990-2040," accessed June 16, 2013 at http://www.eia.gov/forecasts/aeo/er/early_elecgen.cfm; for more optimistic projections, see National Renewable Energy Laboratory, *Renewable Electricity Futures Report*, "Key Findings," at http://www.nrel.gov/analysis/re_futures/ accessed July 10, 2013.

CHAPTER 7

1. Richard Thaler, "Why Gas Prices Are Out of Any President's Control, *New York Times* (New York Edition), April 1, 2012, BU3.

2. PollingReport.com, "Problems and Priorities," accessed January 20, 2012, http://www.pollingreport.com/prioriti.htm.

3. Daniel Yergin, "The Globalization of Energy Demand," *CNBC Megatrends*, June 3, 2013, accessed July 12, 2013, www.cnbc.com/id/100784599.

4. Ibid.

5. The evolving US scientific and political controversy over climate change is summarized in Walter A. Rosenbaum, *Environmental Politics and Policy*, 9th ed. (Washington, DC: CQ Press, 2013), chapter 10. See also Jill Jaeger and Tim O'Riordan, "The History of Climate Change Science and Politics," in *Politics of Climate Change*, ed. Tim O'Riordan and Jill Jaeger (London: Routledge, 1996); Eileen Claussen and Robert W. Fri, *A Climate Policy Framework: Balancing Policy and Politics* (Queenstown, MD: The Aspen Institute, 2004); and Mike Hulme, *Why We Disagree About Climate Change* (New York: Cambridge University Press, 2009).

6. Intergovernmental Panel on Climate Change, "Climate Change 2007: Working Group I: The Physical Science Basis, IPCC Assessments of Climate Change and Uncertainties," 2007, accessed May 15, 2010, www.ipcc.ch/publications_and_data/ar4/wg1/en/ch1s1–6.html.

7. A full profile of Obama's 2013 energy proposals is found at "Climate Change and President Obama's Action Plan," *The White House*, June 25, 2013, accessed July 2, 2013, http://www.whitehouse.gov/blog/2013/06/25/president-obamas-plan-cut-carbon-pollution-and-address-climate-change; and John Miller, "Can Obama's Climate Change Policy Reduce Carbon Emissions?," *The Energy Collective*, July 2, 2013, accessed July 2, 2013, http://theenergycollective.com/jemillerep/244141/how-can-obama-s-climate-policy-successfully-reduce-us-carbon-emissions.

8. Committee on Energy and Commerce, "Climate Change Legislation Design White Paper: Appropriate Roles for Different Levels of Government," (Washington, DC, February 2008), http://energycommerce.house.gov/Climate_Change/white%20paper%20st-lcl%20roles%20final%202-22.pdf.

9. A useful summary of this approach is found in Pew Center on the States, *Climate Change 101: Cap and Trade* (Washington, DC: The Pew Center, 2008), 1–4.

10. Quoted in Susan Lyon, Rebecca Lefton, and Daniel J. Weiss, "Growing Global Oil Demand Harms U.S. Security and Economy," April 23, 2010, accessed July 10, 2013, www.americanprogress.org/issues/green/news/2010/04/23/7657/quenching-our-thirst-for-oil/; see also a useful summary of the vulnerability issue in Rand Corporation, *Does Imported Oil Threaten U.S. National Security?* (Santa Monica, CA: Rand Corporation, 2009).

11. www.iea.org/aboutus/faqs/oil/, FAQs: Oil; see also Kevin Bullis, "Shale Oil Will Boost U.S. Production, But It Won't Bring Energy Independence," *MIT Technology Review*, November 15, 2012, accessed February 20, 2013, http://www.technologyreview.com/news/507446/shale-oil-will-boost-us-production-but-it-wont-bring-energy-independence/.

12. A thorough summary of the important economic and environmental issues associated with fracking can be found in US Government Accountability Office, *Oil and Gas: Information on Shale Resources, Development, and Environmental and Public Health Risks* (Washington, DC: Government Accountability Office, 2012), Publication GAO-12–732.

13. Executive Office of the President, President's Council of Advisors on Science and Technology, ibid. [ibid. in text]

14. National Science Foundation, "Nanotechnology Definition," (February 2000), accessed January 28, 2012, www.nsf.gov/crssprgm/nano/reports/omb_nifty50.jsp.

15. *Nano.gov: National Nanotechnology Initiative*, accessed December 14, 2011, http://www.nano.gov/.

16. Vandana Prakash, "Nanotechnology to Aid the Commercial Viability of Algae Bio-Fuel Production," *QuantumSphere*, April 23, 2009, accessed February 2, 2012, www.qsinano.com/news/newsletters/2009_04/f1.php.

17. Renewable Energy World.com, "Hydrogen Energy," accessed October 15, 2011, www.renewableenergyworld.com/rea/tech/hydrogen.

18. International Energy Agency, *Technology Roadmap: Smart Grids* (Paris, France: International Energy Agency, 2011), 6, accessed February 1, 2012, www.iea.org/papers/2011/smartgrids_roadmap.pdf.

19. Title XIII of EISA (2007) authorized the Department of Energy to initiate new programs to coordinate and improve national grid modernization. President Obama repeatedly urged Congress to authorize and fund an aggressive program of national conversion to a "smart grid" to be completed before the end of the century. Additionally, the American Reinvestment and Recovery Act created $3.4 billion in grants to states and communities to begin development of smart grids.

20. The Barker Institute, Energy Forum, "Energy and Nanotechnology," accessed February 3, 2012, www.rice.edu/energy/research/energyprogram/nanotechnology.html; see also: Neal Lane and Thomas Kalil, "The National Nanotechnology Initiative: Present at the Creation," *Issues in Science and Technology*, Summer 2005, accessed November 10, 2011, www.issues.org/21.4/lane.html; and Robert W. Fri, "From Energy Wish Lists to Technological Realities," *Issues in Science and Technology*, Fall 2006, accessed January 10, 2012, www.issues.org/23.1/fri.html.

21. On hydrogen cell potential, see: The National Academies, "Emerging Technologies: Hydrogen Fuel Cells," accessed October 3, 2011, http://needtoknow.nas.edu/energy/energy-sources/emerging-technologies/hydrogen-fuel-cells.php; and Daniel Sperling and Joan Ogden, "The Hope for Hydrogen," *Issues in Science and Technology*, 20, no. 3 (Spring 2004), accessed February 6, 2012, www.issues.org/20.3/index.html. For the debate over hydrogen technologies, see also Joseph J. Romm, "The Hype About Hydrogen," *Issues in Science and Technology*, 20, no. 3 (Spring 2004), accessed February 7, 2012, www.issues.org/20.3/romm.html#.

INDEX

Allen, Thad, 6
American Recovery and Reinvestment
    Act, 110
Arctic National Wildlife Refuge (ANWR),
    71–73
Atomic Energy Commission (AEC), 133

Biello, David, 106
Biofuels, 152–153
Biogas, 152
Biomass, and renewable energy, 151–153
Bitumen, 74
British Petroleum, 3–5
Browner, Carol, 13
Bupp, Irvin C., 124
Bureau of Land Management (BLM), 17
Bureau of Ocean Energy Management,
    Regulation, and Enforcement
    (BOEMRE), 18–19
Bush, George W., 13, 43–44, 52, 58
  climate change, 39
  coal, 93
  energy future, 41–42
  Energy Policy Act (EPAct), 69–70,
      102, 156
  ethanol, 79
  nuclear energy, 120, 137
  Nuclear Regulatory Commission
      (NRC), 134

Canadian oil shale, 74–75
Cap and trade, 113–115
Cape Wind, 162–164
Carbon capture and sequestration (CCS),
    110–111
Carbon dioxide, and the Clean Air Act,
    113–114
Carbon policy. See Coal; Petroleum and
    natural gas
Carter, Jimmy, 34, 38, 104–105, 177
Casinghead, 81
Cheney, Dick, 58
Chernobyl, 121
Chu, Steven, 22, 130
Clark, Wesley, 81
Clean Air Act, 38, 113–114, 185
Clean coal, search for, 110–112
Clean Energy Superhighway, and the Obama
    administration, 43–46
Clean Water Act Amendments, 38–39
Climate Action Plan, 113
Climate warming, 112–116
Clinton, Bill, 41
Coal, 91–118
  ash, 108–110
  clean, 110–112
  clean water and, 108–110
  climate warming, deadlock, and
      improvisation, 112–116

electric power and, 100
environmental hazards of, 97–98
environmentalism and, 101–102
future (the) and, 116–118
governance, 102–112
industry, 99–100
policy, politics of, 98–102
resource, abundance of, 93–98
Congress, U.S., and energy governance,
     14–15
Constitution, U.S., and energy policy
     politics, 10–11
Crisis, and energy policy, 25
Cronin, Thomas, 30

Deepwater Horizon tragedy, 1–9
Department of Energy (DOE), 16–17,
     29, 38n
Department of the Interior (DOI), 17–19, 70
Derian, Jean-Claude, 124
Dry cask storage, 131
Duffy, Robert, 133
Duty. *See* Tariffs

Earth Day, 38
Economic regulation, 47n
Economics, of nuclear power, 125–126
Economy, and energy policy, 24–25
Electoral cycle, and energy policy, 29–30
Electric power, 165–174
  coal and, 100
  competition and markets, 170–171
  environmental regulations and, 170
  federal regulation and, 169–170
  future sources of, 166
  regulatory federalism and, 169
  Smart Grid and, 171–172
  state and local government initiatives,
       172–174
  state regulation, 170
  See also Renewable energy and electric
       power
Endangerment finding, 113
Energy, managing. *See* Energy policy primer
Energy Independence and Security Act, 43,
     58, 80, 156

Energy policy, U.S. *See* Coal; Energy policy
     politics; Energy policy primer; Global
     energy economy; Nuclear energy;
     Petroleum and natural gas; Renewable
     energy and electric power
Energy Policy Act (EPAct), 42, 58, 69–70, 79,
     102, 156
Energy policy politics, 1–33
  making policy, 9–22
  policy drivers, 22–32
  transformation, 33
  "well from hell," 2–9
Energy policy primer, 34–59
  abundance to insecurity, 34–46
  energy policy options, 46–59
  governed energy marketplace, 59
Energy security, 32
  fracking and, 188
  improving, 186–188
Energy taxes, 50–52
Environment, and natural gas, 83–87
Environmental impact, and natural gas,
     86–87
Environmentalism, 38–39
  coal and, 101–102
  energy policy and, 26–28
  global climate warming, and, 28
Environmental Protection Agency (EPA),
     19–20, 185
Ethanol, 64, 78–81, 156
Executive branch, and energy governance,
     15–17

Federal Energy Regulatory Commission
     (FERC), 16, 19, 169
Federal energy subsidies, by type, 54 (figure)
Federal institutions, and energy policy
     politics, 12–20
Federalism, 11
Federal Power Act, 169
Federal regulation, 48–49
Federal subsidies, and related petroleum
     production incentives, 68–69
Federal support, for the nuclear power
     industry, 124–125
Feed-in-tariff, 172–174

First Assessment Report (Intergovernmental Panel on Climate Change (IPCC), 41
Flex fuel vehicle, 79
Fracking, ix–x, 31, 61, 75–76, 117
  natural gas production and, 84–86
  natural gas supply and, 82
Fukushima Daiichi disaster, 121
Future Gen, future of, 92–93

Genoa, Paul, 132
Geothermal technology, 153
Global energy economy, 176–193
  energy security, improving, 186–188
  global climate change, 181–186
  global imperative, 191–193
  rising demand, 177–181
  technology innovation and, 188–191
Globalization, and energy policy,
    30–31
Global warming, 136–137
Governance, 47–50, 59
Governed energy marketplace, 59
Governing energy, 12–20
  committees, 14
  Congress, 14–15
  Department of the Interior, 17–19
  Environmental Protection Agency,
    19–20
  executive branch, 15–17
  Federal Energy Regulatory Commission
    (FERC), 19
  Nuclear Regulatory Commission
    (NRC), 19
  states and, 20–22
  White House, 13–14
Green Agenda, Obama administration's,
    158–160
Green Power Programs, 155

Hydrologic fracturing, 86, 88
Hydropower, 153, 168

Incrementalism, 12
Interest groups, and energy policy, 28–29
Intergovernmental Panel on Climate Change
    (IPCC), 41

Jones, James, 143
Joskow, Paul L., 40

Kennedy, John F., 34
Kennedy, Ted, 163
Keystone XL project (pipeline), 74–77
Kingston Fossil power plant, 109
Krosnick, Jon, 23

Landrieu, Mary, 15
Lurches (bursts of change), 12

Madison, James, 11
Martinot, Eric, 143
*Massachusetts v. Environmental Protection
    Agency*, 113
Mattern, Rich, 161
McCain, John, 100
McClendon, Aubrey K., 84
Menendez, Robert, 15
Minerals Management Services
    (MMS), 8
Mining, surface, 104–108
Mountaintop removal, 106–108

National Contingency Plan (NCP), 5
National Electric Reliability Council
    (NERC), 169–170
National Energy Plan, 38n
National energy planning, 58–59
National Energy Policy (NEP), 42, 58
National Mining Association (NMA), 99
National security, and energy policy, 32
Natural gas, rewards and risks of, 81–89
  domestic resources, 81–82
  environment (the) and, 83–87
  environmental impact, 86–87
  environmentalists and, 88–89
  fracking, 84–86
  future policy options, 87–89
  supply and demand, 81–82
  versatility of, 82
  See also Petroleum and natural gas
Neustadt, Richard E., 10
Nixon, Richard, 43, 93

Nuclear energy, 119–142
  commercial industry, today, 122–134
  governance, 124–141
  reactors, 123 (figure), 137–138
  rise and decline of, 119–122
  waste material, disposal of, 128–132,
      140–141
Nuclear Regulatory Commission (NRC), 19,
    132–134
Nuclear Waste Policy Act (NWPA), 128

Obama, Barack, 7, 13, 35, 60, 181
  Arctic National Wildlife Refuge (ANWR)
      development, 73
  clean energy programs, 44
  Clean Energy Superhighway, 43–46,
      143–144
  climate legislation, 113
  coal and the "new energy future," 103–104
  coal mining regulation, 100
  Green Agenda, 158–160
  Keystone XL project (pipeline), 76
  natural gas production, 87–88
  nuclear energy, 120–122, 134–135, 137
  renewable energy, 154, 160
OECD (Organization for Economic
    Co-Operation and Development),
    178–179
Office of Surface Mining Control and
    Reclamation Act, 18
Oil consumption, projected for the United
    States, China, and India, 179 (figure)
Oil shale, 73–74
1002 Area, 72–73
Organization of the Petroleum Exporting
    Countries (OPEC), 37
Outer Continental Shelf (OCS) lands,
    exploration and production in, 69–71

Patrick, Deval, 163
Petroleum and natural gas, 60–90
  accelerated domestic production and
      exploration, 69–77
  conservation and substitution, 77–78
  exports and imports, 61–64
    governing, 67–81
    natural gas, 81–89
    politics and, 65–66
    risks and rewards, 64–65
    transformation era, 60–61
Photovoltaic systems, 148
Policy. See Energy policy, U.S.
Political partisanship, and energy policy,
    25–26
Price-Anderson Act, 124
Price controls, 56–57
Progress Energy, and switch to natural
    gas, 82
Public opinion, and energy policy, 23
Public utility commissions, responsibilities
    of, 157
Punctuated equilibrium, 7, 12

Quota, 56–57

Rationing, of energy, 55–56
Raulston, Carol, 107
Reagan, Ronald, 39, 48
Regulation, 48n
Regulatory federalism, 49–50
Reilly, William, 20
Renewable energy, and electric power,
    143–175
  electric power, 165–174
  future of, in the United States, 144–145
  governance, 153–165
  production tax credit, 155
  resources, 145–153
Renewable Portfolio Standard (RPS), 22,
    149, 155, 157, 172–173
Research and development (R&D), 54–55
Restoration, and surface mining, 108

Safety issues, and the nuclear power
    industry, 126–128
Shale oil formations, in the United States,
    85 (figure)
Smart Grid, 171–172, 189
Social regulation, 47n
Solar power, 148–149

Solyndra, 159
Sonoran Solar Energy Project, 158
Spruce Mine project, 107
State initiatives, and greenhouse gas
        emissions, 115–116
Stevens, Ted, 15
Strategic Petroleum Reserve (SPR), 32, 57,
        186n
Subsidies, 52–54
Surface mining, 104–108
Surface Mining Control and Reclamation
        Act, 104–105

Tariffs, 56–57
Technology innovation, and the global
        energy economy, 188–191
Thaler, Richard, 176
Tule Wind Project, 159

United Mine Workers (UMW), 100–101
U.S. Constitution, and energy policy politics,
        10–11

U.S. Energy Information Administration, 64
U.S. energy policy. See Energy
        policy, U.S.

van Doren, Peter, 67
Victor, David, 154

Waste material, nuclear, 128–132,
        140–141
Water, clean, and coal, 108–110
Weeks, Jennifer, 165
White house, and energy governance,
        13–14
Will, George, 28
Wind energy, 150–151
Wind farms, x, 150

Yankelovich, Daniel, 23
Yanosek, Kassia, 154
Yergin, Daniel, 179, 181
Yucca Mountain, and nuclear waste disposal,
        128–131

ABOUT THE AUTHOR

Walter A. Rosenbaum is professor emeritus of political science at the University of Florida and director emeritus of the University of Florida's Bob Graham Center for Public Service. His recent activities include an analysis of the EPA's capacity for climate change regulation, prepared for the Brookings Institution; an examination of the data requirements for a new Federal Environmental Legacy Act; and preparation of an energy policy text for CQ Press. He has also served as a staff member of the US Environmental Protection Agency and an adjunct professor in the School of Public Health, Tulane University Medical College. In addition to his teaching and research, he has been a consultant to the EPA, the US Department of Energy, the Federal Emergency Management Agency, and the South Florida Ecosystem (Everglades) Restoration Project. He is currently the editor-in-chief of the *Journal for Environmental Studies and Sciences*.

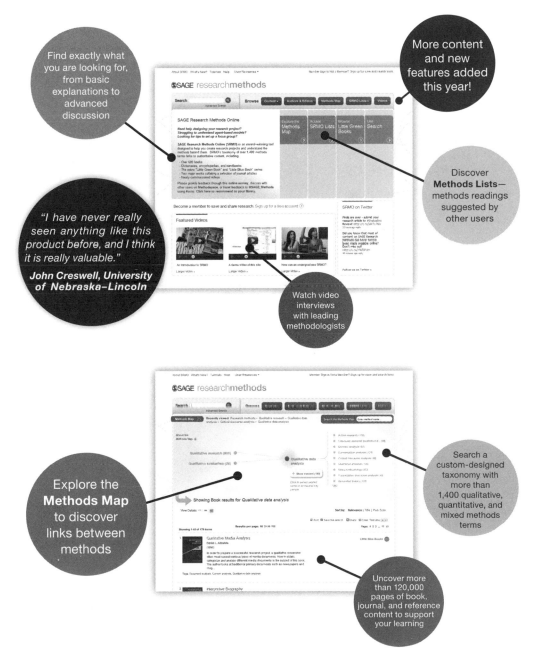

⑤SAGE research**methods**

The essential online tool for researchers from the world's leading methods publisher

Find exactly what you are looking for, from basic explanations to advanced discussion

More content and new features added this year!

Discover **Methods Lists**— methods readings suggested by other users

"I have never really seen anything like this product before, and I think it is really valuable."
John Creswell, University of Nebraska-Lincoln

Watch video interviews with leading methodologists

Explore the **Methods Map** to discover links between methods

Search a custom-designed taxonomy with more than 1,400 qualitative, quantitative, and mixed methods terms

Uncover more than 120,000 pages of book, journal, and reference content to support your learning

Find out more at
www.sageresearchmethods.com